Endorsements

"Andy Och's exploration of the lives of America's First Ladies is as rich and varied as the lives of those women themselves, and as unexpected. His adventurous, even picaresque, experience with the diverse people and places that enhance our appreciation of these extraordinary women, is both informative and engaging, giving us an important behind-the-scenes look at what it takes to be on the front line of history in modern America."

– Taylor Stoermer
Fellow of the Graduate School of Arts and Sciences and
Instructor of Public History at Harvard University

"I've read a score of books on America's First Ladies; however, none from this most unique and interesting vantage point. Half way through the introduction, I knew I wanted to take this journey, crisscrossing the United States, with Andy as my tour guide. With Mr. Och's marvelous story telling ability and extensive research, he transports the reader in time, making history come alive to meet these remarkable women — the person, not her celebrity or fame. A must read for male, female, young and old alike. Be it a professional, novice or skeptic, all will enjoy this delicious adventure. I devoured each chapter and am excitedly awaiting Volume II."

– Jacqueline Berger
National Speaker and Author on America's First Ladies
"The First Ladies Lady"
www.FirstLadiesLady.com

"From spouses who bankrolled their husbands' entire political careers to those who closely guarded potentially damaging family secrets, first ladies have consistently laid the groundwork for the most consequential presidencies in American history. Andy Och makes the case for the personal influence of first ladies in a fun and entertaining manner."

– Lauren A. Wright, PhD
Author of "On Behalf of the President: Presidential Spouses and White House Communications Strategy Today"

i

"Andy Och has given us a fascinating book that is part travelogue, part collective biography. The result of his time spent on the road is a unique history of the First Ladies that will undoubtedly appeal to the broadest audience."

- Dr. Christopher Leahy
Professor of History, Keuka College, Kueka Park, NY
- Sharon Williams Leahy
Founder, HistoryPreserve.com

"No doubt about it! Andy Och is unquestionably the First Ladies Man! Armed with little more than a camera, an open mind toward women and history, and a super imagination which combines all three elements, he has created an epic part-travelogue, part-history, and totally delightful foray into the lives, the times and the places where an amazing assortment of women who became First Lady can take their place on a stage all by themselves!"

- Feather Schwartz Foster
Author of "The First Ladies" and "Mary Lincoln's Flannel Pajamas and Other Stories from the First Ladies' Closet"

"Would have loved being on Andy's fabulous roadshow journey following the interesting society of First Ladies from Martha to Michelle. His insider true stories made them come alive! Our club membership awaits this much anticipated book!"

- Susanne Bradley
Vice President, American Antique Arts Assoc. of Annapolis

"From the very first page you know this is not going to be 'just' another biographical overview of the First Ladies. In fact the very first page tugs you into the stories...the stories of what made the First Ladies 'unusual for their time;' the stories of people, places, and objects associated with these remarkable women; and the stories behind Och's transformation from documentarian to historian because of what he learned. Andrew Och's book is in part history text and travelogue, but refreshingly written from Och's insightful, and frequently humorous perspective. Although written in an easy storytelling manner, the book is rich with new historical detail about the First Ladies. Their lives in the White House are important, but Och also focuses on what came before and after proving their consequence as partners for their presidential husbands and icons for our nation. Thankfully, this is only volume one, we will anticipate and look forward to many more stories as Andrew Och writes his way through the lives of our country's amazing First Ladies.

- Patricia Balderson
Manager, Museum Education, Colonial Williamsburg

Unusual For Their Time
On The Road With America's First Ladies

Andrew Och

Tactical 16, LLC

Unusual For Their Time:
On The Road With America's First Ladies
Copyright © 2016 by Andrew Och

First Edition

Because of the dynamic nature of the internet, any web address or links contained in this book may have changed since publication and may no longer be valid.

Published by Tactical 16, LLC
Colorado Springs, CO

eISBN: 978-1-943226-14-6
ISBN: 978-1-943226-13-9 (hc)
ISBN: 978-1-943226-12-2 (sc)

Printed in the United States of America

This book is dedicated to my mom

JULIE CARROLL OCH
December 5, 1943 – November 17, 2010

She would have loved this project

Thank You

Erik and Kristen Shaw at Tactical 16, Andrea Lea Samari, Bruce Och, Deidra McElroy, Jon Croft, James Rosen, Joe Wilk, Lulu Cohen, J. Eden Gordon and all of the friends, family and fans that followed this amazing journey

Special Thanks

Brian Lamb, Susan Swain, Terry Murphy, Mark Farkas, Peter Slen, Michele Remillard, and everyone at C-SPAN, the White House Historical Association and all of the consulting historians, live guests, authors and experts who contributed to the "FIRST LADIES: Influence and Image" series

Table of Contents

INTRODUCTION

Behind every great man is an even greater woman...or in this case...lady.

If George Washington had never met and married Martha Dandridge Custis, this book would be called something quite different. It may have been written in a different language, or perhaps never written at all.

If George and Martha Washington had never married, America would be a very different place... or quite possibly... not America at all.

Martha Washington was unusual for her time.

*M*y name is Andrew Och and I am the "THE FIRST LADIES MAN". I have completed an unusual journey. This journey gave me the opportunity to learn about every First Lady of the United States from Martha Washington to Michelle Obama. I have traveled to nearly every city, town, village, home, school, church, birthplace, cemetery, train station, farm, plantation, library, museum, general store, town center and cottage that relates to these women, these ladies. I wanted to find out what type of woman grows up to become married to a President of the United States. What I discovered was that many of our Presidents married up. Most of these men would not have made it to the White House without the help, influence, and support of their wives. Nearly all of our Presidents married a woman who was unusual for her time. I have travelled tens of thousands of miles in the lives, footsteps and shoes of these First Ladies, and in this book, you will now get to travel in mine.

In early October 2012, I signed on with a team at C-SPAN, the American cable and satellite television network, to be a series producer for their special television project called "FIRST LADIES: Influence and Image". Little did I know that this project would become an adventure, and a journey that would change my life forever.

When I interviewed for the job, I was asked if I was a television producer that specialized in historical subjects. I said that I was not. They asked me if I had taken a lot of history classes in school, or if I had a special interest in political history or the First Ladies specifically. I said that I did not – nothing out of the ordinary anyway. I was then asked why I should be hired for this position or why I even wanted it. The answer to that question was very simple.

I thrive in the field and "on assignment", and I like a good story. I like to tell good stories, and I like to listen to good stories. These women – these First Ladies – are full of amazing stories. Stories, I feel, not many people have ever heard. That alone intrigued me. I was curious and wanted to know more about these women. More than "her husband was…" or "when she was First Lady she…" I wanted to get to know the women behind the title. This project and this series did just that.

Women have been part of America's history from the very beginning, and they are relatively under-documented and under-credited regarding their contributions. Women have long risen to the challenges before them, often without a vote or public say in matters that directly affected them. In fact, they have experienced many triumphs including legal and social victories as a direct result of their hard work and efforts. Yet, history still files many of their achievements and contributions in the back of storage facilities and bottoms of closets. I wanted to lift the dust cloths and empty out the historical closets. These First Ladies were, and continue to be, an example of how each of us – man, woman and child – can be unusual for our time and make the world around us a better place.

What we typically know best about each of these women (if we know anything at all in some cases) is what they accomplished during their time in the White House as First Lady. Serving as First Lady put each of these women directly into the public eye, and on the world stage, but before they served as First Lady, they were women. They were daughters, sisters, teenagers, cousins, young women, students, successful working women, wives and mothers, and later, after leaving the White House, they went on to be ambassadors, grandmothers, widows, and countless other great things. These are the women I wanted to get to know. Theirs were the personal stories I wanted to tell.

I have been in the room where Edith Wilson was born, and the room where

Lucy Hayes died. I've seen the cradles in which First Ladies have rocked their children to sleep, and the sewing machines used to mend their husband's military uniforms. I have been in the room where Martha Washington said goodbye to her husband, our first President, George Washington. I have stood at the bedside in the room where Dolley Madison nursed her ailing husband, President James Madison, and helped him transcribe the notes of the very first Continental Congress during his dying days.

I have seen Lady Bird Johnson's swimsuits hanging in her walk-in closet at the LBJ ranch outside of Austin, Texas. In Marion, Ohio I saw a lucky four-leaf clover charm given to Florence Harding by a war veteran. It is still in the jewelry box given to her by her father. I have seen Harriet Lane's music book; it still sits on the piano in her presidential uncle's parlor at Wheatland, the James Buchanan House, in Lancaster, Pennsylvania.

I have held earrings woven from Elizabeth Monroe's hair. I have held a letter that Martha Washington wrote to Abigail Adams wishing Mrs. Adams well in her new role as the wife of the second President of the Unites States, John Adams. I have climbed back staircases to private sitting rooms and special places where some of these women chose to be alone with their thoughts.

I have examined Lou Hoover's unique and vast weapons collection in West Branch, Iowa. I have ventured out to the Roosevelt's Pine Knot cabin in Keene, Virginia. I have gone down into the Adams crypt beneath the United First Parish Church in Quincy, Massachusetts, and I have stood on the steps of the Plains United Methodist Church in Plains, Georgia where a young Jimmy Carter asked a teenage Rosalynn Smith out on their first date.

I have learned about gifts of state that First Ladies receive. I have seen gifts from foreign lands, and those more personal gifts from their presidential spouses. I learned that even as frugal as President Calvin Coolidge was, he spared no expense when it came to his wife Grace's wardrobe. I learned that Mary Todd had a rather happy childhood with rare access to her influential father and his political discussions in the family home in Lexington, Kentucky. I have stood in the window where Julia Dent watched a young Ulysses S. Grant walk up to her parent's White Haven plantation house to ask for her hand in marriage.

I have interviewed Harrison Tyler, the living Grandson of President James

Tyler – the tenth President of the Unites States (It's true – I've done the math and traced the history). He lives in his grandparent's Sherwood Forest Estate in Charles City, Virginia. Clifton Truman Daniel gave me a private tour of his grandparent's home (President and Mrs. Truman) in Independence, Missouri where he spent a significant amount of time as a boy. Due to a clumsy television crew, including a nearly disastrous incident involving an elbow and a teacup, my C-SPAN camera was the first allowed in the home in over 30 years. I have seen Mamie Eisenhower's extensive wardrobe, including her shoe and hat collection. Each pair of shoes had a label in them stating that the shoes were made exclusively for First Lady Mamie Eisenhower.

I have been in the private parlors, sitting rooms and libraries, each of which hold personal and professional writings of these women as well as their Presidential husbands. I read letters that I probably wasn't supposed to read. I read letters that no one but the intended was probably supposed to read. I have seen private journals and photo albums of these women and their families showing some of the most private moments in a person's life.

I have walked the hallways of privately owned homes, glided my hands along the handrails and physically followed the footsteps of American History. These are the stories that I wish to share with you. I want you to get to know these First Ladies as well as I have. I want their stories to be told.

I was so very fortunate to have been given an all access, backstage, VIP pass to many of the nation's most treasured collections and historical landmarks. There were very few doors that were closed to me, and even fewer vaults that remained locked. This is not something I took lightly or for granted. I feel a great responsibility to use this access to share the most complete and accurate account of these women and their amazing lives as possible.

Traveling to the many places, seeing all the wonderful collections and getting this unrestricted look at the lives of these women, I could not help but feel a personal connection to all of the First Ladies. I think it's impossible to see and read so much about a person's life and not feel close to them.

When I was hired by C-SPAN as a contracted producer and began my work, I was handed a large red book, about the size of an 80's phone book – it became one of my main resources for historical and locational information about these women. I was told to start reading, outlining and planning, because I would most likely start traveling within a month.

I knew right away that this series was going to be a massive project. I knew that it was going to be important. I didn't know what my exact role was going to be. I had no idea how quickly or how much I was going to have to learn about these women. But maybe most significantly, I had no clue how much I was going to enjoy the subject matter and retain so much of the information and my subsequent research.

What I also didn't know – what none of us on the show knew, I don't think – was that I wasn't going to stop traveling for over a year. And that at the end of the journey, we would be responsible for collecting one of the largest and most comprehensive collections of video, interviews, b-roll (supplemental footage of places and things to use over voices, interviews and narrations) and information on the collective group of American First Ladies that exists in the world today.

The research, planning and studying for this project was so intense, it almost didn't leave me time to think about the big picture or long term implications of the work. It wasn't until people started to tell me – friends, family, strangers I met along the way – how interested in this project they were, that I started to realize its scope.

Looking back, I think I didn't have time to grasp the over all end game, because I was too caught up understanding the material or the woman or the trip that was right in front of me during whatever day, week, show or month I was involved in at that exact moment. I couldn't see the forest for the trees. At its most hectic, my schedule was:

Mon.....edit location pieces and research – live show – guest relations/booking

Tues.....travel and shoot for upcoming shows

Wed.....travel and shoot for upcoming shows

Thurs.....travel – edit – book guests – research next trip/lady

Fri.....edit – book guests – research next trip/lady

Sat/Sun.....more editing and research

REPEAT

This was a pretty consistent schedule for the entire series. It was like that for six weeks straight during the summer of 2013 between seasons 1 & 2 of "FIRST LADIES: Influence and Image". At one point, I was sitting in a hotel room in Plains, Georgia having just shot material for the Rosalynn Carter show, while I was watching the Pat Nixon show live on TV. At a certain point during season 2, gate attendants and TSA agents began to recognize me – and my gear – at Baltimore Washington International Airport.

There were many challenges to my work. I was traveling to places that I had never been to before. At each location I had to work with new people that I had never met face to face. I had to carry and set up all of my gear (video, audio and lighting), scout the location based on information from a phone call or two, maybe a few e-mails, interview experts and historians, film interviews, tour houses and museums, shoot b-roll and scenery as well as any other material that might come in handy for the show. All of this in an eight-hour (or often more) work day. This would be challenging for a crew of five or more. I was a crew of one.

I have to acknowledge the people I met along the way, who have been helpful in gathering information and footage of related locations. Without them, their knowledge and collections, the series and this book would not have been possible. There is a very unique and hard working group of people out there preserving our nation's history. We should be grateful for them, and take full advantage of the work they are doing. We should strive to teach it to our younger generations, and not to leave a single stone unturned as we seek additional information. We should be relentless in our desire to discover new things about historical subject matter, even that which we think has been fully researched. There is almost always more to the story.

People always notice you when you travel with a camera. So, as I went around the country to all of these locations, historical sites, museums, homes and libraries I attracted a lot of attention. I had people come up to me and ask me things like "What are you doing?", "Who do you work for?" and "What show will this be on?" My answer was usually the same or similar. I said that I was "working on a show about the First Ladies". The response was almost always the same – "which one(s)?" And I would say, "all of them!" Invariably, this would prompt a follow up like "Well, sure…but no…which one specifically are you focusing on?" And to this my answer was always the same. "EVERY ONE.

MARTHA TO MICHELLE." The more people were amazed by the thought of this, the more I began to understand that there was something bigger than I realized going on with this project. There was a hunger for this material, and a broad desire to know more about these women.

Another interesting and frequent occurrence was running into people with direct or indirect ties to the First Ladies. A woman came up to me in the gardens of Monticello while I was there researching and filming for the Jefferson women. In our conversation, she told me that her mother had worked for Lady Bird Johnson. While I was filming for the Hoover show, a man in West Branch, Iowa told me about land his family owned that was once owned by President and Mrs. Garfield. In Virginia, I crossed paths multiple times with a couple tracing their family heritage. We spent the better half of a week trading stories about what each of us had learned at a number of locations.

I would also run into colleagues and other TV folks both at home in Washington, D.C. and on the road. When TV people see other TV people they know – there's an unspoken word or look – or the dead giveaway, PortaBrace camera cases and gear bags. We would talk about projects: current, past or future. When they heard what I was doing for the series, the timeframe in which I was doing it, and the fact that I was traveling by myself with no local hired crews, assistance, or built in extra days for site surveys or scouting – they all had similar reactions, they'd say "you're nuts!"

While researching and filming the series, I found myself in a lot of airports, train stations, rental car offices, lounges, restaurants, hotels, bars and cabs. The more I talked to people, the more I was convinced there was interest and excitement about this information. There was a thirst for knowledge about these women that further fascinated me. In most conversations I had, people would bring up the subject of me writing a book or keeping a journal or starting a blog or travelogue. To this I would say I was flattered in their interest and that those were all great suggestions that I would maybe get to down the road, but for the time being, I had my hands full with the television series.

I remember during season 2, being on a plane to Kansas City sitting across from a very nice woman who noticed my odd shaped camera bag as I stowed it above my seat. She asked if it was a dog carrier. You would actually be surprised the number of people who thought my camera bag was a dog. I laughed and told her that A) my dog wouldn't fit in such a small carrier and B) even if he did, I wouldn't put him in overhead storage. We both laughed, and then I explained that it was a video camera. Her reaction was similar to the reactions I described earlier: "What show? What's it about? Who do you work for?"

So, I told her about the C-SPAN project and my role. She took an immediate interest. We talked the entire flight. (Apologies to anyone around us on that flight who may have been trying to sleep or had no interest in the First Ladies). Throughout our discussion, I suggested she could – and should – stop me anytime the conversation got dry or she'd had enough. She never stopped me. Then the plane landed. We chatted all the way up to the baggage claim where she was meeting her estranged half brother for some family business surrounding a sick relative. We exchanged information, because she said she wanted to watch the series and read my book, if I ever wrote one. I hope she's reading this now, and recognizes herself here.

She was one of many significant encounters I had during my travels, leading me to further believe that there was an audience out there for these First Ladies and me, beyond the C-SPAN series. Every trip I took I would find myself sitting on a plane or train, in a bar or hotel, standing in line to pay for a soda at a convenience store, talking to someone about the series, and the reaction was usually the same. First, they seemed very interested in the project, and second they wanted to know when I would be writing a book.

Right about the time I started working on season two of the series, it hit me. All this time, I'd been talking to people all across America about the series and my work. They showed interest in what I had to say and the untold stories of these women. It dawned on me that their stories should be told beyond what we captured in the series. Besides, the information had implanted itself so deeply in my brain; I had no other choice but to continue talking about them, telling their stories.

So, I started to put together a speaking program and began writing my first speech. At first, the plan was to introduce the C-SPAN series and myself. Then, I would talk about Martha Washington because…well, you just have to, she was the first First Lady. After that, I would explain what the series had done for the field of study, and what the journey had done for me, personally. I would then talk about and discuss every first lady from Martha to Michelle. Then, I did the math. That speech would end up being over four hours long. I have no doubt that I could speak to a crowd for over four hours and not run out of things to say, however, I would never put an audience through such an ordeal. After some re-thinking and a few edits, the speaking program now comes in just under an hour (not counting the question and answer portion at the end).

That's when I started to consider a book. A book? A book could be as long or as short as I wanted. A book could – and should – cover every First Lady, all of the related locations I'd scouted, and any and all of my adventures along the way. A book could be that initial speech I wanted to write. It could be a travel guide, with things like "where to eat when you're in Abilene, Kansas." It could be written in first person. It could be informative, a narrative, a collection of short stories, even a textbook! It could be informal; it could be anything I wanted it to be.

Author's Note – Unusual For Their Time

The title and phrase "UNUSUAL FOR THEIR TIME" started out as something I was told about the women I was studying at most of the places I visited. One First Lady was unusual for her time, because she was highly educated or well read – another, because she triumphed over great loss or adversity – and, yet another, because of her musical ability or tastes or a European adventure as a young woman. These women and the people who studied them and kept their collections were all amazing people. But, I started thinking, all of these women can't be unusual if they all are so similar, and have so much in common. Could they be? Of course the people at each location thought their First Lady was something special, that's their job. And they all were and are special, of course. But how were they so unusual for their time? It was said so many times that when I came back to DC, I would say to my colleagues, "You're not gonna believe this...BUT...First Lady X, Y or Z was UNUSUAL FOR HER TIME!" Then my co-workers began to ask me, "Hey, man is so and so UNUSUAL FOR HER TIME?" We even had an "olde tyme" voice that we used for the phrase that also required the person saying it to hook their thumbs into their armpits and rock back and forth on their feet in simulated pontification. The bit was always met with good natured laughter. But then, I started to think. These women weren't necessarily unusual when you put them in a group together as First Ladies. They were all relatively similar in their accomplishments. That's why they were First Ladies. Their uniqueness came when compared to other women of their time (which, I know, was what the historians and curators meant all along). Other men of their time. Heck, they were unusual when compared to just about anyone; man, woman or child – and in many cases this uniqueness spans decades, lifetimes and centuries. These women were indeed, UNUSUAL FOR THEIR TIME. The phrase took on a whole new meaning, and now is the title of this book.

Which brings us here. This is the travelogue of my adventures; the sharing of the information I gathered during my contributions as a producer for the C-SPAN series "FIRST LADIES: Influence and Image". It is a recalling of my journey, which lasted from October 2012 through February 2014, as experienced, documented and chronicled by me. P. Andrew Och. THE FIRST LADIES MAN. Enjoy.

The chapters in this book go in chronological order of First Ladies – there have been more First Ladies and Hostesses than there have been Presidents – therefore the chapter number does not alway coincide with the related President's number in Presidential order and history.

CHAPTER 1
Martha Washington

New Kent County, Virginia – Williamsburg, Virginia – Valley Forge, Pennsylvania – Philadelphia, Pennsylvania – Mount Vernon, Virginia

*M*artha Washington was born Martha Dandridge on June 2, 1731 on her family's Chestnut grove plantation in New Kent County, Virginia. Her parents were John Dandridge and Frances Jones Dandridge. Martha and George Washington were married on January 6, 1759. They had no children together. Martha had four children with her first husband, Daniel Parke Custis. Martha Washington died in Mount Vernon, Virginia on May 22, 1802 at the age of 71.

NEW KENT COUNTY, VIRGINIA

Martha Dandridge Custis Washington and her first husband, Daniel Parke Custis, lived in New Kent County, Virginia on what was known as the White House Plantation. So, perhaps it's fitting that she should end up marrying a second time, to a man who would become the first President of the United States of America. And even though title "FIRST LADY" wasn't coined until after her death, but Martha Washington is considered to be the first First Lady of the United States of America.

Side Note – Build It, They Will Come

The actual White House wasn't built nor was Washington, D.C. the Nation's capital until the Adams Administration.

The Custis family owned the White House Plantation, and while it no longer exists, New Kent County, Virginia does. It was a clear and chilly November morning on the day I drove into New Kent County. The low, rolling hills were frequent as I drove the winding roads. The trees were stripped bare by fall, and there was a distinct smell of water in the air from the local creeks and rivers.

I pulled over to the side of the road and assembled my camera and tripod. With no house or specific location to shoot, this would have to do. We needed some kind of visual to characterize the childhood of the first First Lady.

As I stood there in the middle of a field, waiting to hear someone shouting from a distant farmhouse, "GET OFF MY LAND!" I pictured a young Martha Dandridge growing up and spending her childhood here. We see Martha today in paintings like her official portrait – older, heavy set, grandmotherly – in her bonnet and apron. But, what was she like as a little girl? Where did she run and play? What did her house and room look like?

Looking at these fields and creeks and farms and waterways took on new meaning. An image of a young girl and her friends laughing and playing came to mind. Maybe she was sitting on a rock by a creek in the sun learning how to read or splashing in the water? Maybe she was wandering through the fields and woods? Maybe she was sitting on the front porch of her parent's house, as she liked to do later in life on the promenade of Mount Vernon?

As my camera rolled and I panned and zoomed, this was the scene that played out in my mind when suddenly, a crow cawed overhead and a tractor trailer roared by, bringing me back to modern times. This would be the footage we would use to set the scene for the discussion of Martha's childhood.

Martha was definitely better educated than most young women of her day. Being home schooled by her mother definitely put her at an advantage later in life, however, it wasn't initially enough to impress her first husband's father when the two met in Williamsburg, Virginia. There was more to look at and less left to the imagination about Martha Washington in Williamsburg than there had been in New Kent County.

WILLIAMSBURG, VIRGINIA

Duke of Gloucester Street was bustling with holiday shoppers and tourists when I visited, the day before Thanksgiving. In fact, it was a race to beat the workers installing all of the Christmas decorations around town. I needed to keep the decorations out of my footage to preserve the shelf life of the show, and not have it tied to any specific day, time or season. This was just another added challenge to my daily list of obstacles.

The day started off by conducting sit down interviews with "Martha" and the lead historian for Colonial Williamsburg, Dr. Taylor Stoermer. My hosts had arranged for a small, recreated house to be the set for the interviews. The house had electricity, heat, plenty of space and a bathroom. This would not be the case at many locations during my journey.

The woman who reenacted Martha for visitors was Lee Ann Rose. During my conversation with her, I was amazed by a story that she told about a young Martha Dandridge's conversation with her future Father-in-Law. George Washington was not Martha's first husband. She was first married to, and widowed by Daniel Parke Custis. And, it would seem that Martha was not of the same social standing as the Custis family and John Custis did not approve of his son marrying Martha.

A closed-door meeting between Custis's father, John, and young Martha Dandridge was arranged. Custis went into the meeting with every intention of denying Martha permission to marry his son. When the meeting was over, Custis was said to have completely changed his mind saying something to the effect that he could see his son marrying no one other than Martha Dandridge. No one knows exactly what was said in the meeting, but clearly Martha had the wit and wherewithal to impress John Custis enough that he consented to the marriage.

This is so important in the life of Martha Washington, and so crucial to the story of America, because it is her marriage to Custis, and the wealth she inherited from him, that elevated Martha into a social position that would later become very appealing to a young military man named George, who was, not only looking for a bride, but also, to improve his social standing. Just think if Martha had never married Daniel Custis (which was extremely close to happening), she would have never met and married George Washington. The ripple effect on what we now know as the United States of America is almost unimaginable.

Custis's untimely death left Martha a widow in her early twenties, a mother of two (Martha and Daniel had four children, two died in childhood), and extremely wealthy. Upon her first husband's death, Martha found herself in charge of over 8,000 acres of profitable tobacco fields, the owner of very valuable real estate in Williamsburg and the surrounding area, and in possession of more than three times the Virginia Governor's salary in silver. She had the silver on hand, in the house. Also, contrary to our common perception of Martha based on her portraits as an older woman, recent DNA reconstructive computer imaging shows that Martha, in her early 20's, had been quite attractive. In short, she was young, rich, attractive and one of Williamsburg's most desirable bachelorettes.

Dr. Taylor Stoermer, Williamsburg's leading historian at the time, was the next interview. He was so knowledgeable about not only Martha Washington, but also Martha Jefferson, Martha Jefferson Randolph and Letitia Tyler that he will appear in future chapters of this book as well.

It was Taylor who really brought into perspective the pre-Washington life of Martha Custis for me. Martha's marriage to Custis produced two surviving children who later gave her two grandchildren. These grandchildren would be raised by George and Martha Washington as their own; neither child of Martha and Daniel Custis lived beyond early adulthood. Martha's first marriage produced something else that would endure. Wealth.

Production Note – Live Guest

Dr. Stoermer was also a two time live guest on the series, appearing on the Letitia Tyler and Frances Cleveland episodes.

When Daniel Parke Custis died, Martha became a widow at the age of 26. This left her with land, money, and property in excess, which was especially rare for a woman of her age in the 1700's. One of the first things she did was to contact the principal tobacco purchaser in England. She let him know of Custis's death, and more importantly, she informed the purchaser that she intended to continue growing and shipping tobacco to him at the same price, with the same deal, that he'd had with her husband. This is an important part of the story. Society was not set up for women to be business owners and land operators. Women were not legally allowed to own land. A mother could oversee and take care of land and financial inheritance, but only to keep it intact for their sons or to provide for their families. Many women of the day did not succeed in doing so. Not only did Martha succeed, she thrived.

It would seem Martha had everything. Everything that is, but a husband and a father for her children. Enter George Washington.

George Washington was a young, up and coming military man. He was tall and good-looking, a perfect match for the young and attractive Martha. As the story goes, Martha wasn't terribly interested in George at first. It was his attention to her children that attracted her to him. They began a courtship, and the rest – as they say – is history. So, this is why I say consider what might have happened had Martha NOT married George.

She is the one that brought the social status and significant wealth to the relationship. She is the one that had the tobacco fields and real estate in Williamsburg. She had her financial affairs in order, not that George was a financial wreck, nor was he lazy, however, if Martha had not had her affairs well in order at the beginning of their relationship, George might not have found himself in the enviable position as Martha's husband. George would've had to become a more productive tobacco grower and acquire higher social standing on his own merits. What I'm trying to say is, George Washington married up by taking Martha Custis as a bride. This made it logistically possible for him to initiate and command a revolution that would form a new country.

Historical Note – Custis Graves

You can visit the gravesites of Daniel Parke Custis as well as their children, in Williamsburg. Visitors can trace the lives of the people connected to her first marriage that really launched Martha into the high social circle of Williamsburg and its budding new surrounding territories.

VALLEY FORGE, PENNSYLVANIA

Author and Historian Nancy Loane taught me a very valuable lesson within our first 2 minutes together at Valley Forge. DON'T BELIEVE EVERYTHING YOU READ.

Martha Washington – at great personal risk to her life and safety – came to stay with General George Washington at nearly every winter encampment during the Revolutionary War. Most famously, she stayed at the house in Valley Forge, Pennsylvania. It took Martha 10 days to travel from Mount Vernon in Northern Virginia to Valley Forge. This is a testament to the love George and Martha had for each other, and the need for Washington to have his wife by his side. By all accounts, Martha and George were a love match. She was his closest consult and kept him focused and on task.

I arrived early for our interview to get some footage of Washington's Headquarters and the surrounding area. It was a very cold and windy day in January. I remember I was bundled up in my new wool peacoat thinking how cold I was in my Thinsulate™ lined jacket, wool hat, leather gloves, proper shoes and wool socks (with no holes in them). How in the world did the soldiers of the Revolutionary War do it? Sure, it was cold when I was there, but there wasn't even snow on the ground.

Now for Nancy's history lesson about not believing everything you read. I was very much looking forward to hearing the stories of Martha Washington mending uniforms, tending to the wounds and sicknesses of young soldiers and doing her part for the cause during the war. And that's exactly what I asked Nancy about. Her response took me by surprise. She smiled. She even chuckled. She said something like, "please tell me you don't think that's what happened here". She went on to explain that Martha Washington was the wife of the man that led the revolution against Great Britain. She was not out on the battlefield mopping bloody brows and stitching up flesh wounds. Nor was she sitting by the campfire with needle and thread darning the socks and patching the worn elbows of soldiers' jackets.

The "romaticization" of history has become fairly common in modern day story telling. Nancy told me in very precise words how the story of a nurse's letter made its way through family members and the ages into the hands of an all-too-eager-to-believe person who later authored a fantastical telling of Martha's activities at Valley Forge. Only none of these activities were based in truth. In fact, the dates on the letters were so off that it could only be made up. This is what has been ingrained into public opinion, however historically inaccurate.

I said, "Fair enough. What did she do here?" Nancy knew and she told me.

Martha Washington was very busy at Valley Forge and at all of the winter encampments she visited. Her travels from Mount Vernon, just to get to her husband's side, were difficult in and of themselves. Surely she would need time to recover from the journey each time, and to get things in order in camp and prepare for her time there.

At these encampments, she did what any proper lady of the house, farm, estate or plantation would do. She ran the house and entertained guests. She was the lady of Valley Forge just as she was the lady of Mount Vernon. There were meals and events to run and daily tasks and preparations to tend to, to make sure camp ran as smoothly as possible.

While at Valley Forge, Martha threw elegant dinner parties for visiting

Generals, other military officials, and foreign dignitaries. When I think of Valley Forge the word elegant does not come to mind, but the primary documentation supports it. To support these events, a log hut – that no longer exists – was built off of the kitchen for these dinner parties which Martha said, "made our conditions much more tolerable than they were at first".

She talked with and entertained visitors. Martha went to several worship services there at camp. She once held a celebration of the French alliance on May 6th; over a thousand people were in attendance. We know from written records that the food stock and consumption was something quite different than what the soldiers were eating. During the six-month winter encampment, Martha brought in 2,000 eggs, 750 pounds of butter, at least 1,600 pounds of veal. She commissioned paintings of General Washington and arranged for theatrical performances, including General Washington's favorite play (Addison's 1713 tragedy, *Cato*), to be performed on his birthday.

And as surely as Martha Washington was running the encampment and hosting, she was foremost there as a wife to General Washington. Visitors from Philadelphia were frequent. They had friends and important figures come and stay with them at camp. The British were occupying Philadelphia at the time, and there was always news from the city described to Martha in detail during conversations with female friends who would've brought the latest news.

An original banister exists in Washington's Headquarters at Valley Forge. This was the first time during my travels that I got to run my hand along a piece of furniture, a piece of history that also knew the hand of a significant historical figure. It would not be the last. This trip also taught me to look for accuracy in the romanticized versions, stories and legends. Some would end up being true, as you will read about later. But others, like Martha's supposed activities at Valley Forge, needed to be set right in my work and the C-SPAN series.

PHILADELPHIA, PENNSYLVANIA

The second executive mansion of the President of the United States can be seen though Plexiglas viewing panels in the ground at Independence Park in Philadelphia, Pennsylvania. Martha Washington was the first First Lady. There was no one before her. This entire country was new and so were the roles of its leaders. It's here, in Philadelphia, where Martha developed the role of the wife of the President. At this point and time, she wasn't even called the First Lady. She was referred to as Lady Washington or the President's wife.

As the new country began to take shape and people and places were defined, it's here, at the executive mansion, that Martha and the President would host weekly State dinners on Thursdays. On Friday evenings, Martha organized and held Drawing Room receptions. These weekly Drawing Room Receptions were open to the public and anyone of social standing was welcome to attend. It's here in Philadelphia at these more informal Drawing Room Receptions that we again see evidence of Martha and George's relationship. People would often write or remark that President Washington was always more at ease with Martha by his side.

The story of slavery in the President's home is covered at Independence Park. There were as many as 30 paid, indentured and enslaved people serving in the mansion. One story of particular interest is that of Oney Judge, a female slave and personal maid who had come with Martha from Mount Vernon. Oney ran away to gain her freedom, which upset Martha greatly. It is thought that Oney escaped to avoid being given to Martha's granddaughter once she married. Reports tell that Oney liked working for Mrs. Washington, but was not looking forward to becoming the granddaughter's property. Although not a pleasant part of our history or aspect of some of our founding father's lives, it is necessary and well told in Philadelphia.

Author's Note – Happy Birthday, Jim

It was so good to spend the evening just outside Philly with my good friend Jim Deorio on his birthday. This was the first time I had met his son Jimmy. We ate pizza, had cake and played with Batman action figures. You have to take these opportunities to visit with friends and family when work travel allows.

MOUNT VERNON, VIRGINIA

Mount Vernon is the most visited house and home in the United States. It is rarely closed and the visitor always comes first. So much so, that I was only permitted access before they opened to the public. I loaded up my gear and headed out before the sun came up. My hosts there were very gracious to open the house to me, providing me with a behind-the-scenes look at one of the most well known homes in the world. The Washingtons didn't spend much time together here at Mount Vernon. George was often off on a battlefield or living as the President in New York or Philadelphia. So, even though the property itself belonged to George's family's, to me it seemed as though Martha's story is better told here.

Mount Vernon Curator, Susan Schoelwer, knows a great deal about the life and times of Martha Washington at Mount Vernon and the collection of artifacts at the facility. Martha arrived at Mount Vernon in April of 1759, and there was much to do as she brought 12 house slaves with her from Williamsburg to help manage and run the household. She had the financial resources and managerial skills necessary to oversee the estate, much of which, as I mentioned previously, were gained and developed in Williamsburg. Again, Martha's unique abilities enabled President Washington to carry on with his missions away from home for long periods of time. Schoelwer describes Martha as a "take charge woman" a phrase gleaned from the existing letters, research and what we know about Martha's time at Mount Vernon.

Author's Note – Graceland

The second most visited home in the U.S. is Elvis's Graceland in Memphis, Tennessee and I have been there, too – TWICE.

Martha enjoyed gardens and gardening. She liked to grow vegetables and flowers. She had both gardens off of the kitchen and could easily walk right out to see and choose fresh flowers to be cut for the house or vegetables for any of the daily meals. Mount Vernon was a big operation. It was the center of her life and she was in charge of running the show.

Martha outlived George by less than three years. It was amazing to see the couple's bedroom in such quiet privacy. This was one of the most humanizing moments of the series for me. It is well known that Martha would take daily morning meditations in this room while she and George were living there together. She would sit at her desk surrounded by paintings, etchings, and images of her family. She read her bible, wrote letters or just sat in her chair by the fireplace to quietly think. While Martha took this time to herself, George was be down on the main level, in his office.

We have images of George and Martha Washington. They are old, white haired, powdered wig and wooden toothed grandparent-like figures that do not possess any sense of normalcy or regular life. George may be sitting on a white horse with a sword in his hand, and Martha is usually wearing a bonnet and an apron. At least that's how they appear in my mind.

However, now I imagined a real couple. They were husband and wife. They were parents. They lived together in a house going about their daily routine in the most normal of ways. It was an instant realization and acknowledgement that all of these First Ladies, had similar stories, and I would have an unbridled glimpse into that part of their world. I was sure that the whole story wouldn't just be of their time in the White House as First Lady. Make no mistake, of course that was an important part of their story, no doubt; they did amazing things during that time in their lives. It's why we want to learn about them. But before they were First Ladies, they were the actual people. They were the women. They were the young women that would become the ladies that would marry Presidents.

SUMMARY

What I take away from my travels and research for Martha Washington is that she set the tone. She had to. She was the first. Her traits, characteristics, intelligence, influence and image set the standard against which all who would follow would be judged. Martha Washington was unusual for her time.

She was smarter and better educated than most women of her day. She married a man in a higher social bracket than herself – a man whose father was initially against the union until he met her and she changed his mind. She was widowed at a very early age. She lost two of her four children very early, and the other two in young adulthood. She picked up after her first husband's death and learned how to run and manage the family properties, businesses and fortune.

She then re-married and improved the financial and social standing of her new husband, who later organized and choreographed a revolution, and became the first President of the United States of America. She ran his house and businesses in his absence during times of war and politics. To say that this woman was unusual for her time may be the greatest understatement of this book. This part of my journey taught me not only to not believe everything I read, but also to look for the truth and the facts that tell the stories of our country's history.

The most important thing this first First Lady taught me was that without her, there would be no book to write. There could be no history for a country that doesn't exist. This is a distinct possibility if Martha and George Washington had never gotten married. And quite possibly most amazing of all, is the fact that had young Martha Dandridge not impressed Daniel Parke Custis's father, she would not have been in a position to meet young George Washington. If none of this had happened, the rest (of us) might NOT have been history.

Travelogue Food Tip

Eat at The Cheese Shop on Duke of Gloucester Street in Williamsburg, VA. Their house dressing and fresh sub rolls make any sandwich something special. The roast beef was excellent. I should add here that any and all of these food tips came from friends, family, co-workers, locals or my own exploration and discovery. I did not receive any free food, endorsements or favors for these recommendations. If you go to these places and say my name, I doubt anyone will throw you out. Nor do I think they will give you anything for free. I am expecting you will just get the same fine food and wonderful treatment that I received. ENJOY!

CHAPTER 2
Abigail Adams

*A*bigail Adams was born Abigail Quincy Smith on November 11, 1744 in Weymouth, Massachusetts. Her parents were Reverend William Smith and Elizabeth Quincy Smith. Abigail and John Adams were married on October 25, 1764. Abigail and John had five children together. Abigail Adams died on October 28, 1818 in Quincy, Massachusetts at the age of 74.

WEYMOUTH, MASSACHUSETTS

The C-SPAN series was called "First Ladies: Influence and Image". Image is relatively easy to show in dresses, paintings, china patterns and artifacts. The big question for me was "how do I show influence?" That question was answered as soon as I got to Massachusetts to study Abigail Adams.

When I landed in Boston, after I picked up my rental car and loaded my gear, the first thing I did was to drive to Weymouth. In the middle of a modern residential neighborhood, bordering the water on a busy, two-lane paved road is the childhood home of Abigail Adams. It has been restored to its original wooden clapboard siding with shuttered windows and a chimney. It's here where a young John Adams would "steal kisses" and call Abigail "Miss Adorable", but we'll get to that when we get to the Massachusetts Historical Society.

The home in Weymouth is small. Quaint. Functional. It was late in the evening when I arrived, and the house was closed. But, it was important to see the structure. It was necessary to see what the humble beginnings of such an amazingly influential woman looked like. It was also very interesting to see such a landmark smack dab in the middle of a fully inhabited community of the 21st Century. It was so much so, getting a good 20 or 30 second stretch of video without a vehicle in it was difficult.

I'm glad I took the time to stop and see the place. The footage made the live show, and it added to the journey. It was just a few of the many footsteps I would take in the lives of the First Ladies during this journey.

QUINCY, MASSACHUSETTS

Quincy, Massachusetts is the "hub" of the Adams family. John Adams was born here. He and Abigail lived and raised their children here, until John headed to Philadelphia to join the first Continental Congress, and their efforts to liberate the Colonies from England. Owned and operated by the National Park Service, the original Adams house still stands in Quincy. Only slightly bigger than Abigail's birth home, the Adams farmhouse is where Mrs. Adams raised and taught five children virtually on her own (Abigail and John had six children total, but their last child, Elizabeth was stillborn in 1777). Two original structures remain on the property and a wonderful story of Abigail's independence is told here.

John Adams was away in Philadelphia during the Revolutionary War, and Abigail was letting Colonial soldiers stay on the land to perform drills and train. A young John Quincy Adams is said to have joined the soldiers marching in the yard. A tenant that lived in the back house wasn't pleased about all the military activity. So, Abigail wrote John a letter about the problem. It would seem that this letter (and others like it) was a polite formality to keep her husband in the loop. By the time Abigail received John's response, she had already dealt with the man, and the soldiers were permitted to stay. It was not unusual for Abigail to see a problem, notify her husband, and solve it before he could weigh in with his suggestions and solutions. Abigail Adams was unusual for her time.

Quincy is also the location of the Adams family home, Peacefield. It was a cold winter day when I toured Peacefield. This wouldn't have been an issue, except I was given special access to certain rooms that required me to take off my shoes. Caroline Keinath, the park ranger who showed me around and did on-camera interviews, took her shoes off, too. This is why you never see her feet in the video pieces from Peacefield during the Abigail Adams episode on C-SPAN. She was in her socks. We both were.

It should come as no surprise that Abigail was the one who secured and negotiated the deal for this property and it was Abigail who hired the architects and builders to lower the main floor to give the home higher ceilings. She said the ceilings were so low in the original structure that women – particularly her daughter-in-law, Louisa Catherine – would have to take their hats off before stepping into the parlor.

Four generations of Adamses lived at Peacefield and additions and reno-vations are numerous, including the addition of a family library. However, the integrity and feel of the individual rooms from the time John and Abigail lived there remain.

Portraits of George and Martha Washington were given prominent places on the parlor wall in the Adams home. Abigail had a deep affection for the first President and First Lady of the United States, and it is easy to see this given the size and placement of the paintings. Many other family portraits are placed sporadically around the room, giving a warm homey feel that you might find in anyone's home.

Of particular interest in their residence is Abigail's private bedroom. This was the room in which she lived alone while her husband was away. The Adamses spent a lot of time separated by great distances throughout their lives. She sat at her desk and wrote to John about the goings on or the seasonal flowers and foliage. When I stood in the room at her desk looking out the window, I got a sense of that longing to be together. However, theirs was a life of service and separation, and they knew and embraced it. Keinath pointed out that Abigail was an early riser (5am), and enjoyed her quiet time alone in this room to plan her day. Mrs. Adams, no matter what her title or status, always contributed to chores and work in the kitchen, as well as running the household and family.

This is also the room where Abigail died. She died before John, and once again the Adamses found themselves separated. John said of Abigail's passing, "if only I could lie down beside her and die, too." John Adams also wrote a letter to family friend Thomas Jefferson, and told him of Abigail's passing saying he had "lost his best friend."

Peacefield was the centerpiece of a family separated. It grounded the Adamses and was a necessary and interesting look into John and Abigail's life together as well as their life apart.

John, Abigail, John Quincy and Louisa Catherine are all buried side by side in the basement level of the United First Parish Church in Quincy. When I was first told about and shown the church, everything seemed fairly true to form. It's a beautiful, old church in the center of town. Inside, the pews and decor are what I would call typical. There are plaster wall sconces of the two Presidents, which I expected to see in some form or another. Then the pastor said we would be going downstairs to see the crypt.

We walked around the pulpit, through a door, down a flight of steps, and down a narrow and dimly lit hallway until we came to a gate on the wall to the left. The ceilings were low and it was quiet. It was just the three of us – the pastor, Ranger Keinath and me. The pastor pointed through the gate and said, "There they are. All four of them."

I looked through the gate. It was a room that seemed as if it was carved out under the sanctuary with granite walls, floor and ceiling. It was only slightly brighter than the hallway, and there were four sarcophagi lined up in a row. The individual tombs were large, plain and appeared to be carved from the same granite as the room. Two had American flags laid across them, and two did not. Embossed on the top, about chest level, were the names of the entombed. Those with flags held the former Presidents, and the two without, their wives. I began to set up my tripod and camera at which point the pastor pulled out a set of keys, unlocked the heavy, iron gate and pulled it open, complete with an audible creak. What happened next was a complete surprise.

He stepped back and extended his arm, as if to say "after you." I was stunned. I asked if he meant for me to go in, and he said something like "yes, of course. By all means." I then asked, "just me?" and he nodded. So, I grabbed my camera and tripod and stepped inside.

The ceiling was even lower on this side of the gate. At 5'10", I felt as though my head was just skimming the ceiling. Right to left the order in which they were buried was John, Abigail, John Quincy and Louisa Catherine. I walked over to the corner closest to Louisa Catherine's feet. I set my camera rig down, and took a moment. This was heavy. The granite looked heavy, the sarcophagi lids looked heavy, the small room felt heavy, it smelled heavy. The air was thick, and I knew that something special and significant was happening in my life. It looked, felt, smelled and sounded…like HISTORY. I wasn't sure what (at this point – so early in the project – the First Ladies Man couldn't have been further from my mind), but I knew something was forming. Something was going on inside my head that has now surfaced and manifested itself into what I'm doing as the First Ladies Man.

Historical Note – First Residents

John and Abigail Adams were the first Presidential couple to live in the White House in Washington, D.C. It wasn't even entirely finished during the Adams Administration. D.C. was not much more than a swamp at the time, and Abigail spent most of her time in Quincy during her husband's time as President.

So, I took my moment. I even silently thanked the Adamses for their contributions to the country and asked for forgiveness for my short intrusion upon their rest. I got the footage I needed and took another moment to look around a place where I might never step again. Like I said, this was impressive. I stepped back out into the hallway and thanked my hosts for the amazing and unexpected access.

BOSTON, MASSACHUSETTS

Being raised in and around Washington, D.C., I am no stranger to American history. I am used to cases with old documents held in rooms with long, high dark wooden shelves. I have walked past many large pillars and through equally large and impressive doors. Having been a television producer in the Nation's capital for a number of years, I am even accustomed to having special access to people, places and things. That being said, nothing could prepare me for this series, and I was even less prepared for the letters and writings that are held in the Adams family collection at the Massachusetts Historical Society ("MHS").

Out of respect for my wonderful hosts there, I cannot divulge where in the building this collection is held, but I can tell you that I walked through many locked, coded and barred doors to get there. Once I was there, I was only permitted to film from certain angles with limited wide shots and room pans. The MHS holds four generations worth of the Adams' family papers, which include over 70,000 pages of material. There is so much there, I could write an entire book – several books even – about this collection alone. In fact, the MHS has written several books on it, and they are all fantastic.

It would seem that the Adamses didn't get the historical memo about burning letters that so many other folks in the 1700's got. The Adamses had something in common with the Trumans (which we'll get to in Volume 2), and my late grandfather. THEY KEPT EVERYTHING. While people like Martha Washington and James Monroe were throwing their letters and journals into the fireplace, for the sake of privacy, the Adamses were boxing theirs for posterity and future generations. Thank goodness they did. It's because of their forethought that we now have an original letter from Martha Washington to Abigail Adams in Martha's own handwriting. I held the letter (in a plastic cover inside of a manila folder), and again, I could FEEL History. It was electric.

I mentioned earlier that Abigail was very fond of the Washingtons. It would seem that once her husband had secured the second Presidency of the Unites States, Abigail wrote Martha a letter. The original pencil draft of this letter is held by the MHS. In the letter, Abigail basically says, "Job well done as the first lady of the land. How did you do it? Do you have any helpful hints?" Martha's response is appreciative, humble and polite. She writes something along the lines of "thank you dear friend…I just kind of figured it out…made it up as I went along…I'm sure you'll find your own way and be great." Obviously, I am modernizing and paraphrasing here, but you get the idea. Bottom line, it was incredible to see such correspondence between the two women and in their own handwriting. This was something I had had no idea existed, let alone that I'd see and hold it for myself.

I was sure that reading these letters and seeing these women's handwriting was going to bring me closer to them. These were windows into their souls and their daily lives. It dawned on me that maybe I wasn't supposed to be reading them. It felt intrusive and suddenly, it seemed as if Martha's idea of burning letters had been a good one. If I only knew what was in store for me down the line, having access to the personal letters Presidential wives…WOW…even as recent as the letters between Nancy and Ronald Reagan – but I'm getting way ahead of myself.

You might think holding a letter from Martha Washington to Abigail Adams would be enough for this trip. But it wasn't. There was more to see and do, and I couldn't wait.

It was here at the Massachusetts Historical Society that I would read an early "mash" letter from a young John to a young Abigail. In this earliest letter in the collection from October 1762, John opens and addresses her as "Miss Adorable". He asks to come calling on her again and "steal kisses". He talks about being an accomplished kisser that has given "two or three millions, at least". He continues to flirt with her asking for "as many hours of [her] company after the hour of 9 o'clock". So, in modern terms, he's saying, "Hey, cutie…I'm a good kisser and I want to make out with you after curfew". I don't know about you all, but this is NOT the John and Abigail I was taught about growing up in school. This was great stuff, and it continued to get better with every letter.

In other letters we learn about Abigail's amazingly progressive views on race equality and civil liberties. She writes – very famously – to "remember the ladies" when her husband is legislating. However, still to come would be the most incredible bit of writing – one that seals for me the fact that, given the time in which she lived, and the circumstances of her world, Abigail Adams will always be one of the most influential women in American history.

Once George Washington made known that he would not seek a third term as President, John Adams, as Vice President, was a natural consideration as a successor. At the time, John wrote Abigail, as he often did, to get her thoughts on the matter. He wrote and asked her what she thought about his political future, and what career path he should follow. This alone in the late 1700's should be a bit of a surprise. I mean think about it, women don't get the right to vote until the 1920's, and continue to struggle for equality today. It is Abigail's response that got my respect and attention.

I am paraphrasing here again, but the gist is that she replied something like, running for President is something your heart has to tell you and you are to figure out with God's guidance. She went on to say, "however, if you are asking about another term as Vice President? On that I will give my opinion. I will serve under no man other than George Washington." So, here we see two things. Once again, we see Abigail's admiration for the Washingtons, but more importantly, we see her direct influence on her husband's political career and their future. She basically told John to come home the President or just come home. This is in the 1700's. Abigail Adams was unusual for her time.

Sara Martin was kind enough to share these letters and read them on camera for me. She did such a great job giving Abigail a voice, even though she was working her way through a "wicked bad" head cold. So, I especially appreciate her knowledge and information.

PHILADELPHIA, PENNSYLVANIA

The President's mansion was originally in New York City. A plaque marks the spot, but no building or even foundation remains. During Washington's first term as President, the Adamses had a brownstone on the Hudson River. When the President's mansion moved to Philadelphia, so did the Adamses. Again, Abigail spends much of her time in Quincy at Peacefield, but she is often in Philadelphia for social gatherings and important functions and dinners.

It's here that Abigail attended State dinners and afternoon teas with Mrs.

Washington and some of Philadelphia's elite and upper class. She was right in the mix of the "Who's Who" in this budding new America, and she saw first hand exactly how Martha Washington did it. So, it's not so much what we learn about Abigail's time as First Lady here, but more so the environment in which she was exposed as the wife of the Vice President.

SUMMARY

Abigail Adams was a visionary. She embodied the morals and values upon which America was founded. She was independent, strong and intelligent. We see this in her writing. We see this in the fact that she raised a family – virtually on her own – during violent times of war and uncertainty. She came from humble beginnings and went on to be the first First Lady to live in the White House in Washington, D.C. She had progressive views about women's roles in the world and the civil liberties of people of all colors of skin. As if that wasn't enough – she showed us in her own words the influence she has over her husband's life and career. She wrote, "I will serve under no man other than George Washington." This was one of the most significant letters I came across during the entire series.

Travelogue Food Tip

Take advantage of being in Boston and head down to the waterfront for a cup of New England Clam Chowder and a lobster at The Barking Crab. It has a really cool waterfront/fish market kind of vibe to it.

CHAPTER 3
Martha Jefferson &
Martha Jefferson Randolph

Washington, D.C. – Williamsburg, Virginia – Charlottesville, Virginia

*M*artha Jefferson was born Martha Wayles on October 19, 1748 in Charles City County, Virginia. Her parents were John Wayles and Martha Eppes Wayles. Martha and Thomas Jefferson were married on January 1, 1772. Martha and Thomas had six children together. Martha Jefferson died on September 6, 1782 in Charlottesville, Virginia at the age of 34.

*M*artha "Patsy" Jefferson Randolph was born Martha Jefferson on September 27, 1772 at Monticello in the province of Virginia, British America. Martha and Thomas Mann Randolph, Jr. were married in 1790. Martha and Thomas had 12 children together. Martha Jefferson Randolph died on October 10, 1836 in Albemarle County, Virginia at the age of 64.

WASHINGTON, D.C.

By the time Thomas Jefferson was elected President, he had been a widower for over 20 years. His administration was said to be a "boys club" and his "common man" approach had his White House often compared to a hunting lodge. Two women served as hostesses during his time as President. One was his oldest daughter Martha "Patsy" Jefferson Randolph, and the other was Dolley Madison. When events were held at the White House, it would usually be Jefferson's daughter Patsy that would fulfill the First Lady duties. By all accounts, Jefferson's daughter was well liked and well received by Washington, D.C.

Dolley's husband James Madison was Jefferson's Secretary of State, and many parties and social gatherings took place in the Madison's D.C. home instead of the White House. This is where Dolley really got her feet firmly planted in politics and the Washington scene.

WILLIAMSBURG, VIRGINIA

Before he was President, Thomas Jefferson did have a wife, and during his time as Virginia State Governor in Williamsburg she was his First Lady. She was said to be intelligent, organized and in all likelihood would have made a wonderful presidential First Lady for her husband.

They lived together with their children in the Governor's mansion right off Duke of Gloucester Street in Williamsburg, VA. Martha Jefferson hosted dinners, balls, and receptions there. She oversaw an entire staff of slaves and servants to run a proper household as would have been customary of the time.

In my travels and in my research, I learned something very interesting about Martha and Thomas Jefferson. When Martha knew she would not live much longer, she told her husband not to remarry. A stepmother had raised Martha. It would seem she and her stepmother did not get along, and it was a very unpleasant experience for young Martha. She did not want the same for her two daughters. This being the case, some of Jefferson's promiscuity and relationships might be explained by this deathbed request of his wife. Whatever the reason, Jefferson never remarried, and kept his daughters close to him throughout his life in the White House and at Monticello. In fact, Pasty Jefferson is the first woman to give birth in the White House. Jefferson's grandson, James Madison Randolph, was born in the White House in 1806.

CHARLOTTESVILLE, VIRGINIA

Monticello is a well-visited and remarkable place. Jefferson's inventions, creativity and expansive mind ran wild there. He always kept his large family close, and it could be said that his estate was his own special universe. As it stands today, his wife Martha would not recognize Monticello, the home she knew and loved. Jefferson constantly changed, built and added on to the property after her death, and for the rest of his life.

Martha's first visit to Monticello was a remarkable one, and makes for a good story. Her first trip to Monticello was for her and Thomas's honeymoon. The only building that stood on the property was a two-room, two-story, brick structure, now referred to as the "Honeymoon Suite". This building is not typically open to the public, but my camera and I were granted access.

Thomas Jefferson married Martha Wayles on January 1 in 1772. He then took his new bride up a slippery, snowy hill in a carriage to the brick building at Monticello. The only furniture in the place was a very nice and well-appointed banister bed that Jefferson had purchased in Williamsburg. Thomas and Martha enjoyed a brief stay there before Martha missed the comforts of her wealthy father's estate and asked to be taken back to Charles City, VA.

My time in the Honeymoon suite was noteworthy. It was one of those places that speak to you from the past. I could image the difficult journey up the snow-covered hill. I could smell the fire in the fireplace, and envision the young couple's excitement during their special time together as newlyweds. I can even imagine Martha getting fed up with the sparse amenities and wanting to go home to more comfortable surroundings. I did not take opportunities like this lightly. These were the special places and moments that I felt responsible for sharing with the outside world.

As far as Martha's time and involvement at Monticello, careful records and bookkeeping show that she was an organized and capable woman. Had she survived her illness, she may have been able to keep Jefferson more on track financially, and he might not have died $70,000 dollars in debt (a fortune in those days and a sizable sum of money, even by today's standards). Her true abilities as a First Lady in the White House can only be speculated upon by minimal evidence from her brief time as Jefferson's wife.

Patsy's time with her father is better documented. The parlor at Monticello is littered with books, games and musical instruments. The Jefferson family enjoyed time here together engaging in various activities to pass the time learning about the world around them. Education and exploration was paramount in Jefferson's life.

The most interesting thing I learned here about Patsy Jefferson was that she spent so much time with her father, that her husband often felt ignored, left out, or inferior. Patsy's husband, Thomas Randolph, was a successful planter and they had their own home in Virginia. However, the Randolphs spent much of their time at Monticello while Patsy was an unofficial hostess for her father even outside of the White House. It's no wonder that this caused problems within her marriage. I mean let's face it, not everyone is Thomas Jefferson, and the shadow he cast across his daughter's life must have left Patsy's husband a bit chilly.

However, Patsy and Thomas did survive her relationship with her father. Thomas Jefferson dies in 1826 and is survived by his daughter, Patsy, as well as Patsy's husband Thomas and many of his grandchildren.

SUMMARY

Martha Jefferson was a very capable woman. She kept a proper house for her husband and her family. It is likely that this would have transferred to her time as First Lady in the White House, but it is impossible to know for sure. Jefferson loved his daughters and their families. He kept them close and was very involved in their lives. Patsy Jefferson was the first woman to serve as an official hostess who was not the wife of the President. She filled this role in what was only the third Presidential administration of the United States of America. She was a confident woman who was blazing a new trail that would be followed by other Presidential family members who, due to the lack of a wife of the President, would fill the official role of hostess. It is also during the Jefferson Administration that we see Dolley Madison begin to shine and show her true grit. Dolley Madison's contributions to the role of First Lady, and to the United

States were incomparable and unprecedented, but we'll get to that in the next chapter. It was an unusual time for a young America, and both Martha Jeffersons were unusual for their time.

Travelogue Food Tip

All college towns have good brewpubs and grub. Charlottesville is no different. For great atmosphere and appetizers, hit the South Street Brewery. I sat at the bar and had a bunch of different appetizers and a Caesar salad. The crowd was fun and the music was great. The place was packed on a week night.

CHAPTER 4
Dolley Madison

Philadelphia, Pennsylvania – Washington, D.C. - Orange, Virginia

*D*olley Madison was born Dolley Payne in Guilford County, North Carolina on May 20, 1768. Her parents were John Payne and Mary Coles Payne. Dolley and James Madison were married on September 15, 1794. Dolley and James Madison had no children together. Dolley had two children with her first husband, John Todd, Jr. Dolley Madison died in Washington, D.C. on July 12, 1849 at the age of 81.

PHILADELPHIA, PENNSYLVANIA

Dolley Madison is the quintessential First Lady's First Lady. She had specific influence in the Jefferson, Madison, Van Buren, Tyler and Polk Administrations. She is reportedly, the first woman to be referred to as a "First Lady" by President Zachary Taylor at her funeral in 1849. However, the Dolley Madison story starts way before she got to Washington, D.C. with her second husband, James

Madison.

Dolley's story starts when she was known as Dolley Todd. She was married to her first husband, John Todd and together, they lived in Philadelphia. Dolley's family came to Philadelphia where her father became a starch merchant in the mid 1780's. They moved up from Virginia after emancipating their slaves (as many Quakers did). Dolley's father's business failed and he died in 1792. Dolley's mother ran a boarding house in Philadelphia. Dolley had three sisters and four brothers. It is in Philadelphia where she met and married John Todd in January 1790. Todd was a successful Quaker lawyer.

This is all very important to the Dolley Madison story because her humble beginnings and her first marriage were a stark contrast to what she became as the wife of James Madison. There is nowhere better to learn about this transformation than in Philadelphia, Pennsylvania at the Dolley Todd House just a few blocks away from Independence Park.

Dolley and John had two boys, John Payne and William Temple Todd. Soon after Dolley and John moved into their house, Dolley's young sister Anna moved in with them to help take care of their children. Dolley was not only the caregiver to these three, but she was also their schoolteacher. This is where the picture I had in my mind of Dolley Madison changed.

Similar to the way we always see Martha Washington as a 70 year old grandma in a bonnet and apron, I always thought of Dolley as a turban wearing D.C. socialite throwing the party of the century in the White House ballrooms. However, this new image – this new Dolley – was something quite different. This was a humble, quiet, motherly, schoolmarm who was also the wife of a prominent Quaker lawyer.

Looking at the kitchen of the Todd House, I imagined Dolley and her sister cooking meals or walking through the dining room and pictured the table converted into a school desk and workspace for lessons was a very strange experience. It was definitely something I was not prepared for, and would again show me this journey was going to be full of surprises and teach me quite a bit, even after my extensive research and crash course in First Ladies History.

Dolley's husband and son William were two of the more than 5,000 people who died in the Yellow Fever epidemic of 1793. They died in August of that year. Beyond the loss of her husband and child, the next few months were difficult for Dolley. She had trouble with John Todd's brother over the ownership of her late husband's legal library. As a woman in the 1790's she could not own the house or the inheritance. She was only protecting and managing it for her son John Payne Todd until he became of age.

Dolley was young, fairly well off because of her late husband's law profession, and attractive. She got a lot of attention from men on the streets of Philadelphia. This didn't sit well with the Quakers and Dolley was constantly under the watchful eye of the Quaker community. She even had to go to orphan's court to petition to be the guardian of her own son.

Philadelphia was the Nation's capital at this time. So, politicians, Congressmen and Senators were walking the streets, living and going out around town. This also pumped up the bachelor pool considerably. One of those bachelors was Congressman James Madison. Madison was a friend of lawyer, New York politician and eventual Vice President under Thomas Jefferson, Aaron Burr. Burr was a resident at Dolley Todd's mother's boarding house. It would not take long for James Madison and Dolley Todd to meet. It is believed that the two met on the second floor, in the parlor of the Todd house.

At the time, in the Quaker community, it was customary for a widow to mourn the loss of a husband for at least a year before marrying another man. Dolley and James start a courtship less than a year after the death of John Todd, and were married on September 15, 1794. Madison was not a Quaker and that would be the final straw for Dolley and the Quakers. She was dropped from the community in what is called being drummed "out of meeting".

So, from what I saw, heard and learned at the Todd House in Philadelphia, Dolley Todd walked in one door of the house a modest Quaker housewife who taught her children in the family living room and cooked meals for her lawyer husband – and walked out another door on the arm of Congressman James Madison. James Madison became the fourth President of the United States of America, and Dolley Madison became his First Lady. This transformation was represented and described so clearly in Philadelphia that I could almost imagine it happening right before my eyes. In my mind's eye, I saw Dolley Todd walking in the back door in a plain and somewhat dingy house dress and apron and walking out the front door in a ball gown and turban.

This was one of the most remarkable metamorphoses I learned about in all of my travels. Dolley Madison is one of the most accomplished and remembered First Ladies. Dolley Madison wouldn't be Dolley Madison if Philadelphia hadn't happened. The things that occurred in this house changed the course of American History forever, because what came next was Washington, D.C. and First Lady Dolley Madison.

WASHINGTON, D.C.

Dolley has a lot of history in and around D.C. When the Madisons first came to D.C., James was Secretary of State for the Jefferson Administration. They lived in a house on H Street in Northwest. The house is still there, but the only thing to see is a plaque. I did go by and see it, and shot some footage for the series. Dolley is known for her parties and hostessing skills. So, it's interesting to know the location and see the structure where she threw so many parties during her husband's time in the Jefferson Administration. It's also interesting to think about being born and raised around Washington, D.C. and how many times I have passed that house and had no idea its history.

DUMBARTON HOUSE

The two most significant locations related to Dolley Madison (other than the White House) in Washington, D.C. are the Dumbarton House and the Octagon House. Their stories are related and I visited them both.

Dolley told the story behind these two buildings that starts on August 24, 1814 in a letter to her sister. It was during the War of 1812, and the British were advancing on the White House. James Madison was President and Dolley was First Lady. Mrs. Madison had been instructed to pack her things and vacate the White House. She packed what she could carry, and her belongings were loaded in her carriage. Dolley would not leave the White House until a portrait of George Washington was taken down from the wall and secured. The frame was bolted or screwed to the wall so the painting had to be cut out, broken from the frame and rolled up. It was only after this task had been completed that Dolley made her escape. With her husband in the field, meeting with his Generals, Dolley was whisked away to the Georgetown home of their friend, Charles Carroll, to a place now known as the Dumbarton House.

She waited there for William Jones, the Secretary of the Navy to arrive. He was fleeing the Navy Yard; it had just been burned by British troops. Jones was to collect Mrs. Madison and the Carrolls and get them safely across the Potomac River and into Virginia. It's there, on a farm, where Dolley and President Madison are reunited.

The Carroll's home would go on to become part of the wonderful Dumbarton Oaks Gardens. The home still stands today. Touring the facility, I imagined the First Lady of the United States of America – having just abandoned the White House – waiting for someone to take her across the Potomac River to escape the advancing British troops. It is quite impressive. The second floor is dedicated to telling the story of that harrowing night in 1814. One of the best stories they tell is that Dolley had set the dining room table that night before leaving the White House. She didn't want anyone to think she was a bad hostess or had left in a hurry. When the British troops arrived, it is reported that, they ate dinner, drank wine and toasted Madison's health before burning the White House – nearly to the ground. Which brings us to the next location. The Octagon House.

THE OCTAGON HOUSE

My visit to the Octagon House in Northwest Washington, D.C. was quite informative, and put the puzzle pieces together as to how the Madisons resumed life and business as President and First Lady after they returned to D.C. The Octagon House is two blocks from the White House and a perfect fit for the Madisons as D.C. was rebuilt from the War of 1812. Erica Rioux Gees is the Director there and was kind enough to show me around.

It cannot be mentioned enough times that Dolley Madison loved to entertain. Her passion for conversation and politicking is still virtually unmatched by any other First Lady. She had mastered the art of putting enemies and rivals together in one room – at times, right next to each other. It is obvious just how she accomplished that upon a first step into the Octagon House. The foyer, or receiving area, is a round room. Dolley loved this room because there were no corners. Everyone was equal in this room, as they were introduced, their coats and hats taken and as they prepared for the evening's festivities or meal.

One of the larger rooms on the first floor is where Dolley continued her Wednesday Drawing Rooms, which were later commonly known as "Squeezes" because so many people attended, they had to all try to squeeze into one room for the event. The Octagon was smaller than the White House, but this didn't deter Dolley from entertaining in her typical grand style, nor did it keep her guests from attending these functions.

The dining room was a very important room in the Octagon for Dolley Madison. The country was still at war, and Dolley needed to maintain and show an expected level of decorum for the President and his guests. She oversaw many important dinners with foreign dignitaries; members of Congress and other influential figures who helped put the country back on track in this room.

ORANGE, VIRGINIA

Montpelier is the home of James and Dolley Madison near Orange, VA. It was a vast estate that originally sat on over 4,600 acres owned by Madison's Grandfather. James and Dolley would come to own it and call it home.

After pulling my rental car through the front gates, I drove along the winding road that led to the main drive directly to the Visitor's Center and Mansion. To say it was a long driveway would be an understatement. Let's just say that I wouldn't want to be the one that has to cut this lawn.

I had been invited down on this particular day, because acclaimed Historian; Catherine Allgor was speaking at a luncheon in the Visitor's Center. This was a real treat, because I had the opportunity to interview her in the mansion after her speech. The interview wasn't used in the show, because we ended up having Catherine on as a guest along with Edie Mayo for the Dolley Madison episode. However, what I learned about Dolley from my interview was invaluable, not only for my Dolley research, but also for my continuing adventure.

Sitting down and interviewing an individual with such a wealth of knowledge in Dolley Madison's house – in her parlor – was another one of those enlightening moments in the series that gave me chills. Catherine showed me what it was like to have a passion for these women and their stories. It was a passion that was contagious. Her factual story telling was infectious. Catherine also taught me just what an important woman Dolley was, and how lasting her effect was on the country and the role of First Lady.

The next part of my adventure was a tour of the house led by Lynn Uzzell. Uzzell is a historian and plays the role of Dolley for tours at Montpelier. And who better to show me the house of Dolley Madison than "Dolley" herself. This was a fun shoot, because the dining room was set for a dinner party, and the parlor was just as it would have been if Dolley's were entertaining that very night. We walked out on the front porch, I hit record on my camera and we walked around the house just as if Dolley herself were showing me around the place.

And the tour went a little something like this...

I was shown through the front door and right into the Drawing Room. This room was painted a brilliant red, which was Dolley's favorite color. She had the room painted this way – the same as her "Red Room" in the White House – because she intended to continue her Wednesday Drawing Rooms that had been so popular in D.C. in her post-White House life. Dolley entertained many important people here in this room, including the daughters of Thomas Jefferson who were frequent visitors. Some of her favorite and most frequent guests were family – her sisters, nieces and nephews who often had extended stays at Montpelier.

Once you get past the red walls, the most interesting thing about the room was the items that surrounded me on the walls and tables and shelves. Dolley decorated the room with representation from many important historical eras. A relatively new, but vital American History was represented along with Ancient Greece. A huge painting of Pan and his Nymphs takes up an entire wall next to the fireplace. The beautiful painting was 200 years old when the Madisons purchased it. This mixing of old world and new world history and symbolism was an attempt to place America into the significant societies and happenings of the world. This was the room and the things that guests saw and enjoyed before a proper sit down meal in the dining room. This was the social center of the house.

We then made our way into the dining room. At first glance the dining room was what you would expect it to be. It's a big room elegantly decorated with a long table down the center. However, it's what went on in here and even more importantly how it went on that makes it unusual. Dolley had her own ideas about the seating for meals at Montpelier. Always going against the grain, and

45

mistress of her own events and conversation, she sat at the head of the table, and James sat in the center. This was so Dolley could direct the topics as well as steer conversation, leaving James to comment intimately to the people strategically to his left and right, or more openly to all who were gathered at the table. On any given night the Madisons would serve as many as 20 people during a typical dinner. Many important figures would have dined here with the Madisons including, among others, Thomas Jefferson, James Monroe, General La Fayette, Henry Clay, Andrew Jackson, and the famous Washington writer Margaret Bayard Smith. At one particular dinner, I was told Madison's Vice President, Elbridge Gerry, offered to host the dinner. Mrs. Madison politely declined the offer and said that she could handle the duties "with ease," After the dinner Gerry said it was as though Dolley was born and educated in Versailles.

Side Note – Not A World Traveler

Dolley Madison never traveled outside of the United States. She was said to enjoy the more relaxed atmosphere here at Montpelier to that of Washington, D.C. She said that she was more comfortable serving 100 people at Montpelier than 20 at the White House.

I was then taken into the bedroom on the first floor, which became President James Madison's after he took ill. This room was located right off of the main dining room and is where President Madison would eventually die. It was a small, but comfortable room, duly appointed with a comfortable single bed, a desk and a chair. As Dolley continued to entertain, she would leave the door to James's bedroom open so he could hear the dinner conversation, and to keep up with the latest news. His proximity to the dining room was intentional on the part of Dolley; she had given it careful consideration.

This is the room where Dolley sat with her husband and transcribed the notes that James Madison had taken during the first Continental Congress. These discussions and negotiations that formed the country and government we know today as the United States of America. This amazed me. This was the written story of how our country was formed. A step-by-step instruction book. A *how to start your own new country* manual. For those of you that know the movie "Young Frankenstein", I likened it to Frederick Frankenstein (Gene Wilder) finding his Great Grandfather's book "How I Did It" in his secret laboratory. This effort was intended to help finance Dolley's life after James's death.

The published notes ended up getting her some money, but not nearly what the Madisons had hoped. This was also surprising to me. One would think the notes and backroom discussions of how America was made would be priceless, but not at the time Dolley was trying to sell them.

In any event, this close up look at Montpelier with information provided by the experts made learning about the life of one of the most influential First Ladies of all time both productive and enjoyable. And it wasn't over yet. We then moved on to the Visitor's Center and Museum. Here, I would get a look at a number of artifacts and some amazing recreated dresses that showcased Dolley's flair for fashion.

Among the artifacts in the Museum are Dolley's engagement ring, her family bible, as well as a number of dinner plates and household items. It's always interesting to me to see "regular" every day items that belonged to these women. It's easy to forget they are just people like you and me. They eat, sleep, get married, go to church, read books, play board games and socialize with friends. One of the unique items I saw here was Dolley's snuffbox. We know Dolley was an entertainer and the life of the party, so maybe I shouldn't have been surprised. It just seemed like an unusual item for a former Quaker to have, but she had obviously outgrown that part of her life by the time she got to Montpelier.

One of the more surprising things to me about Montpelier was that excavation and discovery was still in full swing. The folks there had recently discovered that the ice house was under the center piece gazebo. There is reconstruction of the slave quarters going on right now next to the main residence. This showed me that even almost 240 years later, we are still discovering things about our country and her remarkable beginnings. Even for as much as we know about the individuals that started the revolution and birthed this new place called the United States, much is still somewhat unknown. And what this really told me was, if there is so much we don't know about the Presidents, how much is there to learn about their wives? Take it from me the answer is A LOT!

* * *

Historical Note – Jefferson's Walking Stick

Two artifacts that caught my attention at Montpelier didn't have anything to do with Dolley Madison. The items involved a remarkable story about two of our Founding Fathers. When Thomas Jefferson died, he gave James Madison a walking stick. The Jefferson – Madison friendship was a strong one, and has been described as "perfectly balanced". The walking stick was left to Madison in the last Will and Testament of Thomas Jefferson. On display in the museum, was the walking stick and Jefferson's hand written Will. Thomas Jefferson thought very highly of James Madison, and felt their friendship warranted a gift or token of appreciation. It is written clearly in the will that Madison was to receive a gold headed walking stick made of animal horn. At some point over the next couple hundred years, the walking stick's location and existence became unknown.

When I visited Montpelier, the stick had only very recently been discovered. A relative or ancestor of Jefferson or Monroe (I forget which) dug into a closet or an attic, and stumbled upon the piece. They remembered as children it was used as a play sword. The item of affection that had been willed to a former President by another former President, had been passed around and handed down through the years, was used as nothing more than a children's toy with which to play pirates or swashbucklers, and was now on display for all to enjoy. It was so cool to see the walking stick and Jefferson's Will next to each other in the case. The actual walking stick, with Jefferson's Will, combined with the story of how the artifact made its way into the museum's collection made for a very effective exhibit. After hearing this I wanted to go home and dig through my parents' and grandparents' closets, basements and attics

* * *

SUMMARY

To verify so many facts and stories about one of the most well known, influential and beloved First Ladies in American history was quite amazing. To get access to her house, and personal items was genuinely humbling. BUT…to learn something completely new about someone about whom you thought you knew the story? Well, that's where it's at!

My trip to the Dolley Todd house in Philadelphia forever changed the way I looked at Dolley Madison. To be completely honest, I went to Philadelphia for Martha Washington. I was going to get a little bit on Abigail Adams as the wife of the Vice President there, too. And as a little bonus or snippet, I would see a house where Dolley Madison lived when she was young and married to her first husband. It wasn't until I had walked into the back/side door of the house, and gone through it filming and walked out the front door to shoot a conclusion for the piece that I realized what I had just seen.

I remember it very clearly, too. It was just starting to snow, it was cold, I had to drive back to D.C. from Philadelphia, it was almost 5pm and I had been on the road for five days already. The park ranger (The Todd House is owned and operated by the National Park Service) and I had done some good work, and we were trying to wrap things up, but not rush things. We wanted to get it right. And then, right there it dawned on me…Dolley Madison walked in one door one kind of woman, and out another – in the same house – a completely different woman. In one afternoon, I had walked the path that took this woman years to complete – years full of love, heartache, death, rediscovery and eventual reinvention and renewed happiness. I had just traced a story I had no idea I would be tracing and concluded what the ranger agreed was a historical transformation that would change the face of our country forever.

Travelogue Food Tip

I ate my weight a few times over in BBQ during this adventure. While studying Dolley Madison in and around Montpellier I had the pleasure of having dinner at the BBQ Exchange in Gordonsville, VA. There is no finer pulled pork in the land. Thank you, Ben and Jennifer Johnson for the tip, and for joining me. I'm not kidding; this place was so good…I BOUGHT A SHIRT!

CHAPTER 5

Elizabeth Monroe

Fredericksburg, Virginia – Charlottesville, Virginia – Leesburg, Virginia

E lizabeth Monroe was born Elizabeth Kortright on June 30, 1768 in New York, New York. Her parents were Captain Lawrence Kortright and Hannah Aspenwall Kortright. Elizabeth married James Monroe on February 16, 1786. Elizabeth and James had three children together. Elizabeth Monroe died in Loudoun County, Virginia on September 23, 1830 at the age of 62.

FREDERICKSBURG, VIRGINA

Elizabeth Monroe and Fredericksburg will always hold a special place in my First Ladies story. This was the very first stop on the very first trip for the series back in November 2012. It was a five-day trip to cover seven women, and, for me, really got my fieldwork started. Since we still weren't entirely sure what the shows and the series were going to look like – we didn't know what form my pieces and work were going to take and how much or in what part of the show they would be included. There was also the website to consider. How much of what I was doing would make it onto the website? Were we going to do web extras or a travelogue of my trips? So much was up in the air and unknown. At each of these locations I was so hungry for information and content, I was working long days and filming everything I could get my eyes and ears on. In my opinion, you can never have too much footage.

The Monroe Museum in Fredericksburg is located in the old law offices of James Monroe, and accurately boasts one of the largest collections of artifacts from the Monroe's life that exists anywhere in the world. It's through these artifacts that I got to know Elizabeth Monroe. The broad span of her life and locations is well represented in their collection and I spent all day sifting through material and filming.

Fredericksburg is where James Monroe brings his young pregnant wife, Elizabeth. They moved from New York – where the two had met and married – to Fredericksburg where he worked for his uncle, as a young lawyer. Scott Harris and his team were wonderful hosts and they brought in Monroe expert and historian, Daniel Preston from the College of William and Mary for a sit down interview. Preston would also be our live in-studio guest for the Monroe show, and he was instrumental in getting me into the – now privately owned – Oak Hill residence in Loudoun County, Virginia. I owe all of these folks a debt of gratitude for starting me off on the right foot.

As I was just getting cracking on this project as a whole, everything old was new. They showed me some very unique items, including an ivory memo pad about the size of a modern day credit card with each day of the week carved and embossed on each individual card. This is where Elizabeth kept notes, shopping lists and anything you or I might put on a Post-It note. She wrote on the cards with a charcoal pencil. This and other similar artifacts showed that she was an organized and efficient woman.

Music was a big part of Elizabeth Monroe's life. This was the case with most cultured and educated women of her time, and the museum has one of her pianofortes which was believed to have been used in the White House. Women like Mrs. Monroe would play musical instruments, sing and recite poetry for their own pleasure, but would also do so to entertain family and guests.

Because of her upbringing and public status and image, Elizabeth Monroe had a very keen sense of style. Hers was a fashion sense that did not always match her budget. So, she did what many women in her time did. She adapted. Much of her jewelry and clothing was multipurpose. She could change a necklace length or accessorize an outfit to fit many different events and uses. The Monroes did a lot of foreign travel during their public service career and were able to acquire a good amount of items at a good price, keep them in good condition and use them in many ways. This can be seen in much of the Monroe's furniture that they used in multiple houses, including the White House.

It is here in Fredericksburg that I learned about hair jewelry. When I first heard the term "hair jewelry", I thought it was something to be worn in a woman's hair. I figured it to be something that would be similar to a Christmas tree ornament. I don't think I was crazy or a knucklehead to think this either. Tiaras and turbans and all sorts of other brooch style jewelry were all in style, so I didn't think my assumptions were that far off base. How wrong I was when Scott asked me if I would like to hold the hair earrings. I took them (on their protective floss bunting) and said in a brief moment of incorrect clarity "Oh, now I see why you call them hair earrings. Is that really Elizabeth Monroe's hair stuck in there? How would you know that?" He said, "Look closer." Upon further inspection, I discovered that the earrings were woven from what I now understood to be Elizabeth Monroe's hair. I was holding jewelry made from the hair of the fifth First Lady of the United States. Stop one. Trip one. Season one. UNBELIEVABLE.

It turns out that hair jewelry was very popular in the 18th and 19th centuries. In the 1700's it was more of a gift of affection or endearment – something you would give a family member or close friend. Later, in the 1800's, it became a symbol of mourning. Before they put you in your final resting place they snipped a few locks to make into a kind of memorial piece of jewelry. In this case with Monroe's earrings and a ring, they were gifts that Elizabeth had made for one of her sisters. The pieces were interesting, beautiful and to me unusual. The story still gets "OOO's", "AHHH's" and strange faces of disgust when I tell it to people.

As I mentioned, the Editor of the Monroe Papers, Daniel Preston, was on hand for an interview during my visit to Fredericksburg. Dan is a really nice guy and knows more about the Monroes than most. As was the case with Catherine Allgor, since Dan joined us for the live show, his interview never made air. However, all of his information and the time we spent talking was invaluable to my specific knowledge of Elizabeth Monroe.

The one thing that kept popping up in my reading was that Elizabeth was shy or didn't like people. She preferred to speak French around the White House, was most likely afflicted with epilepsy and criticized for not opening the first wedding to be held in the White House to the public. Dan had answers for all of my questions.

It seems that in all likelihood, she did have epilepsy or some similar disease. A seizure or some kind of fit caused her to fall into a hot fireplace and severely burn her face. This could also explain some of her shyness or being aloof after the incident. However, a very simple explanation is that she just didn't like big crowds.

We have to remember that these were real people with the same problems and anxieties, likes and dislikes as you and me. Accounts from others who knew Elizabeth and attended smaller events found her to be quite engaging and a wonderful host. The situation with the wedding is also easily explained.

In the early days of our country and the White House, before Secret Service and events that end up on news outlets like people trying to fly planes into the President's home and jump the fences to do a 50 yard dash, the White House was called the people's house. It's still the people's house, but back then, people took that at face value. People walked in and out of the house like they owned it. Because they did. It would seem that the Monroe's daughter Maria did not want to invite the entire country to her wedding.

One of the more remarkable things I saw and was able to hold (other than the hair earrings – which were hard to top) was the only known letter in existence written by Elizabeth Monroe.

Upon Elizabeth's death, James Monroe did what most folks did in those days. He burned all of his wife's letters, the correspondence that Elizabeth had written and kept. The only letter that has surfaced over these more than 200 years is a letter Elizabeth wrote to a family friend after this young woman's father had died. The letter says what you would expect. She had kind words about the deceased friend and words of condolence to the daughter he left behind. There is no real information about Elizabeth Monroe in this letter. We don't gain insight into her way of thinking or opinions of the political atmosphere or policy of the day. We see a nice woman who does the right thing and writes a kind letter to a family friend who had lost her father.

There was pain on Daniel Preston's face and I could hear the dismay in his voice when he said that he just couldn't imagine that this was the only one. That no one had found anything else in an old trunk in a garage or attic. That no one had come forward with a magic trunk full of journals and letters was truly heart-breaking. I mean, what are the odds that this is the only letter that survives? The thought is mindboggling, but at this point, appears true.

This was also the first letter written by a First Lady that I read. And even if the content of the letter was seemingly expected and run of the mill, I still felt closer to her having read it. I felt a little embarrassed or that I had done some-thing wrong. She wanted all of her letters burned. This one survived and I was reading it against her wishes. However, if we are to learn about these women and preserve and pass on their legacy, some exceptions to feelings like these need to be made. I can tell you this after holding and reading this letter – Elizabeth Monroe had amazing handwriting. She was a small person at 4'11", and her handwriting matched her small stature. But it was perfectly elegant, precise and crisp. So much so that I wish there was a modern day "Elizabeth Monroe" com-puter font. I would've published this book in it.

CHARLOTTESVILLE, VIRGINIA

It shouldn't come as a surprise that when the Monroes moved from Fredericksburg they ended up around Charlottesville. Thomas Jefferson was forming a neat little community (if you can call thousands and thousands of acres little) with a group of friends that lived in the area. It was a real "Who's Who of Founding Fathers and influential Revolutionaries" in that part of town.

The Monroe's new Ash Lawn estate could be seen across the valley from Jefferson's Monticello. In fact, Thomas Jefferson used to ride his horse right up to the front door of the Monroe's for dinners, meetings or other social gatherings. And even though Elizabeth Monroe and Dolley Madison were not the best of friends (though they weren't enemies), reliable stories claim that Dolley much preferred to stay the night at Ash Lawn versus the oddly shaped rooms of Monticello. However, all of these folks and many, many other very influential people of the time were all hanging out together and visiting each other's houses. And since travel was long and arduous during those times, they would often stay for multiple days.

From the 1600's all the way up to the early 1900's the main form of entertaining was the dinner party and the tea luncheon or social. Elizabeth Monroe blossomed at Ash Lawn from a young New York socialite to the Southern Plantation hostess that entertained and organized her husband's political and social events. Before he was President, James Monroe had many cabinet positions in other administrations and he and Elizabeth traveled the world together on many foreign assignments. I got a sense that they were a historical predecessor to Paul and Linda McCartney (during their entire marriage – which was only ended by Linda's death – they rarely, if ever, were apart or slept away from each other).

The most famous story of Elizabeth Monroe's travels was her trip to France in 1794, when her husband was the minister to France (as named by George Washington). Elizabeth was used as a political tool in a huge publicity stunt. It was during the height of the "Reign of Terror". There were massive numbers of people imprisoned and executed. The Marquis was in jail in Austria, his wife – Madame Lafayette was in prison in Paris and her mother had already been executed.

To send in James Monroe would've been too bold a move. Instead, Mrs. Monroe was sent to visit Madam Lafayette. She traveled to the jail in a brightly colored carriage and her arrival was publically announced. The simple gesture of a woman going to visit her friend in jail to console her in her time of need caught everyone's eye. To make a long story short, this move saved Lafayette's life. The plan that the Monroes concocted played on public sympathies and was successful; it goes without saying that the Lafayettes appreciated it. As a gesture of thanks, once the whole situation had resolved itself the Monroes were given two marble mantelpieces currently on display at Ash Lawn – Highland.

By all accounts Elizabeth Monroe settled into her new role at Ash Lawn –

Highland nicely. The house wasn't huge, but they could serve a dinner party of 12 – 20 people and Mrs. Monroe was said to be a more than capable hostess. The majority of her difficulties were finding a good Plantation Manager to keep things running when the Monroes were away on business. There were almost four thousand acres to manage and that was no small task.

The house at Ash Lawn is not massive, but it is well appointed. One of the first things I noticed was the low frame of the front door. Initially, I thought that it was because people were so much shorter back then. I was assured that this was not the case, as James Monroe himself was over six feet tall. Keep in mind that Elizabeth was only 4' 11" and both were considered to be quite attractive. The lack of height in the doorframe was attributed to cost. Taller doors cost more money, and Monroe was said to be a very frugal man. However, their furniture was very nice, and would lead you to believe otherwise.

In fact, much later when Jacqueline Kennedy was restoring the White House and designating it as a museum, she would say that the Monroe furniture was among the finest available to her. (There were also many examples of wonderful Monroe furniture in Fredericksburg). This makes sense though. As previously noted, the Monroes were very well traveled at the expense of the government and were able to collect a lot of items during those travels.

The furniture the Monroes purchased for the White House was another thing for which Mrs. Monroe caught grief. The White House furniture was supposed to be American made, instead, Mrs. Monroe had a French designer make the furniture. She also used the eagle as an image, which had come and gone from French fashion at the time. These things, on top of Mrs. Monroe's affinity for French language and food, led to many calling her "Queen Elizabeth" behind her back.

On the subject of furniture, a dresser in the Monroe's bedroom is a very interesting piece. Not necessarily by design, quality or condition – although all of those are excellent. It is the writing on the underside of the top drawer that makes this piece so unique. In charcoal handwriting it says that the piece is to be delivered to the White House in Washington, D.C. Basically, it was moving and delivery instructions for bringing the dresser to the White House for Monroe's Presidency. When I relayed this story to folks at the White House Historical

Association, it was news to them. There are so many Presidential items out there it is nearly impossible to know where they all are or the stories behind them and how they got to wherever they are.

Both the dining room and the master bedroom are painted blue – Mrs. Monroe's favorite color. The Monroes also created the "Blue Room" that remains in the White House today. The house was delightfully decorated in period fashion as if the Monroes had just stepped out to perhaps visit Mr. Jefferson up the hill. Various knife boxes and china in the dining room lend themselves to the overall authenticity.

The Monroes were the first Presidential couple to have official White House china, which started a very significant White House tradition. My hosts at Ash Lawn – Highland were very eager to point out this fact and show me the original pieces they had – both on the table and in the corner cabinet.

The kitchen is under the main part of the house (a Jefferson concept) to keep the house warm in the winter. This is where Mrs. Monroe spent much of her time overseeing the preparation of meals. This is also where my host and guide – Denis Bigalow – sat by the fireplace and read to me from a handbook which was a kind of "how to" be a proper Plantation Hostess in the 1700's. It gave me a fuller understanding of the language Mrs. Monroe was taught and the expectations relating to tasks that she was expected to perform. As I mentioned, by all accounts, Mrs. Monroe adapted to her role very proficiently.

I was very fortunate to spend the day with Denis Bigalow. Denis is a well-studied historian, the James Monroe reenactor, and a marvelous radio-ready voice. He explained to me that the vast and impressive collection of Monroe items and artifacts on display at the estate were assembled by a number of different avenues. Many items came to Ash Lawn – Highland by donation or loan, which is common for historical sites and museums. Surprisingly, much of the collection was found in places like EBay, auctions or flea markets. Of particular interest to me was the official Monroe White House china on display in a corner cabinet in the dining room at Ash Lawn.

———————————————

Side Note — Collecting Artifacts

At each historical location I expected to learn a significant amount of information about of the First Ladies (after all that was the purpose of the whole project), and a few things about their Presidential husbands and the times in which they both lived. And I did.

One thing I didn't expect to learn about was the science and process by which these locations collect, assemble and present their artifacts and stories. These places really rolled out the red carpet for me, and gave me an all access pass. Looking back now, it makes sense – I mean after all, these folks and I were spending the better half (if not more) of a day together. This was very much the case at Ash Lawn – Highland.

———————————————

It's really astonishing how these collections came to be. From a separate project, I know that a shirt cuff from a Ford Theater actress with the bloodstain of President Lincoln from the night he was shot, was donated to the Smithsonian by a direct relative of the actress who originally wore the cuff. Some collections are incredibly large, and others are surprisingly small. Equally amazing are the things that exist versus the items that have been lost. This is just a random rambling that I felt like sharing with you. Insider baseball, behind the scenes stuff, I guess.

LEESBURG, VIRGINIA

The Oak Hill Estate is in a very small group of homes of Founding Fathers that are now privately owned. Daniel Preston, who I met and interviewed in Fredericksburg, facilitated my visit here. Through his kindness and connection to the owners, and their generosity, the doors of Oak Hill were opened to me. The owner's father purchased the house and land at public auction. It was later passed down and taken over by the current owner and his wife after his father passed away. The couple still lives there today and leases some of the land to local farmers.

Oak Hill was the estate that Elizabeth Monroe always wanted. It was purchased and built by the Monroes during his Presidency. It was the perfect place for them to retire. They could step outside of Washington, but not be too far away from the action. They could still entertain friends and family in a home deserving of a former President and First Lady. The current owners have done a wonderful job of preserving the integrity and staying true to the original time period of the mansion, while still affording themselves a living area with modern conveniences and upgrades for daily life in the 21st century.

The ballrooms, foyer, parlor and dining room were visually stunning and of particular interest. The massive chandeliers are original as are many of the doors, tables and various pieces of furniture. The porches and patios are all where they were during the Monroe's time, as well.

The crowning jewel of the Oak Hill estate is the formal garden. Even though I was there in the winter, it was easy to see its grandeur and imagine the fragrant blossoms and amazing events that would have been held there. The Monroes bedroom windows faced the gardens and as I stood in the window of the master bedroom and drew back the curtains, I was taken back in time, and imagined myself quietly standing next to Elizabeth Monroe as she looked out over her beautiful garden on a spring morning. It is this kind of moment and these types of settings that humbled me, and fueled my unrelenting desire to travel more… see more…and learn more. Gaining access to places like this with wonderful hosts, hostesses and ambassadors to the past is what set this series apart from all others like it. It will not be the last time you hear me thank the amazing people at C-SPAN and all the other people who worked on this project.

SUMMARY

I think Elizabeth Monroe gets unfairly neglected in American History. She was an intelligent and accomplished woman of her time. She doesn't get nearly as much "air time" as her contemporaries. I am often asked about her during my live events and presentations. Some folks will even thank me for mentioning her.

Her involvement in her husband's career and life was clearly influential. It took a bold woman – all four foot eleven of her – to ride down the streets of Paris in a time known as the "Reign of Terror" and knock on the front door of the prison that held the wife of the Marquis de Lafayette, who awaited execution. Her involvement in that political stunt alone should solidify her role in Women's Studies and Early American History lectures and lessons from now until the end of time.

The other area where I think she gets a raw deal is her entertaining and public image. She liked the French. Okay. Remember, we were friends with the French then (not that we aren't now) – they helped us out big time when we were just getting started as a new country. After all, it was the French that helped facilitate the American Revolution, and the British that burned the White House. Not the other way around.

I also think that history is tricky. Let's think about it. None of us were there. I was never invited nor did I attend a function at the White House hosted by the Monroes. We put together stories that are sometimes romanticized or dare I say exaggerated. The stories and facts themselves are often-subjective reviews from letters or reports from people who were there or re-tellings passed down and along through families. We interpret them as best as we can with the information and available evidence. Still, none of us were there. So, when it comes to saying someone like Mrs. Monroe was a snob, or Mary Todd was crazy (which we'll get to later), we have to consider the other side of the story, as Daniel Preston does. Maybe Elizabeth Monroe was self-conscious about her health and didn't care for large crowds. The White House in those days was a madhouse with a virtual revolving door of public access. There was no security and the public thought the White House was (and it is to a certain extent) their property. They ran in and out snatching bits of carpet and curtains and filling their pockets with silverware and souvenirs.

Even one of the biggest events about which Elizabeth Monroe got raked over the coals – her daughter's wedding not being open to the public – I'm told wasn't her decision. The Monroes' daughter didn't want everyone in D.C. walking through the ceremony hooting and hollering and grabbing tablecloths to take home as souvenirs. I can understand that. And the planned public reception that never happened was out of respect for a government official who had recently died in the streets, on the losing end of a pistol duel. All I'm saying is when it comes to some of the stories and popular public opinions (especially when they are negative) let's consider some other possibilities. I feel certain that the truth lies somewhere in between. Especially, when it comes to Elizabeth Monroe.

Travelogue Food Tip

Fredericksburg is a quaint, little, historic town with a lot of neat shops, boutiques and restaurants. We took a break from filming to go to a really cool little Italian place on the corner across the street from the Monroe Museum called Castiglia's. They had fantastic pizza and an amazing Caesar salad. Those who know me well and are reading this know I'm very serious when it comes to my Caesar salad. This one's a winner.

CHAPTER 6

Louisa Catherine Adams

Annapolis, Maryland – Boston, Massachusetts – Quincy, Massachusetts

*L*ouisa Catherine Adams was born Louisa Catherine Johnson on February 12, 1775 in London, England. Her parents were Joshua Johnson and Catherine Nuth Johnson. Louisa Catherine and John Quincy Adams were married on July 26, 1797. Louisa Catherine and John Quincy had four children together. Louisa Catherine Adams died in Washington, D.C. on May 15, 1852 at the age of 76.

ANNAPOLIS, MARYLAND

Louisa Catherine Adams is the only foreign born First Lady in American History. It's funny to think that over 200 years later, if John Kerry had won the 2004 Presidential election, Teresa Heinz Kerry would have been the second. Mrs. Kerry was born in Mozambique. However, Kerry didn't win. I just thought that was an interesting tidbit. In the 2016 Presidential election we had two chances to see this happen again with Jeb Bush's wife, Columba, and Donald Trump's wife, Melania. At the time of the first pressing of this book, Jeb Bush had dropped out of the race. Time will tell how I re-write this chapter for future editions.

Louisa Catherine was born to an English mother and colonist father in London. Her father – Joshua Johnson – was born into a wealthy Maryland family and became a successful merchant for an Annapolis-based company. Johnson was sent by his company to London to manage their interests there.

Her father met her mother in England and they started their family there. So, Louisa primarily grew up in London. During the American Revolution, her parents took refuge in Nantes, France. She was very well educated, intelligent and familiar with European policy and politics.

She met John Quincy Adams in London while he was serving as Minister to Berlin during his father's Presidential administration. The two courted and were married in 1797 having never met Adams' parents or ever having been to America.

***

Historical Note – Political Family

Louisa Catherine Adams's uncle, Thomas Johnson, was a Governor of Maryland and a U.S. Supreme Court Justice.

***

I was born in Bethesda Maryland at Suburban Hospital. I grew up and went to school in Rockville, Maryland. I went to college at University of Maryland in College Park. I currently live in Shady Side, Maryland. I have been going to Annapolis my whole life. It is a neat little waterfront town and the capital of Maryland. I knew it was a historic town. I never knew its relation to Louisa Catherine Adams's story until this project. The courthouse and Governor's offices are right in the center of town. The brick streets, ships in the harbor and sounds of seabirds in the air make it easy to imagine the scene down at the City Dock during her father's time there. There is no specific place or building to visit in Maryland that relates to or tells the story of Louisa Catherine Adams, but it's a fun place to visit and walk the streets to shop and eat.

BOSTON, MASSACHUSETTS

As we discussed in the Abigail Adams chapter, the Massachusetts Historical Society (MHS) holds over 70,000 pages of Adams family papers. I did my Louisa Catherine research at the same time as her First Lady Mother-in-law, Abigail Adams. So, the scene was the same. I had to be taken up backroom elevators and pass through key coded doors to get to some of the files and papers. I lugged my gear through fenced cages and protected areas of the building, and it was great fun to experience the obvious care and protection given to this very important collection.

When the C-SPAN series first aired in 2013, the MHS had just completed two large volumes edited from the diaries and journals of Louisa Catherine Adams. The journals themselves are marvelous – not only in content but the physical journals and handwriting. It was mind-boggling enough to learn about these women by reading their letters, but to see and read their journals and diaries is a whole other level of intimacy and knowledge.

Many of these journals were from Louisa Catherine's childhood and her early teen years. They revealed a thoughtful and intelligent girl from a well-to-do and loving family. She was particularly close to her father and enjoyed reading and writing. It's no wonder she grew up to be the perfect political partner to her Presidential and politically centered husband.

On the subject of John Quincy Adams, many see him as a stuffy, gruff, hard-nosed politician. And he was. But early courting letters show that he had a bit of his father's romance and smooth talking to him, as well. He was 10 years Louisa's senior and she was only 18 when they married, but this was not uncommon for the time.

John Quincy and Louisa Catherine spent a lot of time in Europe and Russia when he served in various roles of American diplomacy. Some of her writings show that Louisa enjoyed this life, and that because of her aristocratic upbringing she was the perfect diplomat's wife. However, along the way and throughout their life together, Louisa suffered six miscarriages – many of which occurred in foreign lands far from home and sometimes even far from her husband, these occasions would cause hardships between them, as well as depression for Mrs. Adams.

Side Note – Martha, Martha, Martha!

The early Presidents, First Ladies and their children get very confusing because everyone is named after someone – mothers and daughters, fathers and sons; someone is always named after George Washington or other early Presidents, and there are too many women named Martha!

One of the most remarkable entries in her adult journals was about her journey from Russia to meet up with her husband in France in 1812. The Adamses had given birth to a daughter in 1811 while they were in Russia. They named her Louisa Catherine.

The birth of this daughter, after the many years, much traveling, and a few miscarriages led to a renewed closeness between John Quincy and Louisa. Adams even wrote in a letter that his wife was a "faithful and affectionate wife, and a tender, indulgent and watchful mother to our children".

This happiness would be short lived as John Quincy was sent off to Ghent on official business, leaving Mrs. Adams behind to look after their son Charles and an ailing baby Louisa Catherine. She was also expected to look after her husband's affairs and wrap up family business before traveling to meet him in France. Their infant daughter didn't survive the illness, and Mrs. Adams was left to grieve by herself.

She sold all the family's furniture, bought a carriage and set out on a journey across Russia behind the French Army, in the middle of winter during an ongoing war. At one point during the journey the carriage wheels were replaced with sled skis. She wrote about the hardships of this trek, and with great detail about getting stuck in ravines, ditches and other obstacles related to their travel.

This was a trip that would be difficult to take today with modern technology and conveniences. Try to imagine what it must have been like for this woman, with a young child and having just lost her infant daughter. The fact that she is even traveling alone, without her husband, made her quite unusual for her time. But Louisa Catherine Adams showed time and time again, that she was not only intelligent, pretty and capable…she was also sturdy and loyal to her husband and her family.

The Massachusetts Historical Society's collection is not comprised only of letters and journals. They also have a number of objects, artifacts and official documents. One such document that they brought out to show me was Louisa Catherine's American passport. It is a large document that is incredibly well preserved. I have traveled shorter distance in great comfort and ruined papers, books, clothes and all kinds of stuff. To think that this woman traveled across Russia and Europe in a carriage on skis with a kid, and has anything left to show for it (not to mention over 200 years later) is nothing short of a miracle.

These journals and volumes are full of remarkably well-written and documented adventures and situations like this. Any fan of early diplomatic history and international affairs would really enjoy the Louisa Catherine papers. Jim Taylor and his staff were again amazingly knowledgeable and informative. In fact, the Louisa Catherine show would be the second time we had an MHS guest on set with us for the live broadcast. Amanda Matthews was the youngest expert and historian to appear on the series. She was great and I appreciate her contributions.

QUINCY, MASSACHUSETTS

The first time Louisa Catherine Adams stepped foot in America she went to the Peacefield Estate in Quincy, Massachusetts to meet her husband's parents. Her in-laws. John Adams has just lost his re-election to Thomas Jefferson and had returned home. Abigail Adams was not a fan of the fact that her son's wife was not born in America. She felt it hurt his budding political career. Louisa Catherine herself said upon going to Peacefield for the first time that she "could not be more astonished if she had stepped onto Noah's Ark".

My tour of Peacefield was just as interesting and remarkable as any of the locations with the addition of a very cold winter day. Remember from the Abigail Adams chapter, that I had to take my shoes off to enter the rooms for interviews and filming. It takes long enough to get through a house as a crew of one to get one woman's story. Then you have to go back and get the b-roll footage and close-ups of the specific items and artifacts. Here at Peacefield, I had to do each of those things twice in my socks. My feet were beyond numb by the time we finished our work there.

Peacefield is more associated and laid out to tell the story of John and Abigail Adams than John Quincy and Louisa Catherine. And this makes sense; after all, Abigail purchased it while John was in New York and Philadelphia. They were the first and primary owners. They lived and died there. John Adams retires there after his term as President, while John Quincy Adams returns to Congress after his Presidency. In fact, he is the only President to do so. However, John Quincy and thus Louisa Catherine do have a story here. They inherited Peacefield after the deaths of Abigail and then John Adams. They primarily used the home in the summertime to escape the heat and the politics of Washington.

So, let's get back to Louisa's relationship with her in-laws. Her father-in-law, the former President John Adams, was apparently a push over and loved her right out of the gate. She was said to be a lovely woman with all the education and manners of a sophisticated lady of her day. So, this makes sense. And while Abigail wasn't as easy a sell as her husband, she eventually came around, too. At one point, Louisa Catherine wrote of her mother-in-law, "she is the planet around which all revolves." Even with relationships getting better, Louisa would always be considered a bit of an outsider having been born and raised in Europe.

This is something that not only plagued Louisa in her new family, but also followed her to Washington. Some people (other than her mother-in-law) thought it hurt her husband's political career. Regardless of which side of the fence you sat on, it was an issue one way or the other. Keep in mind though, we were a young country trying to figure everything out, and I would place into consideration that we still haven't figured out race relations and immigration in the United States, but that's a different discussion for a different day by a different author of a different book. This book is all about the ladies.

One of Louisa Catherine's grandsons, Henry Adams, was very close to her and fondly remembered her in "The Education of Henry Adams". While she was generally considered as the odd person out in the family and a "foreigner", Henry was well traveled and never felt that way about her. He relates in his works that he would often find her sitting in her paneled room entertaining friends and serving tea from her silver tea service. The room, the furniture and the tea service are all still on display at Peacefield. Clearly, Louisa Catherine Adams had a place and played a role at the house.

I think the most memorable thing I learned about Louisa at Peacefield was the wonderful relationship she had with her father-in-law, John Adams. The two wrote many letters to one another and thought very highly of each other. Again, seeing and reading these letters at the Massachusetts Historical Society, and now seeing the rooms, and the desks upon which these thoughts were written, really helped put all the pieces and images together. It was not hard to picture any of the Adamses sitting at any number of original desks there in the house and writing to each other. With so much history, so much writing and so many generations represented, it's hard not to feel connected to the entire Adams family in Quincy.

As I mentioned in the Abigail chapter, the crypt that held both Presidential Adamses and their First Ladies was, and will always be, one of the heaviest, most special and significant moments of this project, for me both personally and professionally.

One relatively unique thing to the Adams family, in Quincy and at Peacefield, was that I learned about two different women at the same places. This was not only a challenge for me as a producer, but for my guide and historian. She told me that I was really challenging her brain to take things and places out of order and out of her usual routine. She liked and appreciated the challenge. Challenging my hosts and myself became a common theme, and I found it to be another fascinating aspect of the project.

The very title of the series "FIRST LADIES: Influence and Image" takes most people and places a little out of their daily routine. These are typically the homes of Presidents. They tell the story of a President at various stages of, if not throughout, his entire life. The First Ladies are a part of that story. I came in and flipped everything around on the people responsible for ushering visitors around and sharing details about the President. Instead of walking into a room and their first words being, "In here President" so and so did this, that and the other, I wanted to hear "The First Lady would" do this; say that, or the other. This was a complete change in routine from what many of these folks have been doing for decades – and many continue to do today. Various people told me that it forced them to relearn the stories of these women, re-familiarize themselves with certain collections and items and adjust the way they presented their anecdotes. I thought this was such a cool thing for everyone involved – right down to the viewers of the series and now in an even different way – you the reader.

SUMMARY

Louisa Catherine Adams was definitely unusual for her time. The story of her journey across Russia and Europe should tell you that. Not only was she mentally and physically strong, but also she was a beautiful and intelligent woman. She – like many of these women – was able to be the mother of large family, and still be effectively involved in her husband's career. In fact, I found throughout the series (especially in the early years of our country) that these First Ladies, with the combined traits of intelligence, having a formal education or otherwise, coupled with strong physical presence and an ability to step outside of traditionally accepted gender roles, were a force behind the success of their men. These men wouldn't have been able to do what they did or become who they became, if they did not have women like Louis Catherine Adams in their corner fighting for and with them.

Travelogue Food Tip

Stay in hotels that offer free continental breakfasts. Even if you don't eat them, coming downstairs in the morning to the smell of fresh waffles and hot cakes is amazing. The added smell of bacon in the air is another perk to starting your day off in these places. They always have a nice fresh fruit selection and an abundance of good proteins like, oatmeal, yogurt and eggs. It's a quick and easy way to get something into your system and get you out the door and on your way.

CHAPTER 7
Rachel Jackson

Nashville, Tennessee

Rachel Jackson was born Rachel Donelson on June 15, 1767 outside of Chatham in Halifax County, Virginia. Her parents were Colonel John Donelson and Rachel Stockley Donelson. Rachel and Andrew Jackson were married on January 7, 1794. Rachel and Andrew had no children together. Rachel Jackson died in Nashville, Tennessee on December 22, 1828 at the age of 61.

Rachel Jackson was never officially a First Lady. She died before her husband was inaugurated as the seventh President of the United States. The campaign between Andrew Jackson and John Quincy Adams was brutal and ruthless, to say the least. Jackson said that it killed his wife. The campaign left Andrew Jackson both a widower and a President-elect, traveling to Washington, D.C. to be inaugurated after he said goodbye and buried his wife at their Hermitage plantation, located outside of Nashville, Tennessee. Some people think that Rachel was buried in the gown she was supposed to wear to the inauguration. The folks at the Hermitage will tell you that there is no credible evidence of this. No matter what you believe, most experts and historians agree that even though Rachel Jackson never stepped foot in the White House as First Lady, her ghost presided over Jackson's two terms as President like a dark cloud that was with him every day.

Historical Note – The Lady Of The House Is Not In

The Jackson Administration starts a twelve-year period in American history where there is no official First Lady. Both Andrew Jackson and his successor Martin Van Buren were widowers. Both had close female relatives serve as hostesses for their presidencies. Jackson's wife's niece Emily Donelson is his hostess. Martin Van Buren enlisted his daughter-in-law Angelica Singleton Van Buren.

NASHVILLE, TENNESSEE

The love story that is Andrew and Rachel starts in the backwoods of Tennessee and could make headlines on the pages of any modern day tabloid magazine. Their story contributed to Rachel's public image as well as the campaign mudslinging – to which Jackson credits her death. Andrew Jackson was not Rachel's first husband, and no one is clear, nor can it be proven, that she ever got legally divorced from her first husband. However, looking back, I feel the criticism and controversy was unfair and unwarranted. But politics is a dirty business, and when mud gets slung…people get dirty.

To make a very long story as short as possible, Rachel Donelson was married when she was a teenager to a man named Lewis Robards. Robards has been described as abusive, tyrannical and jealous. Rachel quickly left that relationship and moved back in with her mother and sister in Nashville. She met a young lawyer named Andrew Jackson in Nashville. Here is where facts get murky. A lot of people related to this story came and went from Kentucky to Tennessee, and it is unclear when some relationships formed and others ended. Robards apparently threatened both Rachel and Andrew. Rachel asked for a divorce. Robards may or may not have granted that divorce. Andrew and Rachel were married. This is what led to the claims of bigamy and loose morals, accusations that plagued the Jacksons, and more specifically Rachel and her reputation to her dying day.

But, let's backtrack a bit. Rachel Donelson had a huge family; Andrew Jackson, an orphan, loved this about Rachel. She provided a love and a family, a sense of belonging that he had never known. In his own right Andrew Jackson had become a successful lawyer and a well-known war hero. He also became the love of Rachel's life and she, his. It is also clear that Rachel preferred her husband to be at home. In the earliest letter in the Hermitage collection, Rachel writes to Andrew in 1796 "My Dearest Heart…do not let fame and fortune blind you to the fact that you have a wife at home".

As Andrew Jackson's fame and fortune grew, he spent more time at home. People came to visit. Their home was always full of friends, family and visitors. By all accounts, Rachel was a wonderful hostess with very nice things and she knew how to throw a good dinner party.

At the Hermitage, they have a number of items on display: silver serving items, china place settings, beautiful dresses and letters from folks who stayed at the Hermitage with the Jacksons, all claiming to have had a wonderful time. Mrs. Jackson's pride and joy was her garden. A newlywed couple passing through Nashville spent part of their honeymoon with the Jacksons at the Hermitage. During their stay, the woman took a long stroll in the garden with Rachel and returned with a lovely arrangement of freshly cut flowers.

So, where did all the gossip about Rachel Jackson originate? Well, as I mentioned earlier, the question of whether or not she was still married to her first husband, and had committed bigamy was always in question. On the public stage Mrs. Jackson was shy, and didn't like the spotlight and fame. She didn't "perform" very well in public, and her large "country" family and "backwards" Southern ways didn't help her public image.

Keep in mind that as a young, budding country, America was still finding its way and looking for its place among well-established countries. As much as we were trying to get away from England, we were also trying to fit in on the international stage. Public appearance was (and still is) very important. Especially, when it came to our leaders. All of our Presidents up to this point had come from Virginia and Massachusetts. So, Andrew Jackson and his wife were considered – even with all of his military accomplishments – for lack of a better term – hillbillies.

Rachel was not a young or particularly attractive woman by popular opinion. She was an accomplished horse rider, which could have been viewed as mannish. She was known to smoke both cigars and a pipe. She was viewed as a bit frumpy or politely put – matronly. This led to the newspapers writing unkindly or unfavorably about her when she would appear publicly or travel with her husband. Remember, politics has always been a dirty business and everything is fair game for the opposition – although, it was fairly uncommon to bring women into it up to this point.

By the time the Presidential election came along in 1828, Rachel had the reputation of being an unrefined, pipe smoking, backwoods, bigamist, hillbilly mountain woman; that didn't play well on the national stage or the campaign trail. But from all the evidence I was shown at the Hermitage, she was just a woman more comfortable at home. She liked to be surrounded by family, friends and loved ones, and every time she stepped out of the house she would get slammed in some newspaper. I would've stayed home, too.

Rachel's health deteriorated during the Presidential campaign. She was laid up in bed when Andrew Jackson was pronounced the winner over John Quincy Adams. Jackson knew his wife's condition was serious, but writes in a letter to a friend as if she will bounce back and travel with him to Washington for the inauguration. Unfortunately, this doesn't happen. In what the Hermitage refers to as the "death letter", Andrew Jackson writes about pains in her left shoulder and breast that lead to her suffocation.

Rachel's death comes quickly on December 22, 1828, and the Hermitage does a remarkable job of telling the tragic story and making it as clear as if it had only recently occurred. A display case in the main museum has many items specifically related to her death. One of the most remarkable items is a cotton lace woven bed bonnet. It is said to be the one Rachel was wearing when she died. Dark red stains on the cap are thought to be Rachel's blood from the final attempts to save her by means of bloodletting. Andrew Jackson was a firm believer in heroic medicine – procedures that either cured or killed you. However, when the bloodletting of Rachel was ordered, it was already too late.

Some of the other items in the display case that explain Rachel's death are Jackson's all black calling cards, which he had printed to indicate his time of mourning. They also have a book called "The Mourner Comforted" which was given to Jackson by a friend. There is a poem written and printed on silk about her death. Andrew Jackson was lost without Rachel; and her items, influence and memory follow him to the White House and are with him for the rest of his life.

Jackson took his favorite portrait of her and had it painted on a small pendant that he kept with him at all times. He set it on his nightstand next to his bed each night as he slept. This pendant is in the collection at the Hermitage. It was remarkable to see this piece, something so important to Jackson, and so representative of his wife's memory. I imagined its weight dropping into my own coat pocket, as it must've each morning for President Jackson. I pictured him looking at it each night as he placed it on his nightstand. This was yet another clear and physical item that made both Andrew and Rachel so very real to me. I definitely took a moment and a deep breath as I locked my camera in for this all-important footage. The loss of Rachel and the impact it had over President Andrew Jackson's life and Presidency cannot be understated.

This same portrait of Rachel would appear in a full size version that would hang in his bedroom in the White House as well as his bedroom at the Hermitage. Jackson said his wife Rachel was the last thing he wanted to see before he went to bed and the first thing he wanted to see as he woke up each day. He also kept Rachel's hand knit covered Book of Psalms. Many such tokens were kept handy as a constant reminder of the wife and partner he had lost, seemingly at the expense of his political career.

The Hermitage is a well-preserved facility outside of Nashville, Tennessee that has become one of my favorite Presidential homes. It sits on a massive amount of land that includes the museum, the main estate, outhouses, slave quarters, gardens, graves, a church and a few cows. My behind the scenes tour was one that I shall never forget.

When you travel and produce television for C-SPAN, you are very well received. C-SPAN has done an amazing job of creating good standing relationships with historical locations across the country and everywhere they go. I was more than ready to continue and build on these relationships and take full advantage of the access that reputation would provide me. The Hermitage was no exception.

When you walk around the Hermitage with its head curator, Marsha Mullin, she who holds all the keys to all the rooms, back doors, closets, storage facilities and vaults, you know you're in for more than a few treats. Marsha unlocked all the closets, opened all the doors, and pulled out all the stops.

When we first entered the main residence she explained that as it stands now, Rachel Jackson wouldn't have recognized the place. The original structure where Rachel lived with Andrew was long gone because of a fire, but that didn't mean that Rachel's influence was absent. As was the case in every other aspect of Jackson's post-Rachel life, the house was rebuilt with Rachel Jackson in mind.

The first thing you see when entering the house into the main foyer is the remarkable fabric wallpaper. This was the identical wallpaper Rachel ordered from Europe for the original house, and Jackson had to have it duplicated and installed in the remodeled house. A beautiful countryside scene with rich blues and greens depicts people walking under trees and lovely streams and ponds throughout. It is a wall-to-wall tribute to Rachel. It is a magnificent way to enter the Jackson home and you immediately feel Rachel's presence. What happened and where we went next, is something that only happened once to me in the entire series and all of my travels. I became part of the exhibit.

Marsha took me outside and around to the side of the house where we entered an almost secret door into the back of the President's bedroom. Most historic houses and museums put carpet runners to take you through the facility and keep you off of the old and rare floors. Some put up velvet ropes to keep you out of the rooms entirely. At the Hermitage, they put floor-to-ceiling Plexiglas, to give visitors an uninhibited view of the room, while keeping them entirely out in the hallways. Marsha, my camera, all of my gear and I were in the rooms inside of the Plexiglas.

We were in Andrew Jackson's bedroom on the first floor recording the video piece about Rachel's portrait, which hung over the fireplace directly across from his bed. I had a perfect view of the room, the painting, his bed and Marsha was in place for her interview. Right about then, a group of tourists walked by the doorway. There were probably about ten of them – all ages – men, women, boys, and girls. They were as surprised to see us, as I was to see them. I went about my business setting up and recording my interview, and they started taking pictures of us. We became the exhibit, not the intended main attraction, which was the President's bedroom.

Anyone who knows me knows that I am not afraid of attention (good thing for my public speaking career, radio show and live music performances). However, I do it on my terms. This was not on my terms. I couldn't control it, and I became very aware of my surroundings, and my actions. I now know what the Silverback Gorillas feel like at the zoo when everyone is staring, pointing and taking pictures of them. It was very unsettling at first. I quickly re-focused on my work, as we had a lot of the house to get through, and we finished up in that room without issue or incident. But, it was a very humbling and strange experience.

After touring the house, we went out into the formal garden. This was a special place for both Andrew and Rachel Jackson, and very fittingly, it is their final resting place. Stories from guests at the Hermitage while Rachel was alive always include a visit or walk through her garden. Later, after Rachel's death, friends and family talk and write about Andrew Jackson going out to the garden to sit and think. There is little doubt that he did this to feel closer to his wife.

SUMMARY

Any time I visit the grave of a First Lady, it is special. After spending as much time researching, traveling, listening, learning and exploring their lives as I did, it seems only fitting to visit with them a little bit on a personal level and to thank them for letting me into their lives, even if for a brief period of time. Many of these First Ladies didn't ask for or want this public life. Most, however, accepted it and shared their husbands and families with the country.

In Rachel's earliest letter to her husband, she is clear that she would rather him stay at home with her. She is not comfortable, nor is she well received, in the public eye. Yet, all accounts by friends and family show her to have been a wonderful hostess at her Hermitage home. She had a large family for whom she cared deeply. She was a loving partner to Andrew Jackson; with a special bond that he carried her physical items and memory to his own grave.

In the end, they both got what they wanted. She got her husband back and he joined his wife in the beautiful gardens of the Tennessee Hermitage home.

Travelogue Food Tip

Go to a place right by Vanderbilt University called South Street Restaurant. They have excellent pulled pork, but the thing to get there is the CRAB & SLAB. It is a platter of various crab legs, a slab of ribs and assorted vegetables. Bring your appetite or bring a friend, because this is a big meal. It's also fun to trace Elvis Presley's life and accomplishments on the mural painted on the wall in the hallway by the bathrooms.

CHAPTER 8

Emily Donelson

Nashville, Tennessee

*E*mily Donelson was born Emily Tennessee Donelson on June 1, 1807 in Donelson, Tennessee. Her father was Rachel Jackson's brother, John Donelson and her mother's name was Mary Purnell Donelson. Emily and Andrew Jackson Donelson were married on September 16, 1824. Emily and Andrew had four children together, three of whom were born in the white house. Emily Donelson died in Nashville, Tennessee on December 19, 1836 at the age of 29.

Rachel Jackson had a very large family. Her family and relatives were always around their Nashville, Tennessee home, the Hermitage. Many of them followed Jackson to Washington, D.C. and became part of his Presidential administration and staff. One such individual was Rachel's nephew, Andrew Jackson Donelson, who they commonly referred to as Andrew Jackson, Jr. Jackson, Jr. was one of

Andrew Jackson's favorites of Rachel's many nephews and nieces. He was a 29-year-old lawyer and West Point graduate when he joined his newly elected Presidential uncle in Washington, serving as his Secretary. Andrew Jackson, Jr. was married to his 21-year-old cousin, Emily Donelson. Emily went along to Washington to serve as hostess for her uncle's White House.

Emily was young, attractive and despite the close familial relations, Washington, D.C. loved her.

Historical Note – It's All Relative

Keep in mind nearly a hundred years later Franklin Delano Roosevelt married his 6th cousin, Eleanor Roosevelt.

Emily had graduated from the Nashville Female Academy and had learned all of the required social graces. Emily was a more than capable hostess and she fit in well with the upper crust in the Nation's capital.

Now, I will attempt to explain and describe a scandal that resulted in one of the largest political group resignations in American History. Back when he was a Senator, President Andrew Jackson met a young woman in Washington, D.C. named Margaret O'Neill. On one of Rachel Jackson's rare trips to D.C., she also met and befriended Margaret (often called Peggy). Peggy's parents owned the boarding house where Jackson stayed when he was in D.C. for government business and Congress.

Peggy was married to a purser in the Navy, John B. Timberlake, and rumors began to circulate about an affair she was having with one of Jackson's friends, a Senator from Tennessee named John Henry Eaton. To make another very long story relatively short, Peggy's sailor husband died at sea, and soon thereafter she married John Eaton. By this time, Rachel Jackson was dead, and Andrew Jackson was President. Thus, the Peggy Eaton scandal was born.

Jackson, already having experienced his wife's tumultuous relationship with the press and the public eye, felt encumbered to save the reputation of this female friend he considered to be unfairly maligned. Jackson tried everything. He instructed his entire cabinet to tell their wives to add Peggy and her husband to the invite lists of parties and social gatherings. He even sent the Eatons away on foreign detail to let the dust settle. Nothing worked. People weren't letting it go. Least of all was his niece and hostess, Emily Donelson, who sided with the gossipy society women against Peggy, and effectively ostracized her from D.C.'s elite society.

Jackson then decided it best to send Emily home in hopes that the scandal involving Peggy Eaton would settle down. There is little doubt he probably felt a bit betrayed by her behavior given what had happened to his wife (Emily's aunt) during his Presidential campaign. Emily and her husband stayed in Nashville through the next Washington, D.C. social season while yet another of Rachel's nieces, Sarah Jackson, served as the White House hostess.

As it turns out, there really wasn't much need for a hostess in the White House; most of the cabinet member's wives were avoiding the White House over the whole Peggy Eaton affair anyway. This is what led to the resigning of nearly every cabinet member in the Jackson Administration aside from Secretary of State, Martin Van Buren. Van Buren had no wife. She had died many years prior to his moving to Washington. Emily would never return as hostess, John Eaton would resign from his post and things would slowly get back to normal in Washington, D.C.

Historical Note – The Petticoat Affair

The effects of the "Petticoat affair" as it would come to be known, continued well into the Hayes Administration. First Lady Lucy Hayes sent flowers to Peggy Eaton's funeral, and in return, received a bit of grief from a few local socialites. These are the same socialites who Rachel Jackson had once referred to as "cave dwellers" after a visit to Washington, D.C.

Emily Donelson's presence at the Hermitage is very easy to feel. They have her official portrait, along with a few needlepoint samplers and other childhood items. She and her family lived nearby and she grew up not far from her Aunt and Uncle's plantation. The Hermitage also has a wonderful portrait of Peggy Eaton that adds to the telling and understanding of the influence this woman had on the Jackson Administration and American Presidential and political history.

While Jackson was President, Andrew Jackson, Jr. had purchased some acreage from his uncle and the overall Hermitage estate. He started building a house of his own there for himself, Emily and their children. Emily fell ill during the construction and died in 1836, the same year the house was finally completed.

Emily, Andrew Jackson, Jr. and their children are buried in the cemetery at the Hermitage church along with other Jackson and Donelson family members.

Side Note – Going For A Drive

I was also able to take a bit of a drive and see my brother's family for dinner in Huntsville, Alabama. This is a wonderful thing about traveling for work – once the work is done, and if you have the added advantage of being prepared for your next day, you can meet up with friends and family all across the country. I did this as often as possible, and in the process, saw many high school and college friends that I hadn't seen in many, many years. I was also able to meet up with colleagues, meet some of their families, and make new friendships with the folks at the places I was filming. All in all it was a great professional and personal adventure.

SUMMARY

Emily Donelson was a young, attractive and well-liked hostess in her uncle's White House. It is unfortunate that she got wrapped up in the Peggy Eaton affair, and even more unfortunate that she didn't side with her uncle, President Andrew, Jackson on the matter. It became and still is one of the most interesting scandals in Washington, D.C. as it resulted in nearly the entire cabinet resigning. This coupled with the fact that it is the beginning of the longest running period of time without an official First Lady made it quite an interesting period in American History – specifically when it came to women's role in early American History and the White House.

However, putting the Peggy Eaton affair aside for a moment, let's look at Emily Donelson for the woman she was, a niece who stepped up and into the role of arguably the most visible woman in America. She certainly didn't solicit that life. She didn't marry a President. She just happened to marry her cousin who was close with her Aunt's husband, a man who would become President. That alone wouldn't have ensured a position of hostess for the President – his wife, her Aunt, had to die in order for the position to be bestowed upon her. She was well taught, well learned and unusual for her time. She was capable of taking on the hostessing and duties of a First Lady, even if that wasn't part of her original plan in life. Who knows what she might have been known for had the whole Peggy Eaton affair not placed her on the wrong side of Jackson's favor? Sometimes all it takes is one little ripple to turn into a tidal wave that changes the entire course of history – and upends the lives of the people who are there when it happens.

Travelogue Food Tip

While not highly recommended for the unusual or remarkable menu, it is in Nashville, Tennessee that I ate at a Jack in the Box for the first time. It's fun to spice things up and try new things when you're on the road.

CHAPTER 9
Hannah Van Buren

Kinderhook, New York

annah Van Buren was born Hannah Hoes on March 8, 1783 in Kinderhook, New York. Her parents were John Dirchsen Hoes and Maria Quachenboss Hoes. Hannah and Martin Van Buren were married on February 21, 1807. Hannah and Martin had five children together. Hannah Hoes Van Buren died in Albany, New York on February 5, 1819 at the age of 35.

KINDERHOOK, NEW YORK

Hannah Van Buren had been dead for about 18 years when Martin Van Buren became President. To learn about his long deceased wife, and his daughter-in-law, Angelica Singleton Van Buren, I traveled to Kinderhook, New York. People often ask me about the order of my studies and travels. The group of women – Jackson, Polk, Van Buren and Fillmore are a perfect example of how out of order things could get because of various factors – show schedule, region, and available locations. I had started this particular week off in Nashville for Jackson, and hit up the Polk ancestral home, which was basically next door, in Columbia, Tennessee. I then went to East Aurora, New York for Fillmore, because it was on the way to Kinderhook where I was scheduled for a visit at the end of the week.

After my work for Sarah Polk in the sunny 70 degrees of Columbia, Tennessee, I was off to the airport, whereupon landing, I went to pick up my rental car and a snow scraper in Albany, New York (this is where a cold starts to set in). I went from getting a trucker's tan in Tennessee (arm out the window and sunroof open) to drifting through the Finger Lakes in a sweater and a snowstorm. I was on my way to East Aurora, New York to visit the Fillmore House and then on over to Kinderhook for a visit to the Van Buren's homestead. I had already covered the Tyler women when I was in Virginia earlier for the first handful of shows, the Anna Harrison and Margaret Taylor stories are minimal at best, and they didn't require travel, so I did some skipping around here. In a project like this, sometimes it just works out that you have to do a lot of driving with a lot of gear (easier than airports, TSA and baggage claim) to many different regions and climates to make it all work and in the end, that's just what I did.

Health Note – A Cold Coming On

Kinderhook was at the end of a long week that had begun with me having a pretty severe cold. Did I mention that at the end of this whole adventure, I had chalked up a bout with walking pneumonia, a couple of run of the mill colds, a need for prescription glasses and a few shots of cortisone in my lower lumbar area and right hip joint? Suffice it to say, I get into my work.

SO...Hannah Van Buren. I will sum it up like this. There ain't much! Many books I read don't even mention Hannah. This includes Martin Van Buren's autobiography. We know from Martha Washington and Elizabeth Monroe, many people burn the letters of their deceased spouses or they burn their own letters themselves when they know the end is near. This is the case for Martin and Hannah Van Buren. But there are a few things that remain, and I was able to find and see those things at the Van Buren's Lindenwald estate. Though Hannah never stepped foot in the house or on the property, some of her items have made their way into the collection there.

The wonderful National Park Service Ranger staff was able to produce a small cameo brooch style pendant of the only known image of Hannah Van Buren for me to capture on video. This was interesting because it was hauntingly similar to Andrew Jackson's pendant of his deceased wife, the one he kept on or near him night and day. So, this meant one of two things. It was either just the "thing to do" in those days, or Van Buren saw Jackson's and got the idea for this sweet yet quiet tribute to his wife. Either way, it exists and they have it at Lindenwald and I was able to see and hold it.

The other thing they have in their collection is Hannah's personal sewing kit. The item itself isn't all that exceptional. It's a small wooden box with needles, thread and other items you would expect to see in any sewing kit. The special-ness of this item comes in the fact that it's all there is. This woman – Hannah Hoes Van Buren – is all but forgotten in the pages of history, reduced to, and remembered by only these two items. Sad? Maybe. Poetic? Maybe that, as well. We don't know the specific stories of these items, or their significance – if any – to her Presidential husband. All we know is that they were hers, and they are basically all we have of her.

There wasn't much to Hannah's story in Kinderhook, but what was there…I got.

SUMMARY

Even the First Ladies history appears to have set aside have a story to tell. Even if that story comes in the form of two small and relatively innocuous items, they still existed. Hannah Van Buren had five sons with her husband. The oldest – Abraham – would marry the woman who became his father's White House hostess. Hannah Van Buren was a part of Martin Van Buren's life and his story, even if it was a story that he didn't need to share with the world.

Travelogue Food Tip

See Angelica Singleton Van Buren (next chapter).

CHAPTER 10

Angelica Singleton Van Buren

Kinderhook, New York

$\mathcal{A}$ ngelica Singleton Van Buren was born Sarah Angelica Singleton on February 13, 1818 in Wedgefield, South Carolina. Her parents were Colonel Richard Singleton and Rebecca Travis Coles. She was the cousin of Senator William C. Preston and First Lady Dolley Madison. Angelica and Abraham Van Buren (President Van Buren's oldest son) were married on November 27, 1838. Angelica and Abraham had four children together. Angelica Singleton Van Buren died on December 29, 1877 in New York, New York at the age of 59.

KINDERHOOK, NEW YORK

Angelica Singleton was born to wealthy plantation owners and tobacco growers in South Carolina. She was well educated, and a very capable woman of her time. She had excellent horseback skills, and would ride with her sister

89

Marion over the acres and acres of their family's property. She was raised in a world of entertaining and privilege. Her family was related or connected to almost every important family in the South. This included a relation by marriage to Dolley Madison. In fact, it's Dolley Madison who introduces her to President Martin Van Buren's oldest son, Abraham.

Fun Fact – Dolley Madison! Drink!

During the research, traveling, recording and live broadcasts of the "FIRST LADIES: Influence and Image", it turns out that Dolley Madison lived so long, and was involved directly or indirectly in so many administrations, that the production team thought college kids would make a Dolley Madison drinking game out of our series. Every time Dolley Madison's name was mentioned in a show – you take a drink, sip, chug or shot.

Angelica was visiting her widowed cousin Dolley Madison in Washington, D.C.; Dolley had just moved back to D.C., and was getting her name back on all the guest lists, and paid a visit to the new President. She brought her sophisticated, pretty and single cousin, Angelica, with her. Angelica Singleton and Abraham Van Buren hit it off, and the rest as they say, is history – which is why we're all here – isn't it?

So, Martin Van Buren needed a hostess, and when the young newlyweds came back from their European honeymoon, Angelica was all too eager to get started. It would seem that the ever-fickle Washington, D.C. society was still reeling from the Jackson Administration and the Peggy Eaton affair. Washington's elite were not welcoming of Angelica. She was a society girl that liked to throw lavish parties, meanwhile, the country, as a whole was not doing well financially. I will say this though, had she not thrown parties, or not thrown the "right" kind of parties, D.C. would have called her a rube and made her a public laughing stock like they did to poor Rachel Jackson. Again, politics is ruthless and not for the faint at heart.

The fact remained that Angelica did return a great deal of pomp and circumstance to the White House in a time when the country might have been looking for a bit of financial restraint. By most accounts, Angelica took this all in stride, and served in her father-in-law's White House very capably as far as her abilities and hostessing skills. Some attributed her lavish style and indulgence to her father-in-law's re-election loss.

Lindenwald is a large estate on a good bit of farmland; President Van Buren purchased it the second year of his Presidency and Angelica, her husband and their three sons would spend summer months there in Kinderhook. When Angelica was there, she filled the role as hostess just as she did in the White House. President Van Buren had a lot of political and personal friends and entertained often. Park Ranger Jim McKay was an excellent resource and a great guide around the estate.

When you walk in the house you are immediately in the large, formal dining room. There is beautiful dark, hardwood furniture all around the room including the huge table, which spans the length of the long room. The room is so big and dark it was difficult to get the lighting right to give the video piece and the viewer an idea of its cavernous dimensions.

Production Note – It's Electric

If you are in an old historic house looking for an electrical outlet, look in the chimneys and the fireplaces. They usually hide them there.

The dining room was appointed with really wild looking green glass bowls and serving pieces. There was also very dramatic and full colored cloth wallpaper similar to Andrew Jackson's home at the Hermitage. Angelica's formal training and travels made her quite the hostess. She knew all the appropriate customs and rules of 19th century sophistication. So much so that the French Ambassador to the U.S. remarked about her wonderful skills and grace as a hostess. This was quite the compliment as the French were said to be highly critical of American customs at the time. So, it's easy to imagine this massive room filled with people and activity as Angelica worked the room and made sure everything was just right for the event. Formal dining rooms are elegant and are full of neat and unusual things to look at, but the real treat for me in these homes is always seeing the private rooms and the family spaces where these folks could be more themselves.

One such room at this house was the breakfast room to the left of the formal dining room; it was located closer to the kitchen. This room was set with the Van Buren daily china. The signature "VB" surrounded by a light green line and a smaller gold line. It was subtle, but elegant daily ware. It was fun to see this smaller nook of a room, and think about the younger Van Buren family visiting and eating here each day.

The parlor or Green Room off to the right of the formal dining room was where Angelica entertained ladies when she and her family were in Kinderhook. This was an ample room with nicely decorated parlor furniture and a period harp. Angelica was formally trained to play the harp in Philadelphia. Playing for her guests would've been one of the many forms of entertainment provided here. The women also recited poetry, made paper flower arrangements and discussed family events and news of the day. It was again nice to see and picture where these women spent their day and what they did to occupy their time.

The private bedrooms upstairs were also a treat. In these bedrooms, I was shown both formal and every day dresses that belonged to Angelica. Among the items in the bedroom was one of Angelica's parasols. It was black lace with ivory handle, and she would no doubt use it on her many strolls over the property. I would guess this would remind her of her outings with her sister back in South Carolina, she clearly enjoyed the outdoors. Overall, the house was very nice with large rooms, and I imagine the Van Burens were very comfortable during their time here.

I was also shown a very personal item to Angelica. It was a daybed style chaise lounge that she wrote about very specifically. Angelica and Abraham had five children together. They had three sons who lived to adulthood, one daughter who died very young and another daughter lost as a result of miscarriage while in

Kinderhook in 1843. In a letter she wrote about recovering from the miscarriage on this very couch, while she watched her sons play outside through a window. These are the kinds of very special artifacts with written evidence as to their significance that give us a window into the lives of these women. The Lindenwald estate in Kinderhook gives a very good personal and public view of the lives of the Van Buren women.

SUMMARY

Angelica Singleton Van Buren was already unusual for her time because of her upbringing and social status. Not everyone goes to Washington, D.C. to stay with their cousin who happens to be Dolley Madison and gets introduced to and marries the President's son. Not only was she raised in good fortune; she had the intelligence to support her privileges and opportunities. On their honeymoon in Europe the young Van Burens were introduced to royalty and attend a number of official events as ambassadors for President Van Buren. Angelica was not only tall and beautiful; she had the social graces of a sophisticated woman of the 19th century. She presented herself in a way that got her the attention and praise of European diplomacy. At this time in our history, that was no small feat. I guess my point is, that on the world's stage, money and beauty will only get you so far. Even if it was to the detriment of her father-in-law's political career, Angelica Singleton Van Buren could walk the walk and talk the talk. And by all accounts President Martin Van Buren cared for her very much.

Travelogue Food Tip

In my travels, I have found that diners always have chef salads on the menu. Every chef salad I have ever ordered in any diner has been fantastic. The Carolina House diner was no exception. I got ranch dressing on mine and had the Snickers cheesecake for dessert.

CHAPTER 11
Anna Harrison

North Bend, Ohio – Vincennes, Indiana – Indianapolis, Indiana

*C*nna Harrison was born Anna Tuthill Symmes on July 25, 1775 in Flatbrook, New Jersey. Her parents were Judge John Cleves Symmes and Anna Tuthill Symmes. Anna and William Harrison were married on November 22, 1795. Anna and William had ten children together. Anna Harrison died on February 25, 1864 in North Bend, Ohio at the age of 88.

This is a tough chapter to write. It is a chapter that will be expanded in future editions of the book. As I have mentioned, the C-SPAN series schedule was tight and rigorous. Difficult decisions had to be made about locations and various First Ladies. The series was called "FIRST LADIES: Influence and Image", and the executive decision was to always take the "FIRST LADY" part of the woman into consideration (which makes sense given the title of the series).

Anna Harrison never stepped foot in Washington, D.C. Anna Harrison's husband – William Henry Harrison – has the distinct notoriety of having the shortest Presidential administration in history. He was the oldest President in U.S. History, having been elected at the age of 68, a record that would hold until Ronald Reagan was sworn in at 76 years in 1981. To prove that he was fit to be President, Harrison declined a ride in a warm carriage and rode his horse down Pennsylvania Avenue in the dead of winter. He then delivered the longest inaugural speech in history on a blustery day without wearing a coat or hat. Shortly after his inauguration he was diagnosed with pneumonia and died 32 days into his Presidency. Anna had stayed behind in Ohio to wait for better weather and to pack up the house. She planned to join her husband in the spring. I heard a story that the last thing Anna said to her husband was to make sure he bought a new suit for the ceremony. One of Harrison's daughters and a daughter-in-law went along with him to represent Mrs. Harrison at the inauguration. Anna Harrison decided not to attend the funeral in Washington, D.C. and tend to things at home, in preparation for a second, more private funeral and burial service.

Due to these circumstances, the series decided to quickly discuss Anna Harrison at the beginning of a show that covered: Anna Harrison, Letitia Tyler and Julia Tyler. I did not travel to learn about or cover Anna Harrison. However, this does not mean that those places do not exist or that I didn't learn about her in my travels.

NORTH BEND, OHIO

Anna Harrison was born in New Jersey, but after the Revolutionary War and the first Continental Congress, Anna's father was in a position to buy one million (yes...ONE MILLION) acres in the territory that is present day Ohio. This is where Anna gets her foothold and beginnings in Ohio. This is where she and William settle down for most of their lives. This is where they are both buried. The tombs are surrounded by a golf course today. There are living ancestors and an active historical society with artifacts and much to tell about Anna Harrison's life in North Bend. So, this is a place I need to go on my own, explore and learn. I did make a few connections and will re-connect with them to expand this chapter in the future.

VINCENNES, INDIANA

Grouseland is the home that Anna and William Harrison had built and shared while he was Governor of Indiana. Since this was an even smaller part of Anna Harrison's life in her limited role as First Lady, this location was also not included in the series or my travels for the series. In my quest to learn everything about all aspects of these women, I will travel here and write up an account of what I see and learn in the next edition.

INDIANAPOLIS, INDIANA

While researching and filming at the Benjamin Harrison House in Indianapolis, Indiana, I was shown a number of family heirlooms and artifacts. Benjamin Harrison was the Grandson of Anna and William Henry Harrison. Therefore, some items were inherited and passed down through the family. The top floor of the house in Indianapolis has been converted into a small museum. They have a wonderful collection, and a number of rotating artifacts on loan. Among these items was some jewelry. This was a really neat thing to see and experience. The shared lives and items in a family of Presidents is a very unique thing. Even though Anna Harrison's stint as First Lady was brief and she never saw the inside of the White House, she and her family are still a part of American History and their lives are well worth learning about.

Fun Facts – First Lady Firsts

The Harrison family has many ties to Mercersburg, PA. President James Buchanan and his niece, Harriet Lane, herself a White House hostess were both born in Mercersburg, PA. I will get to these connections in the Harriet Lane chapter in the Mercersburg section.
Anna Harrison was the oldest First Lady at the age of 65.
Anna Harrison was the first First Lady with a public education.
Anna Harrison was the first First Lady to receive franking privileges (she was permitted to send mail without paying for postage)

SUMMARY

It's too bad Anna Harrison never made it to Washington to fulfill her duties as First Lady. She was described as a smart and politically engaged woman – more so than most women in the 1800's. She probably could've gotten along well with Abigail Adams, Dolley Madison, Sarah Polk, Mary Lincoln, Edith Wilson, Eleanor Roosevelt, Hillary Clinton and any of the other politically astute First Ladies. She continued to use her political savvy and influence long after her husband's death.

Travelogue Food Tip

I'll let you know when I get there!

CHAPTER 12
Letitia Tyler

New Kent County Tidewater, Virginia – Williamsburgh, Virginia – Washington, D.C.

*L*etitia Tyler was born Letitia Christian on November 12, 1790 on the Cedar Grove Plantation in New Kent County Tidewater, Virginia. Her parents were Robert Christian and Mary Browne Christian. Letitia and John Tyler were married in Letitia's parent's Cedar Grove home on March 29, 1813. Letitia and John had nine children together (seven that lived to adulthood). Letitia Tyler died in Washington, D.C. on September 10, 1842 at the age of 51.

NEW KENT COUNTY, VIRGINIA

It was a chilly and windy November day, just before Thanksgiving when I drove down the long winding road that led me to the brick buttress gates of Cedar Grove. This was part of my first trip out for season one of the series. I had set up the visit with the stable manager at the Cedar Grove Plantation. The plantation is now operated as stables and an outdoor location for weddings and private events. The family that owns the property also stays in the main residence from time to time. I was scheduled to meet the current owner here for a private tour. Letitia Tyler was born on this, her family's plantation, and she, along with her family, is buried here.

I was informed by a hired hand that my phone contact had stepped out for the morning and the owner was "on his way" to meet me. I was given permission to get started without him having a look around and getting footage. The owner didn't want to be interviewed on camera, as he didn't consider himself a historian, but was happy to show me around, let me in the house and tell me what he knew. The first thing I did –which was getting to be a standard for me – was to get establishing shots of the front gate and sign for the property.

I was surprised at how much traffic there was on this backwoods two-lane road. There were woods and fields on one side of me and the plantation on the other. I pulled my car inside the gates, took out my gear, got set up and started my routine. After I got enough of the gates and surrounding area, I decided to have a walk around. The house was pretty far down the road, and I knew I would get to that when my host arrived.

As I walked past the first few trees, I saw a small brick wall that formed a relatively small square off to my left. From the looks of things, it could only be one thing. A cemetery. At this point, I knew Letitia was on the plantation, but it was somehow surprising to me that she and her family were just out in the middle of a field behind a small and easily navigable brick wall. There wasn't even a gate. With my camera and tripod slung over my shoulder, I just walked right in. This was my first cemetery of the series. I'm not sure what I was expecting. A gate? A lock? A ticket booth? Something. What I wasn't expecting was nothing. But that's what it was. Nothing big. There was an American flag kind of stuck in the ground and leaning over to the side, blown by the wind. I later found out from the owner that he had no idea who put it there; it just "showed up one day". I pulled the flag out of the ground and placed it to the side for a clear shot of the graves.

Production Note – Put It Back Where You Found It

TV people will come in and rearrange an entire house if you let them. The good ones (of which I consider myself to be) will always ask permission and always put everything back EXACTLY the way they found it. I should reiterate here, that I am welcome back at every place I have visited, I never had to use my insurance and many places said what a pleasure I was to work with unlike many "of those other TV crews" they had dealt with over the years. I have a great respect for these locations, the artifacts, the people who work and study there, and C-SPAN's good name. In fact, working for C-SPAN and this project was such a great experience because of their good name and reputation; I wasn't going to be the one to spoil it.

I set my camera and tripod down in the corner and took a walk around the graves. Some were stand up tombstones, others were ground markers, and the main family members were long full slabs. I found Letitia and her parents. I stopped for a moment to take it all in. Remember, this was my first trip out and my first cemetery. And I had just stumbled upon the graves of a First Lady of the United States and her family. It gave me an early perspective on the significance of this project, the access I was going to have and the rare opportunities that would be presented to me. I realize that I've said this before in this book, and SPOILER ALERT…I will be saying it again.

As I was concluding my recording in the cemetery, I noticed a thumping sound coming closer from up in the air. It was a helicopter flying pretty low, and looking like it was coming in for a landing. Sure enough, the chopper came right over the plantation and set down on a patch of open grass between the main house and the pond. I started walking across the field towards the helicopter as a lone man got out, and set a little dog down on the ground. The pilot was the owner and my host at Cedar Grove. He and his canine co-pilot had flown up from Virginia Beach to give me a tour and repair a fence.

The man was very casually dressed in farm work wear (jeans, flannel shirt and Carhardt work jacket). After quickly introducing ourselves, the man handed me a set of commemorative John and Letitia Tyler coins, which I keep to this day as special mementos of my adventure. I gave him a C-SPAN First Ladies ruler and book mark. With gifts and greetings exchanged we headed off to the main house.

Much of the house was original, but most of it had been carefully modernized and refurbished. As I mentioned, the family does get together, and spend time there multiple times throughout the year. However, there were a few very significant things that were original and specific to Letitia and John Tyler and their lives there.

The house is tall and long but narrow. This original design that had a front and back door directly across an open foyer is an intentional design. In the summer months, the doors were kept open to create a cross breeze through the house to keep things as cool as possible. We opened both sets of doors to get a real feel of the current that could be created. Just standing in this open area between the two doorways gave me a real sense of what the Tylers and their guest would've seen and felt during a stay or attending an event there. The doors were also significant to another story about the property. It only makes sense that my first cemetery would come with my first ghost story.

One winter evening, a caretaker was staying at the residence or working on something in the house. It was snowing pretty heavily outside, and the man heard a knock at the front door. He went to the door, opened it but no one was there. No footprints on the steps, either. Nothing. He thought, as most would, must be the wind or tree branches on the house. Then, he heard a knock at the back door, which faces the cemetery. He slowly opened the back door to again find no one there and no footprints. He reported hearing a woman's voice off in the distance, which again could've been the wind or something outside, but he was now convinced that it was someone knocking on the doors…twice…once at the front and once at the back. I absolutely love stuff like this. And this wouldn't be my last cemetery or ghost story of the series.

After a couple shivers, and the conclusion of the ghost story, we shut the doors and continued the tour.

I was then shown the living room and fireplace, which was also mostly original in layout. This is where John Tyler married Letitia Christian on May 29, 1813. She was a young, attractive and intelligent woman. However, she was not formally educated. She was born to a family of prominent tobacco growers, and John Tyler was an ambitious young lawyer. Sound familiar? Well, it should. This is the formula for many of our country's presidents and men of power. This is not to take anything away from these great men of intelligence and influence who created and lead this great country of ours. I merely and accurately note that the women they chose to marry (more times than not) added financial stability and social status to the man who would be elected President.

This again, was a very cool and special moment. To stand in the place where two people would begin their lives together so long ago. A couple that would go on to be President and First Lady of America. In a house and place that was not typically open to the public. This would've been one of the happiest times of their lives together.

WILLIAMSBURG, VIRGINIA

The Tylers and their nine children (seven lived to adulthood) lived in a modest house in Williamsburg in 1836. John Tyler resigned from the U.S. Senate, and moved his law practice here. Tyler had already enjoyed a successful political career as both a U.S. Senator and Governor of Virginia and here in Williamsburg; he resurrected his career as a lawyer. Always quietly by his side, was Letitia. In 1836, a stroke left Mrs. Tyler wheelchair bound and not well. She still ran the household. She just ran it from her bedroom. His law office has been rebuilt in its original location, in the center of town, near the courthouse. Tyler was in Williamsburg when he became President Harrison's Vice President. In fact, because of Letitia's health, he served in his capacity as Vice President from there.

On April 5, 1841, a messenger arrived with news that President Harrison had died and he was now to fulfill the duties of the President of the United States. This is the first time in U.S. History that a Vice President was "promoted" to President. This also meant that Letitia was now First Lady, and the Tylers had to move to Washington, D.C. and into the White House. The amazing thing that I learned here in Williamsburg, is that the Constitution was written to allow for the Vice President take over the duties of a President, should the sitting President not be able to do so himself; and yet, the terms of the Constitution did not specifically name the Vice President the new President. Tyler didn't wait to hear the specifics and particulars about this discrepancy, and moved right into the White House and assumed the Presidency. In fact, Tyler ignored documents that referred to him as the "Acting President". His claims to the full Presidency were never officially challenged. Congress let him stay, but said there were no rules or provisions to pay him. Thanks to Letitia's family land, businesses and money, Tyler didn't feel he needed a salary and went without pay. This decision and the worries that came along with it, may have contributed to Letitia's declining health while in Washington.

Legal Note – Mr. President?

The U.S. Constitution states that should the president die, become disabled while in office or be removed from office, the "powers and duties" of the office are transferred to the vice president. After no legal challenge to Tyler's claim to the Presidency, the precedent of full succession was established. It wasn't made constitutionally legal until 1967 by the Twenty Fifth Amendment. The Twenty Fifth Amendment makes all issues and situations of succession clear. Some other Presidents to take advantage of the precedent set by Tyler are: Millard Fillmore, Andrew Johnson, Chester Arthur, Theodore Roosevelt, Calvin Coolidge and Lyndon Baines Johnson.

WASHINGTON, D.C.

While in the White House Letitia was very ill and kept to her room on the second floor almost exclusively. One of the only times she made a public appearance was for her daughter Elizabeth's wedding in the East Room in January 1842. This was the second daughter of a Presidential couple to have a wedding in the White House. James and Elizabeth Monroe's daughter, Maria was the first, in 1820. While Letitia was running the White House from her bedroom, Letitia's daughter-in-law Priscilla Cooper Tyler (married to their oldest son, Robert) took care of the public hostessing duties in her Father-in-Law's White House. She was a well-educated actress, and perfect for the role. Priscilla very humbly said of her Mother-In-Law that she "attends to and regulates all so quietly that you can't tell she does it." Which should come as no surprise. Even in poor health back in Williamsburg, she ran the family business with quiet competence and efficiency from her bedroom. In the summer of 1842, after extreme heat and financial stresses, Letitia suffered another stroke. This would ultimately lead to her death on September 10, 1842. Letitia Tyler was the first First Lady to die in the White House.

SUMMARY

Letitia Tyler is a perfect example of a woman, unusual for her time, a woman who stood behind a great man only to make him greater. Her family money and businesses along with her social standing in and around Virginia, elevated an up and coming lawyer and put him in position to have a successful political career. She was not formally educated, but showed signs of high intelligence. Even in the poorest of health, she ran a tight household. She was young, pretty, well liked and produced many children with Tyler. She was the quintessential political wife of the 1800's. There is no telling what she would have been able to do, had she lived a healthier, more public and longer life.

Travelogue Food Tip

The Blue Talon Bistro in Merchant's Square in Williamsburg is some of the finest French cuisine around. I have eaten there on two separate trips, and I plan on eating there again. I got the mussels both times. Their soups are also phenomenal. The first time I ate there, I had the crème brulee ice cream for dessert. BLOWN AWAY. They did not have it on the menu my second go 'round, and I am hoping my third time will also be a charm. Samantha Lacher Lieberson was the first person to take me to the Blue Talon Bistro. I should mention here, that she was also the person that set up all my interviews and tours in Williamsburg that produced so much great material on Martha Washington, both Jefferson women and Letitia Tyler. Thank you, Sam.

CHAPTER 13
Julia Tyler

Charles City, Virginia

Juila Tyler was born Julia Gardiner on May 20, 1820 on Gardiner's Island off the eastern point of New York's Long Island. Her parents were Senator David Gardiner and Julianna Mclachlan Gardiner. Gardiner's Island was purchased seven generations before by Lion Gardiner from the Montauk Indians. It is one of the largest privately owned land masses in the United States, and Gardiner family members still live there to this day. Julia and John Tyler were married on June 26, 1844. Julia and John had seven children together (adding to the nine he had with his first wife). Julia Tyler died on July 10, 1889 in Richmond, Virginia at the age of 69.

Side Note – Spelling Lesson

Per Mrs. Payne (pronounced PAY-NEE) Tyler (relation to be explained later in the chapter), Julia's ancestor Lion Gardiner spelled his name with an "i" like the animal. It wasn't until Julia married John Tyler that the spelling of the family name was changed to Lyon with a "y". A special thanks goes out to my friend Payne for this correction during the final edit of this book. In email correspondence she said that she enjoyed her pre-published read of the Julia Tyler chapter and wished me success. I wish her, her husband, Harrison Tyler, and the entire Tyler family at Sherwood Forest good heath and happy days ahead.

CHARLES CITY, VIRGINIA

The story of how a young 23-year-old Julia Gardiner met a newly widowed 52-year-old President John Tyler is a remarkable one, to say the least. What's even more remarkable is the fact that the story was told to me by Tyler's living grandson, Harrison Ruffin Tyler, while we sat in the living room of his grandfather's house where Harrison Ruffin Tyler and his wife Payne currently live.

President Tyler had more children than any other U.S. President to date. He had two wives, the first of whom died, leaving him a widower. Julia bore his last child, a daughter named Pearl, when President Tyler was 70 years old. Stick with me on this…

Lyon Gardiner Tyler (who went on to become the 17th President of the College of William and Mary) was the fifth born child of Julia and John Tyler. He was born August 24, 1853. Lyon had two wives. Similar to his father, he lost his first wife and remarried. His son, Harrison Ruffin Tyler, was born to his second wife in 1928. Lyon was 75 when Harrison was born. So, here are two men with two wives a piece, both of whom fathered children into their 70's. That is how I ended up sitting in the living room of the 10th President of the United States; interviewing his grandson, Harrison Ruffin Tyler, who was 84 at the time. After our sit down interview, he rushed off to Richmond for his weekly tennis match, and I spent the rest of the afternoon with his lovely wife, Payne

Side Note – All In The Family

I should mention that this is not the only tour of a President's house I received from a Presidential grandchild. It's just the most unique set of circumstances under which such a tour and meeting was conducted. More on that down the road.

Back to Julia Tyler. In 1843, young Julia Gardiner was in Washington, D.C. with her father, New York Senator David Gardiner. Former First Lady Dolley Madison (drink) had set up a trip for the Senator, his daughter (Julia), President Tyler and a few others to go down the Potomac on the new gunboat, named the Princeton.

So, the story as told to me by Tyler's grandson goes like this:

The group was assembled on the Princeton and went down the Potomac to fire the new gun at a barge, which had been moored out in the middle of the river as a dummy target. The demonstration went well and everyone was pleased. As they turned around and headed back to the Navy Yard, they passed Mount Vernon and decided to fire the gun again in honor of George Washington. When the cannon was fired the second time, the right side of the large gun blew out and killed seven people. Among those killed were the Secretary of State, the Secretary of the Navy and Julia's father, Senator Gardiner. Everyone below deck felt the boat shake when the gun misfired, and all the handsome young sailors that were surrounding young Julia ran to get upstairs to see what had happened. President Tyler, who had been trying to get past the young men for Julia's attention, was left alone with Julia. Julia then ran to the stairs to head up, as she knew her father was up on deck, and the President fell in behind her. As Julia and the President headed up, a sailor came running back and said not to let Ms. Gardiner up, that her father had been killed. When Julia heard this, she fainted.

She fell back into the arms of President Tyler who caught her "tenderly and gently". The ship sailed back and docked. President Tyler carried Julia down the gangplank. As she was being carried down the gangplank, she came to and woke up. She would later write her mother that the first thing she remembered was the President carrying her off the ship. Her head had fallen over into the crook of his arm and she was staring up into his eyes. She wrote that it was at this point that she realized that the President "loved her dearly".

I had read this story and numerous similar accounts in many books before my visit to Sherwood Forest; many of the elements did not come as a surprise. But no rendition did it the justice or had the classical romance and flair than the one told to me in person by Harrison Ruffin Tyler. The President's grandson admitted his version was a family story that was based on fact and it had been passed down through the years. With a twinkle in his eye, Harrison said that some of the details might have been embellished through the years. However, he added that he was sure that his grandfather was nothing but a Southern gentleman, and the details could not have been far off the mark. The amazing thing is that even though Harrison never met either of his grandparents, they were still his grandparents, and his rendition was both endearing and charming.

At the conclusion of the story of his grandparent's meeting, Harrison left with his son for his tennis match, and I was left in the very capable hands of his wife, Payne Tyler. Payne led the charge to purchase and refurbish the house in the 70's. She is also quite the historian and tour guide herself. She is also a regular Danica Patrick behind the wheel of a golf cart. We began our afternoon in the same room in which I had interviewed her husband; there I would learn more about Julia, President Tyler and their Sherwood Forest home.

Like many homes and properties during the Civil War, it had changed hands at various times; had been damaged, burned and in some cases, demolished to a certain extent during those occupations. The Tylers purchased the property as President Tyler was leaving the White House and Julia said "the hand of God has been kind to my Sherwood Forest, but I can improve upon it." Julia was very house proud and brought in a number of things from Italy to spruce up the place. The original brass knocker is still on the front door. Even with all the time that has passed, the battles, and the damage done by soldiers and others, remarkably, many original items remain and it is truly like stepping back in time when you visit here.

Julia and her mother were very close, and many letters remain in existence, with details that enabled Payne and husband to not only rebuild the house as it was originally designed, but they also learned about Julia and John Tyler's life together here. Julia often sat on the south side of their home, and overlooked the porch and backyard while she wrote letters to her mother. She often wrote about the President sitting in a chair, reading his newspaper, with his boots casually propped up on the banister. The original banister is still there and when you stand in the middle of the hallway it is easy to imagine the President on one side and Julia on the other, enjoying a summer breeze and each other's company.

These letters that Julia wrote allow us to know about events that happened in the home. Julia threw a ball in honor of her sister Margaret, who visited very frequently. She wrote that the ball started at 9 o'clock and they danced the Virginia reel, a folk dance, and the Waltz until the sun came up. It is also reported that the finest champagne flowed endlessly. Hanging in the main living room is a portrait of Julia and her younger sister Margaret as children. By the ocean in the background, we can only assume that it was painted to represent, Gardiner's Island in New York. Where Julia grew up.

Along with the numerous letters, Julia kept very complete records of all of the purchases for the household, which was very common for a lady of such an estate to do. This confirms the origin and originality of many of the items that remain in the house today. There is an original table upon which President Tyler served Julia breakfast every morning. The President would go for a horseback ride, and then personally bring breakfast in on a tray for him and his wife. In a letter to Julia, her mother writes, "do not take advantage of an elderly man who dotes upon you." Her mother had heard from visitors (perhaps Julia's sister Margaret) that she slept until 9am every morning.

There is also a long mirror that stretches from floor to ceiling, and records show that Julia's brothers were her buying agents; they purchased the mirror from a store called Baudan's and she was upset that the edges of the mirror covered the window facing in the room. Her mother told her not to be concerned with "such minutia." When you have such vivid and complete letters about specific items in a house like this, it really makes them come alive and the stories become that much more real. It was humbling to be reminded that I was in someone's house. They lived here. This was much more than a museum or a Historical landmark. It was a home to Julia and President Tyler and their many children and relatives.

Among the various paintings in the house at Sherwood Forest was a landscape oil painting that confirms a wonderful story that I had read during my research of Julia Tyler. Before Julia met the President, she traveled to Europe as many young women of privilege did in those days. While she was there, a foreign dignitary's son (a Bavarian Baron) took quite a liking to her. Later, when she became First Lady, this man was one of Julia's first guests in the White House, and he brought her this painting as a gift. Things like this really made the story jump off the pages of history and stand boldly right in front of my eyes, and my camera. It was remarkable to see the painting in this home, one that had such a fascinating and spirited story behind it, hanging right within reach on the wall.

Payne related a story to me that topped them all. It was the story of Julia's departure from Sherwood Forest when the fighting during the Civil War intensified.

Historical Note – The War Between The States

I should add here that the Payne and Harrison do not call it the Civil War. Mrs. Tyler was quick to diplomatically tell me they preferred to say the War of Northern Aggression or the War Between the States.

Julia decided to leave the property in the care of a relative, pack up the younger children and head out of town. She gathered her finest dresses, took down the curtains, packed everything and everyone into a carriage and headed for Richmond, Virginia. On the way, she and her sentinel came upon a fierce battle. The sentinel announced the he had the former First Lady of the United States of America and her children with him and they needed safe passage. The fighting stopped, and the small caravan was permitted to pass through. They continued on to Richmond where she sold the dresses and curtains for about $10,000. She took this money and continued on to Wilmington, North Carolina. There she bought cotton and sailed to Bermuda. Julia sold the cotton in Bermuda to cover her daily costs of living. She and her children remained there until the end of the war at which point she sold her remaining cotton in order to sail north to reunite with her mother on Staten Island in New York. It is here where Julia's support of the South and her politics got her in trouble with her brothers and caused such strife that she and her children would return to Richmond, Virginia where she ultimately died on July 10, 1889.

Production Note – Handwriting Only A Mother Could Love (or Read)

My research of these First Ladies did not always take me to a physical place. Such is the case with Julia Tyler and some of her letters. Dr. Christopher Leahy is a Professor of History at Keuka College in Keuka Park, NY and his wife Sharon Williams Leahy is the founder of HistoryPreserve.com. They have both done extensive work with Julia Tyler's letters. They are also friends of Payne and Harrison Tyler. Any friends of the Tylers are friends of mine, and I contacted the Leahys for information. They taught me that Julia would often economize her paper usage by writing across the page (left to right) and then turn the paper 90 degrees and write over what she had just written (again left to right). This made for a crosshatch or checkerboard like letter. Dr. Leahy explained that, unfortunately, Julia did not inherit her father's excellent penmanship. He even said Julia had "handwriting only a mother could love". Dr. Leahy called in for a segment on the live show about Julia Tyler. He and Sharon's contributions to my research and the series will always be appreciated. I look forward to more work together in the future.

Let's think about the details of this amazing journey in the 1860's. She knew the value of her belongings and made a financial plan to get herself to Bermuda to wait out the war. She took her belongings and her children by coach through a war zone. She traveled by boat to and from Bermuda, ending up on Staten Island in New York. This would be a difficult and amazing adventure today, let alone in the mid 1800's.

SUMMARY

Julia Tyler was in the right city at the right time to meet the available widower President. It didn't work out so well for her father, but his job to get her a husband was successful in spite of his untimely demise. Not only did he find her a husband, but he was the 10th President of the United States of America. She was well educated, well traveled and well suited for the duties that would become hers in the White House. The public loves a young First Lady. They set fashion trends and make all the Style section headlines in all the newspapers and magazines.

The public also loves a White House full of children, and the Tylers certainly fulfilled that category. Julia also had a knack for politics. She was pretty and appropriately flirtatious, and helped her husband win votes for many things including the annexation of Texas. Julia ended up on the losing side of the Civil War. Her beliefs and support of her husband's politics ended up causing a rift between her and her family up North. Julia Gardiner Tyler did pretty well for herself, considering many of the obstacles she had to navigate, even though she was born into a wealthy family.

She was the second wife of a Vice-President turned one-term President, who lost her father in a tragic accident. She loved her husband, her children and her life on her beloved Sherwood Forest estate. Her life and adventurous lifestyle make her quite unusual for her time.

Travelogue Food Tip

Payne Tyler not only treated me to a fantastic day at Sherwood Forest, she treated me to lunch. We shared an amazing picnic style pulled pork BBQ with coleslaw and chips sitting at the edge of the pet cemetery at Sherwood Forest. I didn't even tell her how much I loved BBQ! If you find yourself in Charles City, VA or at Sherwood Forest visiting the Tylers, Wilson's BBQ and Grill is the best around.

CHAPTER 14

Sarah Polk

Columbia, Tennessee

Sarah Polk was born Sarah Childress on September 4, 1803 in Murfeesboro, Tennessee. Her parents were Joel Childress and Elizabeth Whitsett Childress. Sarah and James K. Polk were married on January 1, 1824. Sarah and James had no children. Sarah Polk died on August 4, 1891 in Nashville, Tennessee at the age of 87.

COLUMBIA, TENNESSEE

Sarah Polk and James K. Polk were (and still are) considered one of the most powerful political couples in American History. James K. Polk, after a fourteen year run in Congress, including serving as Speaker of the House, was elected to a self-proclaimed one term Presidency. Polk is, thus far, the only Speaker of the House to be elected President. Sarah and James intended to conclude a very successful political career, and retire to Nashville, Tennessee. They built a retirement estate called Polk Place.

Sadly, James K. Polk never got to enjoy Polk Place as he had intended. He died three months after leaving the White House leaving Sarah a widow for forty-two long years. Instead of Polk Place becoming a happy place of relaxation and retirement, it became a place of mourning. It was a well-visited shrine to James K. Polk, where Sarah entertained gracefully, as she had in Washington. She was even visited by both Union and Confederate officials and soldiers during the Civil War. So, what happened to Polk Place and why can't we visit there today?

Tom Price, my host, vault of Polk information and Curator at the Polk Ancestral Home, explained it to me like this…

Sarah and James had no children. After James's death, Sarah took in a young female relative. Sarah became a mother figure and guardian to the young woman. By the time Sarah died, her young ward had married, and did not have the last name Polk. Having no children of their own, Polk Place was willed to family members with the last name of Polk. When the estate came before the court for settlement, close to (if not more than) fifty people with the last name of Polk showed up for their share. Having no clear beneficiary, the judge ruled Polk Place was to be sold and the profit be divided among those who showed up to court and were legitimately named Polk. Polk Place was sold and torn down in 1901, ten years after Sarah died on August 4, 1891. The only real rightful heir was a woman whose last name was not Polk, got nothing, and the house no longer stands.

However, the Polk Ancestral Home in Columbia, Tennessee does still stand, and it's full of items, artifacts and history. In fact, when I got there they were in the middle of a featured exhibit that focused on Sarah Polk's life and style. It was easy to get a sense of the political powerhouse that was the Polks and was very much because of Mrs. Polk.

As I mentioned, Polk was an intentional one-term President. He did not intend to serve more than a term, and stayed true to his word. While the Polks were in the White House, they were collecting furniture and other items for Polk Place, which they were building in Nashville at the time. Much of the furniture still exists today, along with other items, including original photos of some of the rooms.

Road Trip – Dress For The Weather

This was a strange trip for me geographically. I went from driving around Tennessee in a t-shirt with the sunroof open, to rolling through the finger lakes of New York State in a snowstorm during the course of a week. The Weather Channel and apps like Weather Bug can be your friend when you travel. Prepare for anything and everything when it comes to the weather. Getting caught in a rainstorm with no raincoat or a snowstorm with no boots is no fun. Near as I can figure, this is where I began to pick up the walking pneumonia.

The pictures that exist of Polk Place were most likely taken just after Sarah's death in 1891. They show specific pieces of furniture, where they were placed and how they were most likely used. It is so valuable to have these images to help link the past of a place that no longer exists to some of the items in the collection. It makes the people; their lives and their stories come alive. You can now picture them sitting on the sofa in the actual room where it was kept and used.

A set of red velvet chairs and sofas are some of the most stunning items in the collection from Polk Place. They are beautiful and beautifully preserved. They were purchased by the Polks from Alexander Steward's store in New York City and were finely crafted American-made pieces. The detailed rosewood frames and vivid red velvet are striking and provide a regal feel. There are 18 of the original 33 side chairs here. The Polks would frame the room with the chairs while entertaining larger numbers of guests.

Entertaining was, is, and always will be, a large part of politicking. Mrs. Polk knew this as well as anybody. In fact, one of her close friends in Washington was none other than...yep, you guessed it...DOLLEY MADISON! (Drink)

The Polks were big on entertaining, and their china proves it. The Polk china is among the most remarkable of any administration. Dinners at the Polk White

House were served in multiple courses and often went late into the evening. They had white dinner plates, a blue tea set and pale green dessert plates. All of the sets were lined with gold and the Presidential seal. They have many examples displayed on original White House tables and in the original White House cabinets now at the home in Columbia, Tennessee. Sarah Polk hosted lunches twice a week, on Tuesdays and Fridays, with guest lists of 50–75 people who would have enjoyed their meals on these plates.

Many people think Sarah Polk had banned alcohol from the White House during her husband's administration. This wasn't entirely true. Sarah Polk didn't serve whiskey punch at public levees. The Polks served wine at dinners and other social gatherings in the White House. In fact, wine was one of their largest bills during the four years they spent there.

The story I'm told about Mrs. Polk's relationship with spirits is an interesting and understandable one. It seems that Sarah came to live in Washington when James was a Congressman and later Speaker of the House. Like today, many lawmakers get group houses together to ease the financial burden of the districts while they are in D.C. doing business. With no children at home, it was easy for James and Sarah to live together in Washington, D.C. One night during an after dinner card game, Sarah noticed and overheard some of Polk's male politician guests that had gotten fairly drunk and loud. They shared gossip and information through the loose lips born of inebriation. After the guests had left, Sarah told James what she had heard and observed and she informed him that it would be the end of excessive drinking for the Polks (not that they were big drinkers anyway). They would sit back and let everyone else drink, allowing them to reveal their secrets as she and James quietly, and soberly, watched and listened.

Politics was obviously very important and a huge part of Sarah and James's life together. There are numerous portraits at the Polk home that represent a long and successful career. Mrs. Polk was as politically aware and involved as any First Lady before or since. Even prior to her husband being elected, she served him well, both as a sounding board for his speeches and researcher of news and issues. She avidly read the newspaper and highlighted stories about his opponents. She also suggested talking points on issues of the day. At the Polk home they have Mrs. Polk's travel desk, which is beautiful, and obviously well used.

This item represents the many hours she would spend writing and reading on the 30-day trip to Washington, D.C. from Nashville. When Polk was a Congressman, she would write him letters about what was going on back home with constituents in his district. She would find out where her husband's opponents would be headed on campaign stops. Sometimes she could get her husband to these places with his own event before the other candidate had arrived. She was what we, in modern terms, would call "plugged in". As a political partner, Sarah Polk was unusual for her time.

While in Washington, Sarah served as her husband's private secretary. She was an A-list guest at all the top social events and gatherings, and she had a regular seat in the Congressional Gallery. Many First Ladies attended Congressional sessions, however, some were thought to do this as more of a way to be seen and meet people. It has even been suggested that they attended these sessions just to attract attention (can you image?). Sarah Polk paid very close attention to the official business at hand and took very diligent notes. This also meant that Mrs. Polk was in attendance for some of the most famous speeches from the political heavy hitters of her time, like Henry Clay and others.

The Polks were well acquainted with President Andrew Jackson. Polk was Speaker of the House during the Jackson Administration. The Polks were guests at Jackson's Hermitage Plantation. Andrew Jackson was the one who told James Polk to "quit dallying and get married". Then and there, James proposed to Sarah. She accepted the proposal, but wouldn't set a date until he could show her that he could support her. Sarah Polk was a self assured and confident woman of the 1800's. She was definitely unusual for her time. These were the kinds of stories I loved hearing. These were the things I wanted to learn about these First Ladies. This was the part of the lives of these women I wanted to learn about. This is what would allow me to really get inside the mind of the women that would marry the men that would become President.

Part of entertaining and being a public figure is style and looking good. Sarah Polk was at the top of her game in this department, as well. Sarah found a very elegant style and stuck with it. Her dresses, robes and gowns were all very elegant, but not over the top. She was said to be thrifty, as many First Ladies were and had to be working within a budget and many times being in charge and accountable for that budget. She often bought extra cloth and material for her outfits. This allowed her to change and adapt a dress or gown for multiple purposes and various social engagements and seasons. The articles of clothing on display at the Polk home were beautiful and elegant, and really gave me an idea of Sarah's fashion sense and style.

Mrs. Polk was also excellent at accessorizing. She shows this right from the start with a gift from her newly elected Presidential husband. Sarah Polk's inaugural fan is among the most famous and cherished artifacts in American Presidential History. It is written about in almost every book I read about the First Ladies. This may be my opinion, and it may be Historical "insider baseball", but take it from someone who has held this fan (in its protective case, of course). This fan is AMAZING! It is gilt paper over animal bone stiles with lithograph images of every President (Washington – Polk) on one side and the signing of the Declaration of Independence on the other. The new First Lady Sarah Polk carried it with her throughout the entire Inauguration celebration and ceremony. It is immaculately preserved and kept in a beautiful wood and glass case at the Polk home in Columbia, Tennessee for all to see and enjoy. This is an item that irrefutably marks one of the most significant moments in Sarah Polk's life. It made me think of it being used as if the inauguration of her husband were only yesterday.

Sarah Polk also accessorized with handbags, headdresses and jewelry. Gemstone jewelry was not in fashion, so Mrs. Polk chose to go with gold and silver pieces that could easily be worn with today's fashion in mind. Her headdresses were very fancy and well appointed, but delicate with feathers and silks. We are very fortunate to have as many as we do, and from them, we get a sense of how she would top off an ensemble. Her handbags were equally appropriate for each outfit and occasion. One of the more unusual pieces in the collection is a turban style headdress. It's unusual because they were out of style by the time Mrs. Polk is First Lady. One can't help but think that this was a nod to friend and frequent White House guest, Dolley Madison. (Drink)

President Andrew Jackson told Sarah Polk this at one point in time, between his own administration and Polk's, he said, "the scepter shall come back to Tennessee before long and your very own fair self shall be queen." Jackson, as it turns out, was right.

SUMMARY

Sarah Polk was one of the most politically attuned and effective First Ladies of all time. She advanced her husband's political career with her contributions and even though she didn't have the official title, she was his campaign manager. This is an amazing fact given that it was the early to mid 1800's. She was well liked in Washington, stylish and knew how to throw a good party without whiskey. Yet, she is not a First Lady that you typically name (at least I didn't before this project) if you were to tick off ten U.S. First Ladies. She is one of the First Ladies that I think embodies the intent of C-SPAN series, because it's someone I knew about, but didn't know much about.

It was like being reintroduced to someone I had known long ago but forgotten about. She also lives for 42 years as a widow, until her death at the age of 88. This in itself is an accomplishment for a person in the 1800's. She represented her husband well while he was alive and preserved his legacy well after his death. It boggles my mind that any house of any former President is gone and not preserved for future generations. Imagine what we would think and know about James K. and Sarah Polk had he lived as long as she had; Polk Place may have been passed down and saved for us all.

Travelogue Food Tip

BBQ, BBQ, BBQ!! There is a place on the way out of Columbia, TN just outside of town before you get to the highway to go to the Nashville airport called Brickhouse Barbeque. I was surprised that there weren't any pigs on the sign or "cute references" to the Three Little Pigs. It is a no-nonsense brick building that quickly and efficiently serves up great food. It's pretty nondescript, and I almost missed it. Let's just say, I'm glad I made the U-turn. It made the snowstorm I didn't know I was heading into more bearable.

CHAPTER 15
Margaret Taylor

Calvert County, Maryland – Louisville, Kentucky

$\mathcal{M}$argaret Taylor was born Margaret "Peggy" Mackall Smith on September 21, 1788 in Calvert County, Maryland in what is known today as Waldorf. Her parents were Walter Smith and Ann Mackall Smith. Margaret and Zachary Taylor were married on June 21, 1810. Margaret and Zachary had six children together. Margaret Taylor died on august 14, 1852 in East Pascagoula, Mississippi at the age of 63.

I have much more research to do on Margaret Taylor. President Taylor died from a stroke just sixteen months into his term, and Mrs. Taylor was a self-imposed inactive First Lady. Margaret Taylor had her daughter, Mary Elizabeth Taylor Bliss, tend to all of the social duties of the First Lady while she stayed on the second floor, and kept to herself and the immediate family. In fact, at her husband's funeral some folks were surprised to see that she existed at all, having surmised that President Taylor as a widower.

Margaret Taylor, while in this unique sorority of women known as First Ladies, was in a small group within the sorority that didn't want their husbands to be President. Her husband was a military man. As a military wife, Margaret had traveled around and lived in at least eight different states over the years. She felt as though her husband had given enough of himself to the country. So, when the Whig Party nominated him as their candidate for President, she would have rather they left him alone in retirement. Similarly to Anna Harrison (who felt the same of her husband) she would be proven correct in that he would have been better to stay at home and out of politics.

Given the fact that she wasn't in Washington very long and her public appearances were almost as non-existent as her contributions as First Lady, she was lumped into a show that covered three women for the C-SPAN series (Polk, Taylor & Fillmore). This coupled with the fact that her birthplace no longer stands (nor is it marked), the military bases where they were stationed are either gone or don't tell her story, her place of death in Pascagoula, Mississippi is unmarked and her home in Louisville, Kentucky is privately owned, made it difficult for me to drum up stories, artifacts and places to shoot video to represent her life.

Side Note – Maryland Pride

Waldorf, MD is close to where I live now in Shady Side, MD and it shouldn't be too hard to dig up some kind of records that can at least get me to the part of town where she was born and raised. That will at the very least give me an idea about the part of Maryland and the county from which she came.

The fact remains that she was a First Lady and someone; somewhere has to have something to say or show me about her. So, she is another First Lady that I will continue to research and look to expand upon in future editions of this book.

SUMMARY

Margaret Taylor was a special kind of First Lady. She wanted nothing to do with politics or political life. So, she stuck to her guns and stayed out of the public eye. She did this so effectively; many assumed that President Taylor was a widower. She was a devoted military wife that moved many times to be with her husband and keep their family together. She didn't conform to the duties of First Lady, even though her health and abilities would've allowed for it. This alone makes her unusual for her time and different than most of the women that found themselves in her position. Her parents were well to do and she was educated. I will definitely find out more about this elusive First Lady.

Travelogue Food Tip

When I find out exactly where she was raised in Waldorf, MD I will find a restaurant – something other than BBQ (seafood, maybe) and let you know where to go and what to order.

PHOTO ALBUM

All Photos By Andrew Och

The Adams Crypt in Quincy, MA
John, Abigail, John Quincy and Louisa
Catherine are all buried there

Vault at Andrew Johnson National Historic
Site in Greenville, TN

Mary Arthur McElroy dress in the 3rd floor
museum level of the Benjamin Harrison house
in Indianapolis, IN

Lunch at The Cheese Shop on Duke of
Gloucester Street in Williamsburg, VA
reasearching Martha Washington, Martha and
Martha "Patsy" Jefferson Randolph and
Letitia Tyler

Phone interview with Frances Cleveland's living granddaughter Ann Roberts

Beared photo with Benjamin Harrison in Indianapolis, IN

Frances Cleveland's wedding dress in storage at the Smithsonian's National Museum of American History in Washington, D.C.

The First Ladies Man editing location pieces at his desk in Washington, D.C. C-SPAN office

A rare glimpse of The First Ladies Man at his C-SPAN desk in Washington, D.C.

The dining room at Lawnfield in Mentor, OH (Lucretia Garfiled location shoot)

First Ladies Man poses with President Garfiled bust at Garfiled Library in Lawnfild home and historc site in Mentor, OH

Interview with Nancy Loane at Valley Forge, PA

The Garfield's bedroom at Lawnfield in Mentor, OH with Park Ranger Mary Lintern

The First Ladies Man visits Spiegel Grove and Lucy Hayes in Freemont, OH

More fun editing location pieces with The First Ladies Man

First Ladies Man field office at his cousin
Zoey's desk in Beloit, WI

Field office in Galena, IL
(Julia Grant)

The First Ladies Man getting loopy editing at home in Shady Side, MD

Stained glass window dedicated to Ellen Arthur in the Church of the President's in-Washington, D.C. across the street from The White House

End of Season 1 celebration in C-SPAN kitchen

Field office in Springfield, IL (Mary Lincoln)

Field office in St. Louis, MO (Julia Grant)

On Julia Grant's second floor balcony porch at White Haven Plantation in St. Louis, MO

The First Ladies Man standing in the doorway of the vault in the library at Lawnfield in
Mentor, OH (built by Lucretia Garfield after
her husband's death)

Harrison family baptism set with water from
the River Jordan from the late 1800's

Hall's Harley Davidson in Springfilield, IL

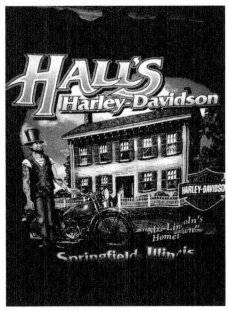

Hall's Harley Davidson Lincoln shirt back –
the best HD shirt find of the whole journey

Location shoot at the Benjamin Harrison House in Indianapolis, IN

The First Ladies Man on the porch of Sherwood Forest with living grandson of President John Tyler - Harrison Ruffin Tyler

Pulling gear behind truck in St. Louis, MO going from White Haven Plantation to Hard Scrabble House on Grant's Farm for Julia Grant location shoot

President Rutherford B. Hayes's gun collection at Spiegel Grove in Freemont, OH

President Rutherford B. Hayes's gun collection at Spiegel Grove in Freemont, OH

President Rutherford B. Hayes's gun collection at Spiegel Grove in Freemont, OH

The First Ladies Man orders "The Dude Abides" at Melt Bar and Grilled in Mentor, OH (Lucretia Garfield)

The First Ladies Man filming at the Hermitage in Nashville, TN home of President and Rachel Jackson

The First Ladies Man at the graves of President and Lucy Hayes at
Spiegel Grove in Freemont, OH

In the archives of the Hermitage in Nashville,
TN home of President and Rachel Jackson

Chili cheese dog horseshoe, a local delicacy in
Springfield, IL (Mary Lincoln)

Filming in the Massachusetts Historical
Society Archives in Boston, MA

Looking at Mary Lincoln artifacts at the
Lincoln Library with Curator James Cornelious

Special C-SPAN sponsored screening of "Lincoln" at the Willard Hotel in Washington, D.C.

The First Ladies Man in the Lincoln's guest room in the Springfield, IL home at the Lincoln historic site

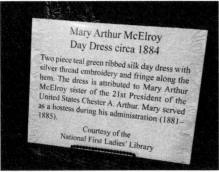

Mary Arthur McElroy dress information at Harrison House Museum in Indianapolis, IN

Filming at the Mary Todd House in Lexington, KY with Director Gwen Thompson

Filming at the Massachusetts Historical Society in Boston, MA

The First Ladies Man at the McKinley House in Canton, OH

Reviewing documents and letters in the Adams family collection at the Massachusetts Historical Society in Boston, MA with series editor Sara Martin

The First Ladies Man at Melt Bar and Grilled in Mentor, OH (Lucretia Garfield)

Outside the Octagon House in NW Washington, D.C. where the Madisons lived after the British burned The White House in The War of 1812. Dolley Madison threw legendary parties while living here.

The First Ladies Man on the road again on his way to the Metro to head out of town

The First Ladies Man gears up to head into a meeting at C-SPAN offices in Washington, D.C.

The First Ladies Man with Millard Fillmore cutout at the Fillmore House in East Aurora, NY

The First Ladies Man filming at the Octagon House in Washington, D.C. for the Dolley Madison show

The First Ladies Man's cat (Dorianne) always wants to hit the road with her dad

The First Ladies Man carries his camera and tripod through the snow in Concord, NH in search of the Pierce graves

Filming the Pierce graves in Concord, NH

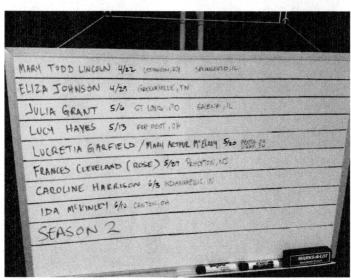

Dry erase board at The First Ladies Man's desk in the C-SPAN offices in Washington, D.C. This board kept track of travels and locations for both seasons of "First Ladies: Influence and Image."

Boarding another plane for another destination along the nationwide trail of the First Ladies of the United States of America

The infamous letter Jane Pierce wrote to her son Benny after his tragic death on file at the New Hampshire Historical Society

Filming interviews at the Pierce Manse in Concord, NH with Peter Wallner and Joan Woodhead

The First Ladies Man enters the Church of the Presidents in Washington, D.C. through the President's special entrance

Driving out of Philly in a snowstorm after filming pieces for Martha Washington, Abigail Adams and Dolley Madison

Season One kick off show with the panel of expert historians and C-SPAN's Steve Scully moderating the live on air discussion

Sarah Polk's jewelry on display at the Polk Ancestoral home in Columbia, TN

Sarah Polk's childhood music book with "Hail to the Chief" sheet music

Fueling the research

Season One kick off show and live on air discussion with a panel of former White House and Staffers from various administrations

The First Ladies Man sitting in the President's pew at the Church of the Presidents in NW Washington, D.C.

The First Ladies Man on one of the many visits to the National Museum of American History to view artifacts on display and in the back storage rooms

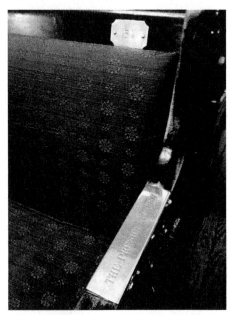

The President's pew at the Church of the Presidents in NW Washington, D.C.

The First Ladies Man with Rutherford B. Hayes at Spiegel Grove in Freemont, OH

Snow storm driving across upstate New York visting Kinderhook, Buffalo and East Aurora

Interview at the Lincoln summer cottage at the Soldier's Home in Washington, D.C.

Steak dinner in Beliot, WI with my cousin Rick after the Galena, IL visit for Julia Grant

The train tracks in Andover, MA that took the life of young Benny Pierce

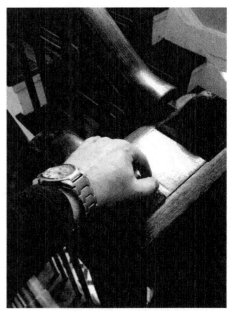

The First Ladies Man with his hand on the original banister post at the Lincoln summer cottage at the Soldier's Home in Washington, D.C.

The First Ladies Man poses with Honest Abe at the Lincoln summer cottage at the Soldier's Home in Washington, D.C.

C-SPAN's "First Ladies: Influence and Image" location shoot travel gear

The First Ladies Man enjoys a cold January afternoon at James Buchanan's Wheatland Estate in Lancaster, PA

CHAPTER 16

Abigail Fillmore

East Aurora, New York

$\mathcal{A}$ bigail Fillmore was born Abigail Powers on March 13, 1798 in Saratoga County, New York. Her parents were Reverend Lemuel Powers and Abigail Newland Powers. Abigail and Millard Fillmore were married on February 5, 1826. Abigail and Millard had two children together. Abigail Fillmore died on March 30, 1853 in the Willard Hotel in Washington, D.C. at the age of 55.

EAST AURORA, NEW YORK

Abigail Fillmore was as unlikely a choice for First Lady as her husband was for President. Neither was raised with wealth or privilege. Mrs. Fillmore has the distinct honor of being the first First Lady with a job. She started teaching in a Cayuga County schoolhouse at the age of sixteen. She's most likely the first First Lady to work outside of the house. In fact, her job is how she met Millard

Fillmore.

Millard was a self-taught man, very interested in reading, and depending on which story you ascribe to, he either met his wife in one of her classes or in the first lending library in the area that Abigail helped establish. Either way, the two met, fell in love and were engaged for seven years while Millard solidified his law career in Buffalo, New York.

When the two finally married, Millard built them a house. When I say Millard built them a house, I mean he built them a house – with his own two hands. It was a small two-story home with only a few rooms. It didn't even have a staircase. They most likely had to climb a wooden ladder to get to the bedroom upstairs. This must've been quite a chore for Abigail in a long housedress. Even more so once she became pregnant and again later, while carrying a young child on each arm. The house was right on Main Street in East Aurora and the Fillmore's were very happy there.

The house now has a staircase and, although you can't really tell from the front, it has been expanded in the back to include a modest museum. The East Aurora Historical Society has done a wonderful job preserving the house, some original Fillmore pieces, and telling the story of Abigail Fillmore.

The great thing about the Fillmore House is that, if you didn't know it was there, you would drive right by it. That's not to say that it's poorly marked or hidden. The house fits right in on Main Street. It belongs there, and really makes the house and the Fillmore's life there come that much more alive. I parked my rental car right out front on the street and walked up and knocked on the door, just like any visitor might have (minus the rental car) back when Abigail and Millard lived here with their two children. My hosts, Kathy Frost and Robert Goller, answered the door. I loaded my gear in across the snow-covered walkway, and we got to work. We started like I did with most houses and locations. I asked Kathy to show me around the place and tell me what Abigail did in each room and what items related directly to Mrs. Fillmore. The house is small, so it didn't take long to get a real feel for the place and what went on here.

The main focus of the house is the front room. It served as the living room, dining room, kitchen, and schoolroom for the students that Mrs. Fillmore tutored. I'm told the fact that Abigail continued to teach and work after she was married was very rare for women at the time. This was yet another sign that Abigail Fillmore was unusual for her time. The front room has a nice fireplace. This is where Abigail would cook the daily meals. She and Millard sat by the fireplace in the evenings while they read and discussed issues of the day. It is also where Mrs. Fillmore held her tutoring sessions. She primarily taught History, but was competent in many other subjects as well. She and Millard kept a small library in the house. This also came in handy when teaching her students.

This room also has some original furniture and one of Abigail's teapots. The Fillmores were well known in the community because of their work, so it's easy to imagine them entertaining many visitors in this humble home that Millard built. Abigail was said to be a very supportive wife, and when he decided to go into politics. There is no doubt that she would do anything to help her husband's star rise.

Our work complete in the original part of the first floor of the house, it was time to lug my gear and haul myself up the narrow stairs to the second floor bedroom.

Production Note – Going Up

The stairs were a modern addition. This is a good thing, because even though my travel kit was small and compact, it still required a tripod, camera, lights and cords that would've been difficult to haul up the original wooden ladder. This was one of the smallest, narrowest and steepest climbs of the entire series. The only place that was smaller was the little elevator that went to the top floor museum of the Benjamin Harrison House in Indianapolis, which is a few chapters off yet.

In the bedroom they have an original bed, and an original chest of drawers. They are both in very good condition and gave me a real sense of how the young, ambitious couple started their life and family together in this tiny house. Another original item here in the Fillmore's bedroom is a quilt that Abigail made. It has a tumbling block pattern and is kept on the bed. This is one of those items that I find truly remarkable for many reasons. First, it was handmade (much like the entire house) and extremely personal. Abigail liked to sew and stitch and quilt. She took great time and care to make this quilt for her and her family's use. She didn't buy it in a store or have it made by servants or slaves. She made it with her own hands, and I could picture her sitting by the fireplace downstairs, talking with Millard while she made the quilt. The other impressive thing is that an item like this still exists and we know its origin.

I know it's not made of tissue paper or balsa wood. It's not a delicate piece of crystal or china. But, I have lost sturdier sweaters to moths or other means of destruction. There are President's houses that have been torn down, and letters that have been burned. So, for as amazed as I am at the things we have lost to time, I am equally amazed at the things that survive. This quilt is one of those things. It provides us with a personal link to the past that is tangible. We can see and hold it. It has texture and a scent and helps bring Abigail Fillmore to life. It makes her real.

The back part of the Fillmore House in East Aurora is an addition that was added as a museum space. The most significant piece here is an original bookcase from the first White House Library. Before the Fillmore Administration, there was no official White House or President's Library. Many assumed that there had been, but no one had brought it to the attention of Congress. No one, that is, until Abigail Fillmore.

Mrs. Fillmore was astonished when she moved into the White House to find that there was no official library. She quickly went to the Library of Congress to find a solution. The Library of Congress made recommendations, and sent her to lawmakers. Ideas, budgets and proposals went back and forth with mild success and attention. It wasn't until Mrs. Fillmore organized a dinner party at the White House for all of those involved that the idea really gained traction and was unanimously approved. In the end, the project was given a $2,000 budget and allowed other libraries to share and supply copies of public Congressional documents to the newly established White House Library. With this victory under her belt, Abigail confidently lobbied Congress to install indoor plumbing in the White House. She said that she had found the White House "without a Bible or a bathtub".

Other items in the museum include various musical instruments. They have a harp that belonged to the Fillmore's daughter, Mary. Abigail Fillmore was often not in the best of health and she sometimes avoided public events. In these times, the hostessing duties fell on her daughter Mary. Mary would often play the harp or piano to entertain guests and small groups at the White House. Items such as this, from the White House years, are always welcome additions to smaller museums. They give visitors an idea what life was like for the family while they occupied the most well known house in America.

SUMMARY

Abigail Fillmore is another great example of a First Lady who didn't make a huge splash on Washington's social scene. Nor is she on the tip of anyone's tongue when First Ladies are the topic of conversation at a cocktail party or around the water cooler (that's kind of a joke. I know First Ladies aren't a typical topic of every day conversation). However, her First Lady firsts are undeniable. They are significant, and they are relevant in modern times. Surely, the White House would've gotten indoor plumbing eventually, but it's Abigail who gets it done. The White House Library is obviously her crowning achievement, but if you asked someone randomly walking down the street who came up with the idea, I doubt they would be able to tell you it was Abigail Fillmore who not only came up with the idea, but went to Congress to make it happen. She was the first First Lady with a day job outside of the home. This speaks volumes to the changing times in our country and with our leadership. Power to the people. It also says a lot about Mrs. Fillmore. She continued to work after getting married, which went against societal norms of the day. Abigail Powers Fillmore was indeed unusual for her time.

ANDREW OCH

Travelogue Food Tip

All of these small towns have really neat little diners, bars, lounges and "Mom & Pop Shops". Take advantage of them when you travel. My hosts from the Aurora Historical Society took me to a neat little joint called The Bar Bill Tavern. Two of my staples on the road (and at home – who am I kidding) are wings and a Caesar salad. It's a safe bet. You can get it in most restaurants and airports, and it's usually hard to mess up. The Bar Bill Tavern had both. The food and service were both excellent and friendly.

CHAPTER 17
Jane Pierce

Concord, New Hampshire – Andover, Massachusetts

*J*ane Pierce was born Jane Means Appleton on March 12, 1806 in Hampton, New Hampshire. Her parents were Reverend Jesse Appleton and Elizabeth Means Appleton. Jane and Franklin Pierce were married on November 19, 1834. Jane and Franklin had three children together. Jane Pierce died on Decemebr 2, 1863 in Andover, Massachusetts at the age of 57.

CONCORD, NEW HAMPSHIRE

The amazing thing about the Pierce Manse in Concord, New Hampshire is that if it weren't for the ladies of the Pierce Brigade, the house would have been torn down to make room for "progress" and modern development. Yup, we almost lost another one. This is one of those "I really can't believe it" moments of my adventure. To think that any house of a former President and First Lady would be destroyed or torn down is well beyond me. I've said it before and I'll say it again…I am amazed at the places, letters, artifacts and items that survive time, but I am equally amazed at the ones that don't. In any event, we have these women to thank for preserving this home and the stories of the lives of the Pierce family that live on within its walls. Thank you Pierce Brigade!

Jane Pierce is fascinating to me for many reasons. She is not a very public First Lady or woman. She didn't care for politics, and she didn't want to move to Washington, D.C. Her husband served two House terms, one Senate term, became a brigadier general in the war with Mexico, established a fairly successful law career, and was elected the 14th President of the United States. Jane didn't seem to be a fan of any of his endeavors that took him away from Concord.

She has a silent beauty in her pictures. And her life story is rather tragic. I think that much of her public persona and reputation is unjustly unfavorable. After reading about her in so many books, I was anxious to get to Concord and get the real story. What I learned was incredible and put the dark figure of Jane Pierce in a whole new light.

There was snow on the ground, but a crystal clear blue sky on the January day I drove from Quincy, Massachusetts to Concord, New Hampshire. This was one of those early trips that had me covering some of these ladies out of order. This is another time it made sense to pick up another lady, because I was "in the neighborhood". I was in Quincy studying and filming for Abigail and Louisa Catherine Adams, so I figured, "why not hit Concord, New Hampshire and Andover, Massachusetts to get Jane Pierce as well?"

Travel Tip – Boots On The Ground

When Traveling in New England in the winter, wear boots and pack warm socks. You never know when you're going to be trudging through snow in a graveyard.

The Pierce Manse is well preserved, and does an excellent job of incorporating the actual living spaces with artifacts that depict life for the Pierces with the more modern features of a museum and gift shop. One of the most memorable features of the house, are the original pine knot floorboards. Joan Woodhead was the President of the Pierce Brigade at the time of my visit and showed me around the place.

For me it is something special to walk on the actual floors of history. The boards were light in color, full of knots and texture, and they were wide 12 inch boards, as was the typical of the day. It is a very impressive, and beautiful floor. I ran my hand along the smooth, textured boards and imagined Jane walking, pacing or standing on them. In many cases she stood at the bedside of one of her children or outside of a bedroom, and waited for a doctor to tell her his thoughts about a sick child. Maybe she would have been standing at a window, while she waited for Franklin to return home from a war, a work trip or a political journey. In many of Mrs. Pierce's letters it is obvious that she was not a terribly happy or healthy person, and her life was surrounded by death.

The Pierces had a total of three children. Their first-born son was named Franklin, Jr. and only lived a few days after his birth in February 1836. Frank Robert Pierce was born in 1839, and Benjamin (Benny) came along in 1841. Tragedy struck once again when Frank died of Typhus at the age of four in 1843. We will discuss Benny's gruesome demise in a bit.

It seems Jane was never happier than when she had her whole family at home. She sought a simple life with her husband, children, immediate family and her church. Jane's father was a minister, and when she married Franklin, she thought she could change him, and make him more of a religious man. Unfortunately, it was death and loss that would change them both.

As I was given my usual initial tour of the facility to discuss the plan, the topics and items we discussed on the phone in our "pre-interview", it was easy to see that Jane made a humble home, and lived a fairly simple life. She didn't entertain much, and the furniture was such that a small family would be comfortably served in the activities of daily life. There is a couch that they had brought with them to the White House. Jane wrote to Franklin about spending much of her time on this couch, not feeling well and waiting for him to return home.

Like most folks of her day, Jane was an avid letter writer. We are fortunate to have many of these letters, and her small traveling desk. It is a basic, black, enameled wooden box with a small, flat desktop that flips up to reveal an open compartment for writing supplies. She kept her paper, ink, pens and pencils in the box and used the desktop to write while the box sat in her lap on trips. It's nice to have this significant piece of Jane's, because she was such a fan of letter writing. It is her letters that clearly reveal to us how she and her son Benny felt about Washington, D.C. and Franklin's Presidential election. Again, we will get to the details of that story in a bit. Remember, I am a television writer who fully understands the "art of the tease"!

Another interesting item in the house was a small side chair that she had borrowed from her sister to help furnish the White House. This was just a very vivid and physical example of the kind of woman Jane was, and the times in which she lived. Can you imagine nowadays if a First Lady went to her sister and said, "Hey, sis can I borrow a chair for the Blue Room? There's a corner in there that needs something, and I just don't have anything for it".

The main meal of the day was served in the Pierce house at noon, and the current day dining room is set to represent this. Mrs. Pierce always kept sugar cookies around and on the table, as they were one of Franklin's favorites. This is another little fact I learned that made Jane that much more real to me. In my house, my mother didn't keep too many sweets around, but we always had a bag of Pecan Sandies for my dad.

I set up in the main parlor or living room to conduct my interview Peter Wallner to learn all I could about Jane and her life here in Concord. It was during this interview that I mentioned reading about Jane writing letters to her dead children while in the White House. Peter quickly corrected me and told me that it was really only one letter. My jaw dropped. As it turns out, the rumors and stories were only half true. Jane hadn't written multiple letters to all three of her dead children. She had written one. It was to Benny, it was in the New Hampshire Historical Society's possession, and I was going to get to see it. For me, this was like finding the Holy Grail. However, this would not happen before finishing our interview and taking a look at the bedrooms upstairs. So, you're going to have to wait a little bit longer for that story.

When you have a woman as private as Jane Pierce was, and knowing how important her children were and the circumstances of her losses, it was extra special to see the private rooms of the house. As I mentioned, Jane didn't entertain much (if at all). Her main activities consisted of going across the street to church and visiting her sister in Andover, Massachusetts. Seeing where so much time was spent and such significant moments of her life took place was crucial to the telling of her story.

The bedrooms (like the rest of the house) were simple, clean and functional. It was easy to imagine the family there spending time watching over sick children or laughing with them in the short time they had together. Jane spent a lot of time in her room alone while Franklin was out of town. She wrote letters there. She prayed there. She recovered from illnesses there. These were important rooms to her, and therefore important rooms to me.

Peter explained to me that from her letters we can conclude Jane was a bit self-centered and potentially, a hypochondriac. She certainly had ailments and heath issues, like anyone else, but hers may have been a bit over-played or exaggerated. While Franklin was off fighting in the Mexican-American War in 1847, he was shot and wrote home to tell his wife about the incident. In a letter she responds, only mentioning that she had not been feeling well, suffering from sinus issues and having to spend a lot of time in bed. There is no mention of her husband's injury, health or well being.

NEW HAMPSHIRE HISTORICAL SOCIETY

It's always good to know people. It's even better to know the right people. In this instance, I just asked the right person the right question, and the next thing you know, I'm holding letters written by Jane and Benny Pierce. In this case, Peter Wallner was the right person. This was one of the more memorable moments in my travels (and YES, I know I say that a lot – it was the adventure of a lifetime). When you read something historical and remarkable in a book, you want to verify or substantiate it. At least, I do.

Most of the books I read portrayed Jane Pierce as a recluse in the White House. They told stories about a couple of sisters that used to visit Mrs. Pierce behind closed doors, dressed in all black. The tales consisted of séances and crystal balls, contacting the spirit world and writing letters to her dead children. When I heard that there was, in fact, a letter written to Benny...I had to see it.

Production Note – Little Genies

Television (and life, really) is a constant work in progress. When you treat life as being organic, you can adjust your plan and come out for the better. It's not whether you have a Plan B. It's whether you have a PLAN C through Z. Especially, when you are on the road in locations you've never been to, working with people you've never met or worked with before. You never know what little gem might turn up. A producer friend of mine, Andrew Wallworth calls them "little genies".

The story of Benny's death has been told many different ways, by many different people in many different arenas. Here is my version based on the many different books, places and people I encountered in my research:

When Franklin Pierce went to the 1852 Democratic National Convention in Baltimore, Jane Pierce thought her husband was going to nominate a Presidential candidate, not to BE NOMINATED the candidate. She certainly didn't want him to win and be elected President. But he did get nominated and he did win the election. It is unclear how much she knew about his plans or the whole nomination, but it is clear that she was not happy. By this time the Pierces had lost two children and were left with one son – Benny. Benny was Jane's world. She only let him out of her sight to go and stay with her sister in Andover, Massachusetts. He enjoyed his time there with his aunt, uncle and cousins.

When Franklin Pierce won the election they had to pack up their belongings and get to Washington, D.C. for the inauguration. Tragedy and death struck again. Jane's uncle died, and they had to go to his funeral in Boston. So, they left Benny in Andover with her sister and travel to the funeral. They came back to Andover to pick up Benny, and head back to Concord to pack for the move to the White House.

The train was not five miles out of town, when an axel broke on the car that carried the Pierces. The train derailed and the Pierces car broke off and rolled down a hill. When the car came to an eventual stop, and everything settled, Benny was found virtually decapitated. He was the only fatality in the accident. Mrs. Pierce either saw this happen or saw him just after he was killed; she passed out. Franklin Pierce covered his son's head with his jacket and carried him back down the train tracks to Jane's sister's house. They had the funeral service in the living room of her sister's house.

So, to review…Jane and her husband are coming back from a funeral to pick up their only surviving child, in order to go back to Concord, to pack up their house, to move to Washington, D.C., where Franklin will be President, and Benny is killed right in front of his parent's eyes. Jane blamed Franklin's deceit about the election for God's vengeance on their child. The accident was something for which Jane Pierce never forgave her husband.

So, that's the story of Benny's death as compiled by my research, and here is what I saw at the New Hampshire Historical Society that relates to the incident.

There is a letter that Benny wrote to his mother from his aunt's house in Andover, Massachusetts. The letter is dated June 1852 and reads, "Dear Mother…I hope he won't be elected for I would not like to live in Washington, and I know you would not like to either."

So, it is clear that Jane and Benny talked about the election, the Presidency and the possibility of moving to Washington, D.C. It is also clear that neither of them wanted this to happen. This isn't surprising given Jane's opinions about Franklin's political career and the amount of time Jane and Benny spend together. Mrs. Pierce clearly had her son's ear on this matter.

Now, for the issue of the letters (multiple…with an "S") she wrote and sent to her dead children (plural) when she was in the White House.

First, there are not multiple letters. There is one letter. I saw it. I held it. I read it. It's not even a letter really. It's written in pencil. It can be thought of as more of a journal entry. Letters written in pencil were drafts, and weren't sent until they were rewritten in ink. Where would she send it anyway?

Second, it wasn't even written in Washington, D.C., let alone the White House. The letter is dated January 1853 from Concord, New Hampshire. Mrs. Pierce was far too grief stricken to go to D.C. for the inauguration. In fact, there were no balls or celebrations of any kind, as Franklin was understandably torn up over the loss of his only remaining child. The Pierce Administration was under the black cloud of death from the very beginning. Some reports have Mrs. Pierce leaving black curtains and bunting up at the White House for two years. The acceptable period of mourning for the time was one year. This extended mourning period did not help Jane's public image.

I'm not sure how people found out about this, or heard about any letters. Maybe they didn't. Maybe they made it up. Nonetheless, the word spread around town that crazy Jane Pierce was locked up in an secret room in the White House writing letters to her dead children with a couple of witches.

Here is how a grief stricken and inconsolable mother…who had now lost every child she brought into this world…wrote in pencil in January 1853…began her words to her son, Benny:

"My precious child I must write to you although you are never to know or see it…"

Her words went on to say what a horrible mother she was to have not been able to protect her son, and many other self-deprecating sentiments. She poured her heart out, and I'm fairly sure no one was ever meant to read this letter. It is one of the most moving things I have ever read. I cannot imagine her pain. I do not know this kind of pain or loss. It has to be immeasurable. It's bad enough to have lost one child. Jane lost all three. The last death happened right in front of her. Unfathomable. The specifics of his death pushed it over the edge of imagination. Keep in mind this happened in a time with no counseling or support groups. There may not have even been the concept of treatable depression, or proper medicines. She basically went through this on her own, in the public eye. Attention was the last thing she wanted from the world. This was on top of the fact that she already felt as though her husband had deceived her in the first place. When I tell this story in public, it is hard not to tear up.

This is why I say that much of her public persona and reputation is unjustly unfavorable, whether she was often in poor health or not. Selfish hypochondriac, maybe? Put yourself in Jane Pierce's shoes. What would you have done? What would people think and say about you?

OLD NORTH CEMETERY

I had one more stop to make in Concord, before I headed back to Quincy. Peter had offered to drive me to the cemetery where the Pierces and their children are buried. The Pierces are buried not very far from the Historical Society in downtown Concord. It seemed fitting to visit the people who had just indirectly shared their entire lives with me. I drove out through a snow and ice covered road that was not much more than a dirt path. I gathered my camera gear and trudged out into the snow to "meet" the Pierces.

It was a respectable and clean looking gravesite and markers. I was actually surprised by the lack of fanfare. If you didn't know it was there, you seriously might miss it, or not even realize that it is the final resting place of a former President of the United States of America and his family. Granted, there was a good amount of snow on the ground, but I could tell by the lack of fences and other security measures, that anyone could just walk right up and touch their final resting places. I like that you can get this close to history.

ANDOVER, MASSACHUSETTS

I couldn't close the chapter on Jane Pierce without a trip to Andover. It's such an important and significant part of her story. There were so many good times for Jane there, but ultimately it would be the location of her greatest sorrow. The hurdle with the house in Andover is that it is privately owned and the interior has been updated to support the modern life of the family that lives there. I cannot thank Debbie DeSmet and the Andover Historical Society enough for arranging my access. The family was friendly, gracious and opened their home up to my camera and me.

The story with Jane's sister's house, beyond what I've already told you, is that during the Pierce Administration it was called the Summer White House. It was (and is) located at 48 Central Street, and the White House staff would occupy the house across the street at 47 Central Street when the Pierces were in Andover. Jane was close with her sister, and they spent a lot of time there.

It is a big house with many rooms, located right in the center of town on the main drag – hence, Central Street. There are high ceilings and even though it has been modernized, it is easy to see why the Pierces enjoyed staying there. It is a lovely, homey house and a very quaint town, even by today's standards.

The house is located right down the street from a church that Jane attended (which is still there), and the train station (which is no longer there). After the accident that killed Benny, this house is where they brought his body. This is where Franklin came as he walked his dead son down the train tracks. Benny's funeral was held in the living room. Ten years later in 1863, Jane's funeral was held in the same room. It is said that Jane carried with her Benny's Bible and locks of hair from all of her family members who had passed on before her until the day she died. Her life, it would seem, was both surrounded and consumed by death.

Standing in the living room where the two funerals took place was heavy. I could look past the new furniture and TV to see in my mind the small coffin for Benny and later the larger one for Jane. When looking at the life of a historical figure like this, I find it a huge dose of reality to see not only where it all began, but also where it ended. When you look back this far in history, the figures seem almost mythical (at least they do to me). But, when you know there is an end, and hear the stories of how it ended, and then see the place where life's motion stopped…they become real. And, that was what I wanted for my contributions to this series. That was what I continue to want out of my live events and presentations and that is what I want out of this book. I want these people to jump off the pages of history. I want them to step out of the oil paintings and photographs. I want them to become real people. Because they were, and they are.

When I finished at the house, I went to the Andover Historical Society and got one more version of Benny's story, and what Andover meant to Jane Pierce. It was a valuable stop, and it helped formulate my version as I have described here in this book. I also wanted to, once again, thank the Andover Historical Society for arranging my access to the house. This kind of access and special tours of private homes and places really set the series and my journey apart from any similar projects.

I then grabbed a late lunch, and got some footage of the town and the church across the street from 48 Central. As I hopped in my car and headed out of town, I noticed train tracks to my left. I found a place to pull over and got out of my car. I stood there for a while; not even noticing that the sun was fading and the temperature was dropping. These tracks lead right back into or out of town. I know that the station had been moved, and likely, the tracks, too. They would have at least had to been adjusted or shifted to accommodate the new station location and modern trains. Then again, maybe not. These were as close as I could get to the actual tracks that took Benny's life. I was about a mile out of town. I had to be close to where the accident took place. So, I went back to my car and got my camera. I took a good long and careful look and listened up and down the train tracks before getting into position for my shots. This footage made it into the final cut for my Andover piece and it made the show. How could it not. It was a significant way to close the books on Andover, Benny and Jane as I packed up my gear and headed back to my hotel in Quincy.

SUMMARY

Jane Pierce was unusual for her time. She didn't like politics. She didn't like Washington, D.C. and she didn't want her husband to be President. Life didn't go as Jane planned or expected. She was a homebody. She loved her family, and she loved the church. History tells us she came out of her shell a little bit during the second half of her husband's presidency, but not much. And surely not enough to pull her out of the darkness in which most books describe her. I still believe that she is remembered a bit unfairly. All of her children were taken from her, the last in the most gruesome of circumstances. She didn't ask to be in the spotlight of the public eye. In fact, she tried to duck out of it entirely at nearly every turn, and pleaded with her husband to do the same. She didn't directly make huge contributions to our country or the role of First Lady. However, indirectly she gave almost everything to it. Jane Pierce's losses are unusual for any time.

Travelogue Food Tip

The Shawsheen Luncheonette is right in the heart of town, and has fantastic homemade soups and sandwiches. I had a grilled cheese with bacon and a bowl of tomato basil soup. It was a quiet and perfect meal for a cold and cloud covered day in Andover.

CHAPTER 18
Harriet Lane

Mercerburg, Pennsylvania – Lancaster, Pennsylvania

*H*arriet Rebecca Lane was born on May 9, 1830 in Mercersburg, PA. Her parents were Elliot Tole Lane and Jane Buchanan Lane. Harriet's uncle James Buchanan became her legally appointed guardian when she was nine years old. Harriet Lane was one of seven children. Harriet Lane was the only official hostess for her uncle's administration from 1857 – 1861. Harriet Lane married Henry Elliot Johnson on January 11, 1866. Harriet and Henry had two children together. Harriet Lane died on July 3, 1903 in Narragansett, Rhode Island at the age of 73.

MERCERSBURG, PENNSYLVANIA

Life for one of the most well known, well liked and influential First Ladies who wasn't an actual First Lady begins in Mercersburg, Pennsylvania. Harriet Lane was the niece and ward of the only bachelor President in our nation's history. Grover Cleveland entered the White House a bachelor, but got married during his presidency (the only President and First Lady to do so), which we will get to in the Frances Folsom Cleveland chapter. James Buchanan was in love an Irish girl named Anne. James and Anne were engaged. She broke off the engagement, and died before Buchanan could reconcile with her. He said that his heart was so broken he could not love another woman. He remained a bachelor for his entire life. However, this single lifestyle of President Buchanan would benefit the country in the form of his niece, Harriet Lane.

Washington was ready for a breath of fresh air. Some had considered Sarah Polk to be strict and stuffy, neither Margaret Taylor nor Abigail Fillmore were very social women on the grand political scale, and Jane Pierce was consumed by death and mourning. Harriet Lane's life was filled with death and tragedy, too, but she handled it much differently than Mrs. Pierce and many of her contemporaries. Harriet was young and vivacious. She had a desire to live life to the fullest. Harriet Lane was unusual for her time.

Harriet Lane is adopted and in her uncle's care because both of her parents had died by the time she was nine years old. She lost three siblings when they were very young, the other three would die in their 30's. In her childhood home, her bedroom window looked out towards the alley where her grandfather was thrown from a horse cart and died, her two children died very young, her husband died before her, and of course she lost her Uncle James Buchanan eventually to natural causes. Despite being surrounded by death and tragedy, Harriet Lane rises to the top of the national and international scene. She is the first woman to be referred to in print as the First Lady. Thus, it is during the Buchanan Administration that First Lady becomes a part of the common vernacular.

I left D.C., heading for Mercersburg on Monday the 21st of January 2013. It was Martin Luther King, Jr. Day and the day of the second Inauguration of President Barack Obama. It was impossible not to think of the significance of the day, and how far our country had come since 1776 as I prepared for this trip. I gathered my seven bags, made my way through the crowds across Capitol Hill, rented a car at Union Station and headed northwest out of the city. I was actually happy to be getting out of town. Inaugurations are fun and all, but I've seen more than a few in my day, and D.C. turns upside down during all the celebrations and festivities. It makes it hard for those of us who live and work there to go about our normal every day business. So, this extended trip across Pennsylvania was a welcomed escape. It also gave me time to drive and think about the way things were for the people I was studying. Harriet Lane and many others had to make a similar journey from Pennsylvania to Washington, D.C. by coach.

Side Note – Who's On First

There are many First Lady "firsts" that overlap, or are attributed to more than one First Lady and are disputed, discussed and argued. This is one of them. In my opinion and my studies I found that Harriet Lane is the first woman – albeit not a wife – related to a President's administration or time in the White House that is referred to as First Lady. However, because she is not Buchanan's wife, I can see why some people take issue with this term being attributed to her.

This was a fun part of driving certain legs of my journey. It just gave me more perspective on the distances that separated people and the lengths to which people went to get around the country. It makes me sound soft comparatively, but this travel was very difficult, and I had a GPS, gasoline car, planes, electricity, indoor plumbing and all the other modern conveniences.

I rolled into Mercersburg early that evening, and checked into the Mercersburg Inn Bed and Breakfast. The innkeepers were very friendly, and like most folks, curious about my gear and what had brought me to their little town. I told them about the C-SPAN series, and my travels, which had really just begun at this point.

The innkeeper, Gerald Lute, gave me an autographed copy of his book ("The Life and Legacy of John L. Grove") that he had written about a local industrialist, and his wife Pam made a fantastic red velvet cake. I keep the book in my home office as one of many wonderful souvenirs I acquired on my amazing adventure pursuing the First Ladies.

Travel Note – You're Out Of Order

I was picking up the Harriet Lane story out of order and early, because I was headed to Valley Forge, PA and Philly for stories about Martha Washington, Abigail Adams and Dolley Madison.

Tuesday morning I got started early at the Fendrick Library on North Main Street, right in the heart of Mercersburg. My hosts were ready for me and eager to show me their town and their First Lady. Walking the streets of Mercersburg and hearing about the tragic nature of Harriet's early life there was significant. To think that young Harriet knew so much death by the age of nine is staggering.

When I think back on my visit here, two things stick out. The first was my tour of the house in which Harriet spent those first nine years of her life. The house is right next door to the Fendrick Library and it is privately owned. My hosts had arranged for me to gain access with its current owner and resident.

The original structure and layout hasn't changed much since Harriet lived there. The dining room was in the same place. The courtyard in back was still there. Most importantly, one of the upstairs bedrooms, Harriet's bedroom, was still a bedroom. This was the room that faced the alley across Main Street where her grandfather was thrown from a cart and died. There was even some original furniture and china in the house that gave the place a truly historic feel.

This home was important, because it was where Harriet spent the first nine years of her life. These were the years in which she saw both of her parents and three of her siblings die. These were the types of tragedies that were so common during this period in history. These were the types of events that debilitated some people. However, they did not have that effect on Harriet Lane. It was her ability to rise above them and live a full life that made her so appealing and successful. She outshined all of the gloom that surrounded those years in her early life.

The second place that stands out in Mercersburg is the Presbyterian Church on Upper West Concord Street. This was the church where Harriet's parents were married, and the church where Harriet was baptized. They even have the pewter baptism set from the time Harriet and her family worshiped there. It is, in all likelihood, the same baptism set that was used in Harriet's ceremony. There were many other etchings, pictures and artifacts from the time period in the church that helped set the historic tone.

Harriet's father was a prominent figure in town. She was raised in a nice house. She was baptized in a respectable church. Her uncle was a rising figure in the Democrat Party on a national level. It's interesting to think about what path she would've taken had her parents not died when she was so young. But, it's equally (if not more) interesting to now know what she did become under the guidance and supervision of her uncle James Buchanan.

Before I left town, I had the good fortune of being taken to the James Buchanan birthplace memorial. It's out in the woods and off the beaten path. Luckily, my host and historian was from a local family, native to these parts and had no problem taking me there. It is a pyramid structure made from all local materials. It was Harriet Lane that commissioned the monument. Harriet was an art lover. She went to the Visitation Convent School in the Georgetown neighborhood of Washington, D.C. She studied and traveled abroad. She knew much about the finer things in life, and by all accounts, had excellent taste. She is the reason and inspiration behind what is now the National Gallery of Art. This monument to her uncle's legacy was a perfect way to finish my visit to Mercersburg. It was a poignant symbol of the love and enduring gratitude Harriet Lane had for her uncle and his legacy. He stepped in and took over her life where death had tried to strip her of it.

This foundation of knowledge and reference that I gained in Mercersburg was necessary to better comprehend the next stop in my trip – Wheatland in Lancaster, Pennsylvania.

Side Note - Back To Mercersburg

I have since returned to Mercersburg and the Fendrick Library to visit with my hosts and friends. I gave a speech there in July 2015. One thing I always mention in my presentations is that we have barely scratched the surface when it comes to these women. As in-depth and complete as the C-SPAN series was, and as wide and far as my travels were, each location could have a 90 minute show of its own. Every location holds a wealth of artifacts and information about each of these First Ladies. It was on my return visit to Mercersburg that I learned that the town has significant ties to many women related to the William Henry Harrison Administration and the Benjamin Harrison Administration. You just never know who is going to be in the crowd at a speech, and have some question or comment or piece of literature that will add another puzzle piece to the big picture of the First Ladies of the United States of America. Mercersburg is a treasure trove of history for First Ladies, Presidents and many other aspects of American History. I know I will return there soon and often and recommend the same for all readers of this book.

LANCASTER, PENNSYLVANIA

James Buchanan's Wheatland Estate is a remarkable place. I learned just how remarkable in the first few minutes setting up for recording in the very first room in which we worked – the parlor. I was setting up my lights and camera when I asked my host, Jennifer Walton, if I could adjust the blinds for lighting (remember – always ask before you touch in these places). She said I could but to be careful. So, I reached for the draw strings, as she continued that they were original blinds. I froze. I asked if she meant that they were original from when James Buchanan and Harriet Lane lived there in the 1800's, and she said yes. In fact, she told me that the house was somewhere between 70% and 75% original. That was just amazing to me. Another interesting fact about the house was that Harriet Lane was married in the house when she was 36, and she inherited the house from her uncle when he died in 1868.

As I mentioned we started our work in the parlor or the living room. The parlor is a great place to start, because Harriet was such an accomplished hostess both here in her uncle's house, and later in the White House. There are a number of pieces in this room that highlight this aspect of her life.

The main piece and focal point in this room is the piano. It was bought for Harriet by her uncle. The piano was made in Boston in the mid- to late 1850's. One of their favorite activities here at Wheatland was to sit and entertain guests with Harriet playing the piano and singing religious hymns or patriotic songs. Sitting on the piano is a music book with her name on the cover in gold leaf lettering. This combination of the music book and her piano makes the room look and feel as if Harriet might walk in at any minute, sit down and begin to entertain guests, holding court in the room just as she did so many years ago.

Visitors can also get a good sense of Harriet's travels and foreign appeal here in this room. They have a beautiful gown on display that she might have worn in her meeting with Queen Victoria. There is a bracelet given to her by Queen Victoria in 1857, and a lithograph of Prince Albert that she had hanging in the White House. She entertained Japanese diplomats and dignitaries that visited the White House in 1860, and there are many artifacts and gifts from those visitors, including some origami and her Japanese to English dictionary.

Also on display in the parlor is an original tea set that represents her love of entertaining and generous hostessing abilities, and there is a desk that shows her passion for letter writing and keeping in touch with friends and associates before, during and after her time in the White House. Harriet kept finches while she was at Wheatland, and an old birdcage from the 1800's is right beside her writing desk where she sat and composed any number of writings. She was said to love nature and enjoyed bringing some of the wildlife that the Wheatland Estate had to offer inside to enjoy.

Upstairs, the bedroom is furnished with a mix of Harriet's belongings from her time at Wheatland and later in life when she lived in Baltimore, MD. The majority of her furniture was European fashion and handmade in Paris. She had many gowns, also European or New England-made with low necklines. Her low necklines were a bit racy for the times, but the times soon adjusted to her style. Soon, women all over Washington, D.C. and across the country (as limited as that was at the time) were wearing similar dresses and gowns. In fact, women were copying her style of jewelry and the way she wore her hair, too.

There is also an embroidered tabletop with her mother's hymnal in this bedroom. Harriet kept many remembrances of those family members she had lost with her at all times. Another writing desk is here in her bedroom; she used it when she was in the White House.

One of the more unusual and – if I'm being honest – CREEPY items in the room is a beeswax Harriet Lane doll. It is remarkably accurate and well crafted. It looked exactly like her. It's an unusual piece that was crafted for her when she was First Lady.

Another piece in the room that shows her affection and appreciation for her uncle and the life he gave her is the bed. It's not her bed, but a bed she had made for her uncle. At six feet, James Buchanan was a tall man. Most early leaders of our country were six feet or taller. Thus, the bed was custom made to fit his tall frame.

Production Note – Waiter, There's A Hair In My Jewelry

I would like to take this opportunity to again thank Scott Harris and the folks at the Monroe Museum in Fredericksburg for teaching me about hair jewelry on my first trip, so I didn't look like as much of a knucklehead when other folks broke out their follicle finery.

The most interesting and significant piece in the room was Harriet Lane's jewelry box – or more accurately stated, the items in her jewelry box. Remember way back in Fredericksburg, Virginia when I was gathering material and footage for Elizabeth Monroe? Remember her hair earrings? Well, Elizabeth Monroe had nothing on Harriet Lane when it came to hair jewelry. However, now we are in the 1800's and hair jewelry has taken on a different meaning. Instead of a sign of affection, this kind of jewelry was now a token of mourning. So, before they dropped you in the ground, they snipped off a few locks to remember you by. It only stands to reason, that because there was so much death and loss in Harriet's life that there would be a fair amount of hair jewelry in her collection.

The first piece I was shown was a two-sided locket that opened on both sides, front and back. On one side was a picture of her sister Mary Lane Baker. This sister had died just before Harriet returned from a trip to Europe. The other side opens to reveal a picture of her brother Elliot Eskridge Lane who died right after James Buchanan's inauguration. He was supposed to be Buchanan's personal secretary, but along with many other guests at the National Hotel in Washington, D.C., he caught a severe case of dysentery that eventually took his life.

The next piece was also a locket that could be used as a pin or brooch and contained an intricate pattern of woven hair from three of her nieces and nephews each of whom died very young. The backside contained more hair in an almost swirled pattern. The names and dates of death for all were engraved there, too.

Certainly one of the most unusual and intricate pieces of jewelry that I was to see during the whole series was Harriet Lane's mourning locket globe. This piece was gorgeous and masterfully crafted. Kept closed and worn around her neck, this would have looked like a golden globe or ball pendant. However, the globe opened to reveal a smaller sphere that actually spun around on a tiny axis. Each side contained the hair and engraves names and death dates of her mother, her father and three of her siblings. Each glass window that displayed the family member's hair was only about a ¼ of an inch or smaller. The intricate craftsmanship was truly one of a kind.

The last and probably most significant piece in Harriet Lane's Wheatland jewelry box was the bracelet that commemorated her dear uncle's death. It was a gold band with a beautiful cameo on the front. Similar to the globe locket, this could be worn without a hint of its true meaning to the unknowing observer. However, the backside that faced the wrist contained a lock of President Buchanan's hair and ferns clipped from the grounds of Wheatland on the day he died (June 1, 1868) pressed under a piece of rectangular glass with rounded edges about the size of a quarter. Engraved along the inside of the band of the bracelet were the last words President James Buchanan uttered in life, "Oh, Lord God Almighty as thou wilt".

The last artifact we looked at in the bedroom really put a punctuation and finality on the many losses suffered by Harriet in her lifetime. Hanging there in her bedroom at Wheatland was a painting of her two sons, James Buchanan Johnston (1868-1881) and Henry Elliot Johnston (1869-1882). Both of her sons died in their teens around the same time from Rheumatic fever. The boys are painted against a rocky seascape to symbolize death and moving on, dressed in nice clothes with some of their favorite possessions. This memorial painting is yet another of Harriet Lane's items that symbolizes perhaps the most devastating losses in her life, those of her children.

Location Note – Home Grown

My host and guide at Wheatland was Assistant Director, Jennifer Walton. Not only was Jennifer extremely knowledgeable, easy to work with and very natural on camera, she was a local. She told me that it was Harriet Lane that influenced her college studies and major. It was also Harriet Lane that inspired her to do what she does and work there at Wheatland. She is truly happy in her work and in her dream job. The video pieces at Wheatland definitely reflected her passion for the subject matter.

SUMMARY

Harriet Lane was one of the most popular and celebrated First Ladies or hostesses that was not married to a President. Her influence on style and culture was significant. She set fashion trends, pushed the limits and injected a youthful spirit into the White House and Washington. She was the first woman to be referred to in print as "First Lady". Her love for the arts was the inspiration for the National Gallery of Art. After the death of her two sons she was the driving force behind what is now the Children's Medical Center at Johns Hopkins. She was known and loved nationally and internationally. She achieved all of this, despite tremendous loss during her entire life. It was an enormous amount of loss even for that day and age.

Harriet Lane lost all six of her brothers and sisters. Her bedroom window overlooked the alley where her grandfather was killed. Her parents died by the time she was nine. She lost nieces and nephews far too early in their lives. She was at her Uncle Buchanan's bedside when he dies at the age of 77. Then her children died an untimely death in their teens within a year of each other. Finally, her husband died two years after their second son passed away. In circumstances beyond what devastated other people and First Ladies before and after her, Harriet Lane shines through the gloom and lived her life to the fullest. She left behind marvelous institutions that we still enjoy and take advantage of today. Harriet Lanes was unusual for her time.

Travelogue Food Tip

Amazingly enough, I didn't eat BBQ or Caesar salad every day at every meal. In fact, sushi was a pretty regular thing, when I got a good recommendation. Bad fish is NOT something you want when you're on the road (or anywhere really). It's fun to try new places and explore when you're traveling by yourself. I enjoy it, anyway (I kind of had to...what choice did I have). Jennifer suggested a place called Blue Pacific Sushi & Grill that was not too far from Wheatland, and it happened to be near a Harley Davidson dealer (see next chapter for why THAT is important). The sashimi was fresh, the special rolls were imaginative with tasty sauces, and there was a giant fish tank in the middle of the place that kept my attention throughout the meal.

Bonus Fish Fact – Go Fish!

The fish tank's primary resident at Blue Pacific was a Silver Arowana fish that was about a foot and a half long. Arowanas can grow to 3 feet in captivity and even longer in the wild. They are a fresh water fish and different varieties can be found in Asia, Indonesia and Australia. The Silver Arowana is native to South America and the Amazon River. These fish are jumpers. They are silver in color with large eyes and scales. They can jump as high as 6 feet out of the water and snatch food (insects, small birds, lizards and even mammals) out of the air and low hanging trees. They also eat other smaller fish. I have had a few of these in tanks in my house over the years. They are beautiful fish and a lot of fun.

CHAPTER 19

Mary Lincoln

Lexington, Kentucky – Springfield, Illinois – Washington, D.C.

*M*ary Lincoln was born Mary Ann Todd on December 13, 1818 in Lexington, Kentucky. Her parents were Robert Smith Todd and Eliza Ann Parker Todd. Mary and Abraham Lincoln were married on November 4, 1842. The Lincolns had four children together. Mary Lincoln died on July 16, 1882 in Springfiled, Illinois at the age of 63.

LEXINGTON, KENTUCKY

Mary Ann Todd was born to a prominent family in Lexington, Kentucky. The house she was born in no longer stands, but the house she grew up in does. It's right on West Main Street near the center of town, and the schools where Mary went as a little girl and young woman. In fact, many people came to Lexington for culture and education in the South during the early 1800's. It's here in Lexington, and at the Mary Todd House, where I got a glimpse of the

179

Mary that most of the world doesn't know and has never seen. The Mary Lincoln I got to know was a well educated, well liked, fun loving, and even precocious young woman.

When I set out to begin my research on Mary Lincoln, I was a bit hesitant. No. Hesitant isn't the right word. I don't know if I know the right word to describe what I was feeling. Mary Lincoln seemed monumental to me in so many ways. Larger than life. I thought to myself, how do you teach people about someone A) they already know about, or about whom they think they know the whole story and B) about whom they have already formed opinions? When I speak, at least one person in the crowd asks "was Mary Lincoln really crazy?" or "how crazy was Mary Lincoln?" I'm not a doctor or a psychologist, nor did I know Mrs. Lincoln or young Mary Todd personally (obviously), however, what I saw and learned in Lexington, and in Springfield, sheds a new light on Mary. I hope this chapter does for you, too.

Before I go any further, I must jump ahead a bit in the story and address an issue. *Mary Todd Lincoln.* She never went by that name. Growing up she was Mary Todd, and after she was married, she was Mary Lincoln. Mary Todd Lincoln is a 20th century adaptation, invention, incarnation and inaccuracy. I will get into specifics later in this chapter. Now that we're all clear on her name, let's get back to Mary Todd and Lexington, Kentucky.

Mary lived in the Todd house between the ages of 12 and 21, and Director Gwen Thompson was the perfect person to show me around and teach me about Mary's life growing up in Lexington. She lived there with brothers and sisters, stepbrothers and stepsisters, and even a few cousins at times. Her mother died when she was six. Her father remarried two years later. The Todd House was an active one. It is well known and documented that Mary had a difficult relationship with her stepmother. There are journals and letters to friends that indicate Mary was often not pleased or not getting along with her stepmother. I would submit that this is not unusual (there are fairy tales and Disney movies about this very subject). In fact, I will go further by asking, what child didn't have problems with his or her parents (let alone stepparents) at some point or another growing up? If you combine this with our modern interpretation of the flowery language of the day, and the fact that young people and especially teenagers can be overly dramatic, we might see Mary's youth and relationship with her stepmother a little differently. I'm not saying she didn't have some issues and instability. But at her childhood home I was shown a life full of activity, privilege, family and every advantage a girl might need to succeed in life in the 1800's.

The house in Lexington is big. It has three stories, two large parlors, an ample dining room and a number of bedrooms. Sometimes Mary would have her own room, and sometimes she would share with her sisters and female cousins. In either case she had a nice sized room and beautiful furniture and furnishings. In her bedroom there was a small lithograph of Madame Mantelle who ran the finishing school Mary attended in Lexington, Kentucky.

Mary was very well educated for her time. I already mentioned that Lexington was a hub of education and culture, and that Mary was privileged and from a prominent family. So, it would stand to reason that Mary would have been able to take advantage of this in her schooling, as well. She attended two schools in Lexington. She went to Madame Mantelle's Academy and before that, she went to Ward's Academy. Both of these institutions taught her the usual finishing skills (like needlepoint and dancing) that a proper young lady was taught in those days, but she also learned French, literature and arithmetic. She was a highly educated woman of her time. And her education didn't stop at formal schools. It continued at home with her family.

In the Todd house in Lexington there are many rooms and items that represent just how privileged and unusual her upbringing was. When you first enter through the front door there is a long hallway down the center of the house and large rooms to either side. Let's start, as I did, to the right. This room was the formal parlor. Guests of all sorts were entertained here. Most interesting in this room, is a portrait of her grandmother, Mary Brown Humphreys. This was the mother of her stepmother. This woman was a great influence and role model for Mary.

Mary's grandmother, or should I say her grandmothers (plural) were both strong women that outlived their husbands and did very well for themselves. Mary was close to them and would have seen the examples they set for being independent women of means that could take care of themselves in a man's world. Mary's grandmother Humphreys showed Mary something else. She showed her a different perspective on slavery. Mary Humphreys freed her slaves in her will, in what was known as gradual emancipation. Now, today this might seem just as wrong and barbaric as slavery itself, but for Lexington, Kentucky in the early 1800's, this was considered extremely progressive.

Mary's family owned slaves. There were as many as six in the house at a time. Mary was no stranger to slavery, but she was also no stranger to new and different ways of thinking about slavery. This brings us to the next couple of rooms, where Mary would have also been exposed to prominent members of society and helped her father entertain and engage in political conversations of the day. The room connected to the parlor, is the dining room.

The Todd's neighbor and good friend was Henry Clay. He was a leader in the Whig party of which Robert Todd (Mary's father) was also a member. The two men were highly in favor of the colonization of American slaves to Liberia. Mary was special to her father, and her father was special to her. Mary always wanted to spend time with her father and had an unusual appetite for politics for a young woman, or any woman for that time. Mary was permitted to stay at the dining room table and sit in on conversations that were typically reserved for the men.

Beyond the conversations, the dining room was very well appointed, hutches and china cabinets surround the room with wonderful pieces from the Todd family and the period. It is easy to see that Mary and her family were well to do, and knew how to entertain. The conversations that were held there would carry over into the next room. This was a room that was usually exclusively reserved for men, called the gentlemen's parlor.

It was a beautiful room with dark hard wood and deep colors. It had everything you might expect to see in such a room, where important men made important decisions and smoked cigars and pipes and laughed and drank brandy. In the middle of all this "mannery" sat young Mary Todd. She listened, but also contributed. One time, Mary told Henry Clay that she wished him to be President so that she could live in the White House with him. She even worked on his failed Presidential campaign in 1840 when she was only 22.

The other rooms and decor of the house are equally impressive and elegant. Amazing family portraits hang in every room. The living room adjacent to the gentlemen's parlor has a feminine tone to it. Mary would have spent time in here playing with her siblings and cousins. There is a fantastic guest room upstairs where later she and her husband would sleep when they came to visit Mary's family. The upstairs dormer and smaller bedrooms were wonderful accommodations for her younger family members. These rooms only further showcased an upper class home full of life and activity. On the third floor there are modern display cases that have been built to hold a number of fascinating artifacts of the 1800's owned by the museum. These items include a finely made pipe and a number of books and printed material.

I was told stories of Mary playing in the creek behind the house, and at one time owning a pony to ride around town. She and her cousin took branches from the backyard and made hoop skirts for church. There are family bibles, knick-knacks and finery in every nook and cranny of the house. It looks as though Mary's childhood here was anything but the gloom and doom that her adult life would hold for her.

Before I left Lexington, I did get a preview of that gloom and doom in the form of the local cemetery. Mary's family was split by the Civil War, as many families were. She had brothers who fought for the Confederacy and brothers who fought for the Union. Her brothers, along with her parents and other family members, are buried here in Lexington.

SPRINGFIELD, ILLINOIS

Mary Todd met Abraham Lincoln in Springfield, Illinois. She was visiting her sister in the summer of 1836. This was a common practice among families at the time. A younger sister would go off to the "big city" and stay with an older married sibling (typically, a sister and her husband). They were usually there on a "husband hunting" expedition. In Mary's case it was more to get involved in politics. Although from an early age, she had told family and friends that she would marry a man who would one day be President.

The Lincoln home in Springfield is a National Historic Site run by the National Park Service and the head curator Susan Haake was there to show me around and teach me everything should could about Mary Lincoln's time in Springfield. The whole surrounding area is preserved to look as it did when the

Lincolns lived here. When they moved into the house it was a one story dwelling in a lower middle class neighborhood. The Lincolns added onto the house making it a two story home as the neighborhood improved, meanwhile, Lincoln's career as a corporate lawyer for the railroads continued to improve, as well. Here I learned that from very early on in their life together Mary didn't want to just "keep up with the Joneses," she wanted to BE the Joneses. Sometimes this meant living beyond their means and got them into financial issues, but for the most part it did advance Abraham's career, and thus, the Lincoln's social status. It was the only house that the Lincolns ever owned. They lived there for seventeen years.

The home is beautifully and accurately preserved, and looks as though the Lincolns might walk through the front door at any minute. The home served many purposes, both public and private. There are many original artifacts, and the entire house tells a complete story of the family's time here. Let's start with the public side of things; since that's the first part of the house I saw when I walked in the front door.

In the early days, Mary was one of the best political partners of any of the First Ladies. She was brought up in an upper class family and educated in some of the finest schools in the country, and she brought that (for lack of a better word) knowledge with her to Springfield. When she redesigned the house, she added a second parlor like her home in Lexington. When she held receptions, the layout and flow of the first floor was such that guests entered the front door, were greeted by Mary in the living room or parlor to the right, and then moved through to the dining room for food and refreshment. The dining room was formal. Mary grew up in a house with a formal dining room, and she would not do without one here. She would teach her husband and her children etiquette in this room. It also served them well for social gatherings and important dinner guests. During receptions after some light refreshments, guests passed around into the second formal parlor to have a word with Abraham Lincoln.

The whole house was very well decorated and appointed. However, the formal parlor was something extraordinary. The furniture was plush velvet with beautifully lacquered hard wood. There were marble top tables, brass valences on the windows, gold candlesticks, and I'm told Mary spared no expense when it came to this room. This room also contained a walnut knickknack shelf with a number of interesting items owned by the Lincolns. A bust of Abraham Lincoln that Mary had commissioned and displayed while they were living there was featured in the parlor. My hosts made sure to highlight this item. This bust was in the house when the Lincolns were living there. This is important, because it kind of falls in line with the whole "dress for the job you want, not the job you have" theory to which Mrs. Lincoln subscribed. Mary decked the place out to promote her husband. She wanted to show the man he had become, while not letting anyone forget from where he had come. It is important to note, she helped build and create the public image of her husband. Her husband was a man who would become President. Just like she told her friends and family back home in Kentucky. This bust was a symbol of that greatness and political potential.

Mary also held social events in the house called "strawberries and cream" parties. She had a famous white cake recipe, and we know from bills and record keeping that she often shopped at Watkins Confectionary in town. A specialty known as a macaroon pyramid was also often served at social gatherings at the Lincoln's house in Springfield. One of Mary's prize possessions was her Royal Oak stove. This stove was made in Buffalo, New York, and cost the Lincolns somewhere between $20 and $25 dollars. Keep in mind the average income at this time was $500 a year. This was an expensive item, and a source of great pride and status for Mary. She even wanted to take the stove with her to the White House. As the story goes, Mr. Lincoln explained to his wife that not only did the White House already have a perfectly good stove, but also she would not be doing much cooking there.

Having covered the first floor, it was time to head upstairs to see the bedrooms and private quarters of the Lincoln home.

The home has a number of bedrooms on the second floor including a private bedroom for Mary. This would have been considered extremely luxurious, and unusual for the time. It would also be very beneficial for a woman in a house full of men. There were other factors at play, too. Mary suffered from migraine headaches and Mr. Lincoln often stayed up late working or meeting with clients and business associates. Mary would have gained much needed relief in her private bedroom. The one thing about the room that baffled me, to the point of mentioning it here and there in the house, was the wallpaper in Mrs. Lincoln's bedroom. It was crazy. The intensely intricate filigreed patterns and harsh purple and gilded colors were making my head hurt and causing me to go a little batty, and I was only in there for about 30-45 minutes. I'm not kidding…this wallpaper was wild. I'm sure, knowing Mary, that it was the height of fashion, good taste and popularity. I'm also fairly certain that it wasn't cheap. I can't see how this pattern would help a migraine, but I'm sure the peace and solitude the room afforded Mrs. Lincoln was valuable.

Production Note – Spring Break

I was in Springfield during the Spring Break season for many schools. Over 400 people came through the Lincoln house while we were filming and working. I was not allowed nor did I want to interrupt the tours or the experience for the visitors. So, I would have to set up, tear down and move all of my gear in between tour groups. Even as good as my hosts and I were and as smoothly as the day went, this was a remarkably time consuming endeavor to an already physically and mentally exhausting process. Walking through one of these houses and not damaging, bumping into, knocking over or dropping anything is a job in and of itself. It was equally difficult for one person to set up and move the gear while processing what was going on technically, and to make sure everything was being covered editorially. It adds a whole new twist to do it without intermittently disturbing and staying out of the way of over 400 people. The park rangers giving the tours would yell through the house that a tour was coming and it was like a verbal water brigade or telephone game throughout the house to let me know that another tour was about to come through the part of the house where we were working. Everyone had a good time with it, and it actually became laughable throughout the day.

Mrs. Lincoln's room had a large comfortable and well-appointed bed. She had beautiful furniture in the latest style of the day, and all of the comforts that the era provided. She even had a beautifully crafted mahogany chamber pot seat.

She spent many hours here in this room doing needlepoint, getting ready at the beginning or end of her day or just simply resting in times of poor health.

The boys all had rooms throughout the second floor; the rooms were not huge, but were more than ample. As the oldest, Robert even had his own room. The boys' rooms were decorated very simply and appropriately for a young person's room of the time: furnished with a bed, a desk and a dresser. Each of the rooms had toy soldiers, games and other items of the period that you would expect to find in a boy's room. Above the kitchen, by the back steps there was a room for the hired girl, who the Lincolns employed as a live-in helper to Mrs. Lincoln.

The Lincolns also had a guest room at the front of the second floor. The interesting thing about this room was that it was furnished with things from the Lincoln's old apartment. This was very cool to me, and it was one of the most significant things in my Lincoln related travels that made them "real people". I never knew when or where this feeling or realization would strike me, but it happened with each of the First Ladies (especially the ones that were from the past and not from my lifetime). This was something that I had done. I imagine that most people have done this in some form or another. I'm talking about the transferring and transitioning of furniture.

When I moved out of my parent's house the summer after 11th grade to live at the beach (the specifics of this are another story for another book…or perhaps a "coming of age" movie like "Fast Times at Ridgemont High") I took a dresser and a mattress with me. These items later followed me to college, and eventually ended up in the guest room of my first house. I am the main occupant and part-time resident of a family lake house that still utilizes the silverware and plates from the house in which I grew up. The house I live in now has older dressers from my grandparent's house in the guest room. The point here is, that the Lincolns did in the 1800's what people still very commonly do today with their furniture and old household items.

Visitor Interaction Note – Bottoms Up

When I was shooting b-roll footage of the guest room, a call came down the hallway from one of the park rangers. A tour group was coming through the part of the house where we were working. So, I folded up my camera and tripod, moved my lights, and stepped to the side of the room. I was off to the side and out of the way. Or so I thought. A woman leaned in the room over the velvet rope to get a better look at the room. I stood there quietly enough for a while looking straight ahead, catching the woman in my peripheral vision. She turned and looked right at me. So, I turned and looked at her. She jumped and let out a startled "GASP." I apologized for startling her, and she laughed, explaining that at first she had just thought I was an inanimate mannequin, and part of the exhibit. I told her who I was and what I was doing, and she (like most folks I encountered on the road) was fascinated and wanted to hear more about the series. She then asked me if I knew anything about the room in which I was standing. I proceeded to tell her everything I knew about the room, and my thoughts, which I have just explained here, about the repurposing of the furniture making Mary Lincoln a real person. She agreed and asked if she could take a picture. I said certainly, and tried to step further out of the way, so as not to be in her picture. I told her that I hoped I had stepped far enough out of the way. She said she thought she might have got a bit of my rear end in the picture, but added with a wink that that wouldn't ruin her picture. She and her group were from Austin, TX. She was fun, and I hope she is reading this and remembering the incident – and still has the picture of the room with a little bit of my rear end! After the exchange and the group had moved on, Susan said my interpretation and explanation of the room was spot on, and if I needed a job after the C-SPAN series was over to come back and she'd hire me. Now that I write this, it may have been here in the Lincoln house in Springfield that the first thoughts of a speaking program and tour entered the back of my mind.

THE ABRAHAM LINCOLN PRESIDENTIAL LIBRARY
AND MUSEUM

After over 400 people, one spirited lady from Texas, at least ten rooms on two floors and some chilly and overcast outdoor filming in the street, it was getting late and I wasn't finished in Springfield. We made our way across town and over to the Abraham Lincoln Presidential Library and Museum to get a look at some of the most rare and most valuable Lincoln items in existence. The Library and Museum themselves are impressive buildings with well done exhibits and displays, however, this Indiana Jones of First Ladies (that's me) headed straight for the basement.

I set up my gear in a conference room in the lower level of the library offices where Lincoln Collection Curator James Cornelius had carts and carts of artifacts waiting for me. Our focus of study and period of artifacts was centered on her time in the White House. However, some of the things and information carried over into her post-White House years.

This is where I learned that Mary Lincoln never used Mary Todd Lincoln. It was all in her signature. She had signed her name in all of her books. In this case it was a few volumes from what is believed to have been originally a 27 set collection of the works of Sir Edward Bulwer Litton. The books were signed "Mary Lincoln 1864". They also have her personal letter seal with the initials "ML" that she owned and used in the White House. Cornelius explained that she "never ever" called herself Mary Todd Lincoln or Mary T. Lincoln. She was always Mary Lincoln, Mrs. Abraham Lincoln or Mrs. President Lincoln.

Many people who have been to the Smithsonian or other museums will have seen the Lincolns' White House china. Here at the Lincoln Library in Springfield, they had soup terrines and other pieces from the Lincoln's personal, "every day" china that they brought with them to the White House. There were also letters that Mary wrote to various people in Washington and in the administration that indicated she was beginning to have problems with some of the people and officials in Washington. She wrote letters asking for favors with the promise never to ask again. Her reputation suffered because of these letters and requests. One such letter was to the Assistant Secretary of the Treasury, Mr. George Harrington, asking if he could find a job for her friend Elizabeth Keckley as a dressmaker, because she had fired her old dressmaker Ellen Sheehan. Now, again, this could be just an every day hiring and firing, or maybe Sheehan did something really bad or made a crummy dress that got her fired. We don't know. We weren't there. However, given Mrs. Lincoln's history and other known behaviors, it seems that rational action is not always in her wheelhouse.

Some items made all too clear the loss that Mary suffered. The greatest of which, in the White House, was the death of their son, Willie. Just before my visit, the Library and Museum had recently acquired a piece of very rare sheet music. The sheet music is a tribute piece, a ballad called "Little Willie's Grave." At the top of the sheet music it reads, "To Mrs. Abraham Lincoln." The poetry is attributed to a WM. Ross Wallace and the music is by J.R. Thomas. A substantial New York publisher published it at the time by the name of William Hall & Son.

Historical Note – What's Old Is New Again

This is yet another example of my mind being a bit blown away by a recent discovery. I was in the Lincoln Library. Abraham Lincoln is one of the most well known faces around the world, and one of the most celebrated Presidents in the history of our country. How is it that we are still to this day, unearthing "new" artifacts and information about him? These newly found national treasures reinforce the significance of this television series, and continues to reinforce the driving force behind my speaking program and future books. There is still so much to learn and discover about these Presidential families, especially the First Ladies, who we so often know so much less about than their husbands.

Mr. Lincoln gave Mrs. Lincoln many gifts during their time together. Many of these gifts are on display at the Library and Museum. One such gift was a very interesting music box. It is made of dark wood and is about two feet long by half a foot tall and another half a foot wide. It is very plain, but well made and beautiful. So well made, in fact that it still plays. There is a small crank that goes into a hole on the side of the box, and it plays show tunes. Mr. and Mrs. Lincoln were big fans of the theater (which for obvious reasons is sadly ironic). The saddest part about this music box is that it plays a song from "Our American Cousins", the last play that the Lincolns would see together. Mary listened to this music box often around the anniversary of her husband's death, and sink into deep bouts of depression.

The Library also has a fascinating collection or postcards, pictures, journals, letters and souvenirs from some rather extensive traveling that Mary Lincoln, and her son, Tad, did after President Lincoln's death. This is rather remarkable to me, based on the stories of financial ruin, depression, odd behavior and insanity that surround Mary Lincoln in her later years. It would seem from the pictures that there was some bit of money, happiness and normality in Mrs. Lincoln's life after her husband was assassinated. This brief stint of good time would soon be overshadowed by Tad's death in 1871.

Not all of the items I was shown had ties to death or depression. Mr. Lincoln had (in my humble opinion) excellent taste in jewelry, and similar to his wife, didn't seem to spare any expense in this department. One such item was a rather large gold heart pendant that was covered on both sides with diamonds. Judging from the approximate date it was given to Mary, and the extravagance of the piece, it was likely to have been an anniversary or Christmas present during their time in the White House.

The next thing I learned came out of nowhere as we were looking over some of the other papers and folders on the carts. Much has been written about Mary Lincoln's sanity (or lack thereof), and her son Robert's role in her institution-alization. Robert is often portrayed as a bit of a villain, only looking out for himself, and his own financial gain. Given what has been known up to this point, and again, our modern interpretation of the language used in writing of the day, it was reasonable to think those things are accurate. However, here is another way of looking at it.

The library has letters and receipts from when Mrs. Lincoln was living by herself in Chicago after the deaths of her husband, and their son, Tad. By this time, Robert was married and also living in Chicago. Mrs. Lincoln was living in a high-rise hotel or apartment building. She had reportedly been acting erratically in public and making strange purchases all over town. For instance, she lived in an apartment that was completely furnished. Yet, she bought a lot of new furniture, signed the bills of sale, but never paid for or picked up the furniture. The Library has the bills of sale and receipts, as well as letters between Robert Lincoln and the storeowners to corroborate these reports. Robert had to go all over town and settle his mother's accounts and disputes. The final straw came after the great Chicago fire of 1871. Mrs. Lincoln was found delirious and wandering the streets saying that her apartment was on fire. There was no fire in her apartment, and doctors determined that she was hallucinating and very fortunate not to have jumped out of her window to escape the imagined flames. This scared Robert into institutionalizing his mother to protect her from herself. Unfortunately, Mary was not given the chance to speak for herself on the matter, which didn't help the public opinion on the matter, nor how future generations would come to view Robert's decision. However, given that research has shown, and evidence has come to light regarding the basis for her institutionalization, we are presented with a different side of the story; one that perhaps supports Robert's decision based out of genuine care for his mother, not financial gain. He quite possibly saved his mother's life.

About four months after being admitted to Bellevue Place, a private sanitarium outside of Chicago, Mrs. Lincoln was released and allowed to live with her sister back in Springfield. Five months thereafter, she was found by a court to be "restored to reason." Based on what I have seen, researched and read, it is my opinion (keep in mind that not only am I not a doctor…I don't even play one on TV) that overmedicating herself during fits of depression combined with mental instability may have led to her unreasonable and dangerous behavior. I will continue to theorize by saying that MAYBE after getting into a facility where she was monitored and properly cared for, she "sobered up," rekindled a relationship with her sister, and was able to mentally stabilize herself. It's just a thought.

Author's Note – T-Shirt Collection

I collect Harley Davidson dealer t-shirts. The first thing I did on each trip after researching, filming and learning everything I could about each of these First Ladies was to Google the nearest Harley dealer and scoot on over to pick up a shirt. Harley Davidson dealers all have custom designs on the back of their shirts unique to their store and location. One of the best shirts from my travels came from Hall's Harley Davidson in Springfield, IL. The back of the shirt has Abe Lincoln (top hat and all) bare armed in a black leather vest with a full sleeve of tattoos standing next to his Fat Boy Harley parked out in front of his Springfield home. The artwork and specificity to the store's location is outstanding. This trip added a number of new states to my collection and about 30 shirts. There are close to 200 in the collection. Note to self: count Harley shirts.

WASHINGTON, D.C.

I think you can tell a lot about a person when you look at the places they go when they're happy and the places they go when they're sad. I mean the physical places, the retreats and the vacation homes. For Mary Lincoln, her retreat was a cottage on the grounds of what is now known as the Armed Forces Retirement Home. It is a beautiful home tucked in between what I call the Hospital District in upper side of Northwest Washington, D.C. off of North Capitol Street. I traveled here one afternoon to see President Lincoln's Cottage at the Soldiers' Home. The attraction here is the structure. The rooms are fairly bare, and flat screen TVs tell the story of the cottage's significance very well. One of the really neat things about this house is an original banister in a back staircase. This is similar to the winter encampment headquarters of George Washington in York, Pennsylvania. I ran my hand along the banister just as I had done in York. It's incredible to think of the hands of Mary and Abraham Lincoln moving along the same piece of wood. Something about the actual touch and feel of it brings them that much closer and makes them that much more real.

I was there to talk about Mary Lincoln, so I was shown to a very special room that is not open to the public. The room is called the Mary Lincoln Room. They call it this because Mrs. Lincoln most likely spent a lot of time here recovering from a carriage accident in 1863. They think this because it is the only room in the home with windows on three walls, and the cross breezes would have been very nice and relaxing for her. It is also one of the more isolated rooms on the second floor.

The carriage accident was thought to be an early assassination attempt on President Lincoln. Lincoln's carriage had apparently been tampered with or sabotaged and the horses got spooked when the driver's seat separated from the carriage causing it career out of control. Mrs. Lincoln jumped from the carriage and hit her head on a rock. She was treated at the White House and then taken to the cottage, which, at the time, was just outside of the city, a quieter place to rest and recuperate.

The cottage had also served as a place of solitude for Mary after the death of their son Willie in 1862. It was a place she could be alone and grieve. She even hosted a séance there. President Lincoln had suspicions that his wife was being taken advantage of so he had his friend and colleague, Noah Brooks sit in on the séance. Lincoln thought that the medium may have been trying to blackmail his wife, so he needed a guy on the inside. Lincoln was right and the man was proven to be a phony, using tricks to make noises and other effects. This is another case where history treats Mary a bit unfairly. She is portrayed as a bit of a kook for her beliefs in the supernatural. What people today don't always understand is that many people bought into this kind of thinking. Death was all around and a part of every day life. This was especially true during the Civil War. It seems like everyone was dying and the average life expectancy was not very high. Many people were trying to connect with the dead in the afterlife, and the supernatural was very popular at the time.

Even though she used it as a place to mourn the death of her son Willie in 1862, and to recover from the carriage accident in 1863, Mary Lincoln often writes about the beauty of the cottage and what a nice place it was to visit. It was an escape from the political pressures and oppressive summer weather of Washington, D.C. Most if not all Presidential couples had and continue to have summer homes and favorite vacation spots. The cottage was that place and that home for the Lincolns.

SUMMARY

One of the challenges with a woman like Mary Lincoln is revealing or teaching something that hasn't already been seen or wasn't already known. As I've mentioned multiple times in this chapter, Mary Lincoln's mental health was always in question. People ask me at nearly every live event about her. She and her husband for both good and bad reasons are of great interest to people. So, was Mary Lincoln crazy?

Many aspects of Mary's life were tragic. There is no doubt about that. She suffered great loss. Many people were suffering great losses at the time. There was no penicillin and death and war were all around. In some aspects, Mary's life was unfortunately fairly typical for the time, in that she lost many children and family members. Her life was equally typical, in that her husband died. It was extremely atypical in the fact that her husband was the President of the United States and he was shot in the head while sitting next to her at a play. Do I feel sorry for Mary Lincoln? Yes, of course I do. I feel sorry for all of the unnecessary and tragic loss. I feel especially sorry for the lives of the children. Many people could have been saved by simply drinking water and staying hydrated. However, it was an unfortunate circumstance of the day and age.

We need not go back any further than the previous chapter and administration to see just as much (if not more) loss people experienced in their lives. Harriet Lane dealt with her loss very differently. If we go all the way back to Martha Washington, we can see another woman who dealt with great loss very differently. Martha and Harriet lost all of their children and their husbands. So, it stands to reason that Mary Lincoln may have been a little off, and unable to deal with what was not unheard of circumstances. In this way she is similar to Jane Pierce. Death and tragic loss got the better of her. So, why do I feel worse for Jane than I do Mary? That's easy.

Mary wanted the public life that she got. She wanted to marry a President. She wanted to be involved in politics. She wanted that fame and notoriety. Then, when she got it and things didn't go as she planned, she didn't deal with it very well. Jane Pierce wanted anything but the public life that was thrust upon her by her husband. Now, again, this is not to say that Mary didn't have some mental issues and some very tragic and unusual specifics to her loss. However, she intentionally chose and put herself into the public eye, and then didn't handle that lifestyle very well. I think it overwhelmed her. But let's go back to her childhood and upbringing to see just how unusual Mary Lincoln was for her time.

She was the apple of her father's eye and he gave her privileges that were not afforded to most children, let alone girls, during that time period. She was remarkably well educated. She had amazingly strong female role models despite losing her mother at an early age. She said she was going to marry a man who would become President, and she did. I compare this to Babe Ruth calling his home run hit before the pitch. Mary Todd, who would later in life become Mary Lincoln, was indeed unusual for her time.

Side Note – So, What Have We All Learned From This?

There were many components to my journey and my specific visits. Each one was as important as the next. That goes for each location, each person, each artifact, each letter, and each conversation. There was no way to include everything I saw and learned while on the road in each episode. This is why I continue my travels, continue my research, continue my writing and continue my speaking. We still have so much to learn about these women.

I had a gauge for the success of a show after it aired live. If after all of my research, all of my travels, all of the pre-interviewing of guests, all of the show prep with the host and guests, all of the work and research of the other producers and all of the live calls from viewers…after all of that and the show was said and done…did something new and unexpected come out? In every case, in every show, with every First Lady…the answer was "yes".

In the green room after the Mary Lincoln show, I had a conversation with Historian and series co-creator, Richard Norton Smith. We were discussing exactly what I have just explained in the previous paragraph. I was saying that it was a good show, because something I hadn't heard, something that wasn't planned or discussed before the show had been brought up. I remember saying that I thought it was quite remarkable that we could still teach people about someone as well known and as widely studied as

Mary Lincoln. Richard agreed, and said to think about next week when we got to teach people who the heck Eliza Johnson was!

Travelogue Food Tip

Springfield, Illinois has a local specialty called a "horseshoe". A horseshoe is a plate of meat covered with French fries, cheese and other toppings. I went to D'Arcy's Irish Pub to get mine, and it was excellent. I ordered the chili cheese dog horseshoe. It was amazing. The chili was fantastic and the thin crinkle fries and white cheese topped off an incredible plate of food. I offer many thanks to my C-SPAN colleague Laura Finch for introducing me to this local delicacy.

CHAPTER 20

Eliza Johnson

Greenville, Tennessee

$\mathcal{E}$ liza Johnson was born Eliza McCardle on October 4, 1810 in Leesburg, Tennessee. Her parents were John McCardle and Sarah Phillips McCardle. Eliza and Andrew Johnson were married on May 17, 1827. Eliza and Andrew had five children together. Eliza Johnson died on January 15, 1876 in Carter Station, Tennessee at the age of 63.

GREENEVILLE, TENNESSEE

My travel schedule during this project was tight. There is no doubt about that. However, sometimes there was a little breathing room on the front or back end of a trip that allowed me to relax a bit and enjoy the town and or location. When I landed in Tennessee, I drove to Greenville, and checked into the historic General Morgan Inn. The hotel was beautiful with an exquisite lobby. My room was large and well accommodated while still retaining its historic feel. I was very fortunate to stay in a number of historic hotels and buildings during my travels. I was also fortunate enough to get into town in time to have dinner with the Superintendent of the Andrew Johnson National Historic Site, Lizzie Watts.

Lizzie has been with the National Park Service for a number of years. Before the Park Service, she worked with President and Mrs. Carter at the Carter Center in Atlanta, Georgia. We talked about the plan for the next day's work together as it related to Eliza Johnson, her work with the Carters, and the ladies that I had already studied and covered for the series. It was a really nice break, and a very calm evening of interesting conversation. It gave me a much needed break from the usual routine of running around from town to town and eating my meals alone.

There are three main facilities at the Andrew Johnson National Historic Site. Eliza Johnson's life with Andrew and their children is covered from the time they met through the Civil War and into their post White House years. Because of this organization and availability of artifacts, I will approach this chapter much in the same chronological order.

Production Note – Featured Items

In my pre-interview phone calls to each location, I would start out asking the similar questions. It seemed to make the most sense to me to find out what we could learn about each woman's life before, during and after the White House. The stories I covered and came back with were based on the items, artifacts and evidence each location had to support them. There were usually a few items that I discovered once I got to the location (little gems and rarities or things that were unique and unusual). Many times, those pick ups were the "Featured Item" on that particular First Lady's webpage that we promoted during the live shows.

Eliza Johnson has an accomplishment to her credit that no other First Lady can claim. She taught her husband and future President of the United States of America how to read and write. When the Johnsons were first married in

1827, Andrew was a tailor. He had purchased a tailor shop right in the center of town at an auction. That very same tailor shop has been lifted, preserved and moved into the Memorial Building in Greenville. The original sign that reads "A JOHNSON TAILOR" still hangs on the outside of the relocated building. Eliza would read to, and teach her husband, in the evenings in his tailor shop, while he did his work and made suits for the men in town. The Memorial Building has some of Eliza's original books that she used to teach him how to read and write. To get a real feel for the scene we did something very special. Similarly to the Adams' Peacefield home in Quincy, Massachusetts, I took off my boots, loaded up a minimal amount of gear, ducked under the velvet ropes and very carefully climbed up into Andrew Johnson's tailor shop. Needless to say, this was not part of the usual tour given in the Memorial Building. Once again, with C-SPAN's good name as my gateway to privilege, I was doing something that few (if any) people have done. Once again, I found myself standing on the actual floorboards of history, and I took a moment to think about what had taken place here over 180 years ago.

We assembled Eliza's books on the table in the middle of the shop and set up the shot to record the piece about this remarkable story. My on-camera host for most of the day would be Park Ranger, Kendra Hinkle. Kendra also was an in studio guest on the Eliza Johnson live show from Washington, D.C. She was born and raised in Greeneville, and few know Eliza's story or the details of the collection better than she does. She was also great to work with, and a natural on camera.

Production Note – What's On The Tube?

I watched the Eliza Johnson live show from my hotel in Mentor (pronounced MEH-nor), Ohio having just completed my work at the Lawnfield estate for the Lucretia Garfield show. I was keeping about three ladies ahead of the game at this point.

The books I was shown to illustrate Eliza's teaching of Andrew were "The

Teacher's Assistant: System of Practical Arithmetic" which was compiled by a Stephen Pike and "English Grammar to Different Classes of Learners." The fact that the Johnsons kept these of these books showed their respect and reverence for education. They most likely knew the significance of the work they had done together in the shop. It is also here in the shop where Andrew began to gain notoriety for being an excellent debater and skilled public speaker. Crowds of men began to gather in the tailor shop to have conversations with Andrew or just to hear him speak on matters or the town and the day. The humble tailor that Eliza tutored, was becoming a local celebrity. This would take me to the next building that told the tale of the Johnson's early life, in their first home together.

The Johnsons lived in their first house in the early 1830's all the way up until they bought their homestead in 1851. It was a small but comfortable house in the center of town, and it's where the Johnsons had four of their five children. It is also where Mrs. Johnson learned to entertain for her rising star politician husband. Andrew Johnson was elected both an Alderman of the town and Mayor before he hit the national stage. The kitchen and dining area of the house was where the story of slavery as it relates to the Johnsons was told. Although Johnson would later side with the North in the Civil War, and would be an advocate for emancipation, the Johnsons did own two slaves in Greeneville. Their names were Dolly and her ½ brother Sam, and they helped with domestic chores and the children. Andrew Johnson was 18 and Eliza was just 16 when they were married and their marriage license is on display there in the house.

Mrs. Johnson suffered from consumption (now known to be tuberculosis) for most of her adult life. When the Johnsons arrived at the White House in Washington, D.C. the press corps greeted Mrs. Johnson as she got out of her carriage for comment. She told them that she was an invalid and had nothing to say. She had gray hair by this time, and could barely walk up the front steps. Mrs. Johnson kept a low profile during her time in the White House, and stayed mainly in a room on the second floor across from her husband's office. He would visit with her every morning after breakfast, and again in the evenings after his workday was complete. Mrs. Johnson may not have been physically well, but her mind was sound. Many people think that Mrs. Johnson was an influential voice in her husband's administration, as she ran most of the family's personal affairs from her bedroom.

The items that relate to their time in the White House are dispersed between the museum portion of the Memorial Building and the homestead across town. In the museum, I was shown a very unique gift Mrs. Johnson received while she was First Lady. Queen Emma of the Sandwich Islands (now the Hawaiian Islands) was the first queen to visit the White House. She brought Mrs. Johnson an intricately crafted ivory basket. Other items of Mrs. Johnson's on display in the museum were a simple black and gold cross necklace, one of her sewing cases and a photograph of one of the first Easter Egg Rolls that was held on the White House grounds.

The Easter Egg Rolls originally took place on the lawn of the Capitol Building during the Madison Administration, but that stopped when the lawn was getting ruined. They were all but cancelled during the Civil War, and it is thought primarily the Johnson family held them on the White House lawn, so Mrs. Johnson could watch her grandchildren from the window.

Andrew Johnson was the first President to be impeached. The charges were brought against him for the circumstances surrounding the removal of the Secretary of War (Edwin M. Stanton) and a violation of the Tenure of Office Act. Johnson was acquitted and an aide ran back to the White House to tell Mrs. Johnson. When he arrived, Mrs. Johnson sat quietly knitting in her room and said, "I knew he would be acquitted. I knew it. Thank you for coming to tell me." She reportedly had a tear in her eye as she offered her thanks. There is an original ticket that was sold to attend the impeachment hearings on display in the museum.

After President Johnson's term was over in March 1869, the Johnsons came back home to Greeneville. They had sent their daughter ahead of them to be in charge of restoring the house. Greeneville had changed hands at least 26 times during the Civil War, going back and forth from Union to Confederate control. The Johnsons' home suffered from the numerous changes in command. Soldiers used their home for many things during the war, including a hospital and barracks for the soldiers. Graffiti on the walls of some of the closets remains to this day. There are soldiers' names and unit numbers from both the North and the

South etched into the plaster. Many soldiers wrote the names of their mothers, sisters, wives or girlfriends back home. One of the largest examples is in Mrs. Johnson's closet and reads, "Andrew Johnson the Old Traitor". It's crazy to think that people were doing stuff like that even way back in the 1800's let alone to think that it is still there and legible after all this time.

It was mind blowing to stand there with my camera and document the graffiti of Civil War soldiers on the wall of a former First Lady's closet. It is one thing to be told over the phone that there is some "Civil War graffiti on the walls in the house," and a whole other thing to be staring at it close up with my own eyes. The whole scene and situation was just very surreal.

After her time in the White House, Mrs. Johnson returns to her old room in their house on the Greeneville homestead. She kept a room upstairs on the second floor across from her two daughters, and President Johnson had his room on the first floor. This distance was probably because of Mrs. Johnson's illness and a desire to not keep her husband up at night with her coughing and spitting. Her bed and much of her original furniture is still there in her room. Her illness also required she have a few special items including a spittoon and an invalid's chair. The chair was basically a recliner that could be raised to help a person in and out of it. It also had a footrest that moved up and down. In her room, Mrs. Johnson had a water basin and chamber pot that was painted pink. President Johnson had a matching set that was painted blue. I don't use this word often, but I found this to be…"cute."

Mrs. Johnson loved sewing and embroidery, poetry and scrapbooking. Items related to these activities are on display all around her room. There is a brass sewing bird clamped to the side table next to her chair. To answer the question in many of your minds (and mine at the time), a sewing bird is a decorative accessory that holds hems, pincushions and thread. There is a Bible that belonged to Mrs. Johnson on her nightstand and a book of poetry in which she marked several favorite poems. One such marked page was the poem "Love and Adversary". This poem seems to encapsulate the ups and downs of the Johnsons lives during the Civil War and their time in the White House:

> "That thorny path, those stormy skies
> Have drawn our spirits nearer

And render'd us by sorrow's ties

Each to the other nearer."

Mrs. Johnson was a scrapbooker, or I guess it's more accurate to say that she made a scrapbook of her husband's political career. The scrapbook primarily contained newspaper clippings from the 1850's through the 1880's. Since Eliza Johnson died in 1876 and Andrew Johnson died in 1875, it stands to reason that one or both of their daughters or another family member kept up the scrapbook. One of the pages that was specifically marked in the scrapbook had an article from when Johnson retired from the White House in 1869. There are other articles about Johnson becoming a U.S. Senator representing his home state of Tennessee in March 1875. He is the only President to later become a Senator in the history of the United States. The really cool thing about this scrapbook is that it is not normally kept in Mrs. Johnson's bedroom. We had to bring it there for our video piece from a vault hidden in the administrative offices at the Historic Site. To answer another question that many of you may be wondering, yes. I was allowed to go into the vault, and yes, it was very cool.

Some other items of note in Eliza Johnson's bedroom were portraits and pictures of her children and grandchildren, various combs, brushes and beauty tools, a brooch and assorted jewelry, pincushions and other sewing instruments, and her calling card. I know that Eliza Johnson isn't the most well known First Lady, nor is she probably someone most folks recognize. However, if you have seen a painting or image of her, I can almost guarantee she was wearing a lace cap. I would say it's kind of her "thing". Well, they have a couple of her caps there in the room. This is a nice touch. It's like seeing Abraham Lincoln's top hat. It just brings the story together. Again, it makes her real. It is also nice to see a room like this of a person, who because of medical conditions spent so much time there. It really gives you the feeling that the person is still there and you can imagine it in use.

When Mrs. Johnson left Washington and the White House, she brought a number of gifts and items home with her to Tennessee. One of the most famous authors of the day was Charles Dickens. He visited the Johnsons when they lived in the White House. Mrs. Johnson had an original copy of "A Christmas Carol" that she kept as a memento. She also had a large porcelain box that her children called the bon-bon box. A French dignitary gave the box to her, and it came filled with 50 pounds of chocolate. We know this because of letters that were written by her children about going to their mother's room to get candy from the box. Another beautiful piece that Mrs. Johnson brought with her from the White House was a beautiful gaming table made of 500 interlocking pieces of wood. The people of Ireland gave it to her and they would use it to play card games like Eucher. The children of Philadelphia gave her a sort of case to keep and display fruit that she must have been attached to, because that came back to Tennessee with her as well.

By the time her husband, President (then Senator) Johnson died on July 31, 1875, Eliza Johnson was too ill to travel and attend the funeral. She stayed at home with one of her daughters. She stayed in the house until her death not six months later on January 15, 1876.

SUMMARY

Probably because of her poor health and lack of a public persona, Eliza Johnson gets lost to the ages in most cases. However, she taught her husband, a President of the United States of America, how to read and write. She was displaced by the Civil War with serious health issues; when one has to imagine that staying in the comfort of her own home had been much better and more desirable for her. She willingly gave her husband up for public service, when a simple life in the little tailor shop may have been more her speed. Despite her illness, she ran the family, had five children, many grandchildren, and was in all likelihood a sounding board and confidante to her husband in his political career. My time spent in her home and among her things in Greeneville, Tennessee left me with no doubt, that Eliza Johnson was unusual for her time.

Travelogue Food Tip

When traveling by yourself, always accept an invitation from a local to go to eat. They always know the best places to eat and usually know a lot of people who will also be dining there (especially in small towns). Kendra, her co-workers and I had lunch at Tipton's Café in downtown Greenville. They had excellent sandwiches and homemade soups. It was a neat little local hangout, and it was packed at lunchtime.

CHAPTER 21
Julia Grant

St. Louis, Missouri – Galena, Illinois

*J*ulia Grant was born Julia Boggs Dent on January 26, 1826 outside of St. Louis, Missouri. Her parents were Frederick Dent and Bray Wrenshall Dent. Julia and Ulysses S. Grant were married on August 22, 1848. Julia and Ulysses had five children together. Julia Grant died on December 14, 1902 in Washington, D.C. at the age of 76.

ST. LOUIS, MISSOURI

Much of what we know about Julia Grant we know, because she told us in her memoirs. She is the first First Lady to publish one. She was born in the city of St. Louis, but in her writings she devotes much of her childhood to the Dent family plantation of White Haven and its 850 acres of land. The White Haven property is just outside of St. Louis, and the location of one of her earliest childhood memories. She wrote that her father held her up over his head and told her that the trees were "waving and welcoming" her back to her summer home. She was about two years old at the time. The Grants were an affluent family of the times, and it showed in their homes, their properties and the education of their children. It is even said that Julia had a pony to ride around the property, into town and to school while she lived on the farm. Julia Grant appreciated the finer things in life and that would be obvious throughout her life, and in her husband's White House. Julia referred to her childhood as "one long summer of sunshine, flowers, and smiles."

The first thing I noticed about the White Haven house was its unusual green paint. It reminded me of the dining room at Mount Vernon. I thought to myself that it was probably a very stylish color for the time. My host and guide, Park Ranger Pamela Sanfilippo, said that is was indeed a very expensive and popular color during the time the Grants lived there, after their time in the White House. The house is intentionally bare with flat screen monitors that take the viewer through the Grant's life and times here. The house itself is a very well preserved structure.

When I walked up to the front walk, the main things I noticed (once I got past the color of the house) were the beautiful porches that go across the first and second floors of the front of the house. It is easy to imagine the entire Dent family sitting on the front porch listening to Julia sing and her sister play the guitar.

I entered the house by walking up a short, but steep, set of stairs and going through the front door located in the middle of the house. It is a typical set up with a hallway down the middle of the house, which leads to a staircase that takes you upstairs, and rooms to either side of the hallway. On the main floor, to the right, is the parlor. This is where guests were treated to drinks, light refreshments and conversation. This is also where Julia saw her mother perform hostessing duties, and maybe received a few social lessons of her own.

The formal dining room is where the Dents had all of their meals. Julia shared fond memories of family time here eating and spending time together. She recalled white china with gold trim and cut glass being used to serve meals. One of the particular food items she mentioned is Maryland Biscuits. The Dents were slave owners, and had as many as eighteen slaves at one time. A specific slave named Kitty is fondly remembered in Julia's memoirs.

Because I Was Born & Raise In Maryland Note –
Oh, Biscuits!

Maryland Beaten Biscuits are a round golf ball sized piece of bread that originated on the Eastern Shores of Southern Maryland during the days of plantations and manors. Before cooking, the biscuits are beaten with a special ax to trap air inside to get them to rise. This was originally necessary, because of a lack of leavening. This technique may have been learned from the Native Americans. Each roll is shaped and smoothed by hand and baked.

The sitting room was next as I continued my walk, and work, around the house. This room was reserved for close friends and family. A period game table in the corner suggested that checkers and chess were played in here. Julia and her sisters also played with dolls and other toys in this room. The family was very educated, so reading would have been done in here, as well.

Upstairs there are two bedrooms. One was Julia's parents and the other for her and her sisters. I was told that the brothers slept out on the second floor porch during the summer and nicer weather. This was apparently a common practice in the 19th century in situations like this. It is because of one of Julia's brothers that she met and eventually married a man named Ulysses who would become a Civil War hero and President of the United States of America.

Julia's brother Fred attended West Point Military Academy in New York. His roommate was a young man named Ulysses S. Grant. Fred and Ulysses visited the Dent family at White Haven during the summer and on holiday breaks. This made Julia and Ulysses very real to me. I've gone to college roommate's homes over holidays, and had roommates come to my family's house, as well. I can remember one Thanksgiving in particular when my friend Ryan Vener came to my parent's house in Rockville, Maryland with his girlfriend and his brother Randy. We had a blast, and my parent's were wonderful hosts. This is a very "real" thing to do. I'm sure many of you reading this have done the same thing.

Soon after Ulysses began these regular visits, it became obvious that it was Julia he was coming to see. Julia and her mother thought very highly of young Ulysses. Her father did not feel the same way. Julia's father and Grant did not see eye to eye on slavery. The Dents were slave owners and Ulysses opposed slavery. This made for heated dinner conversations and a difficult courtship for Julia and Ulysses. However, Mr. Dent finally conceded to the engagement in 1845, if the young couple would wait for Grant to return from the Mexican War. They did, and the engagement lasted three years. A letter to a friend later in life reveals that Grant saved Julia's brother's life on the battlefield in the Mexican War, which, no doubt, further endeared Ulysses to the Dent family. Julia Dent and Ulysses S. Grant were married at White Haven on August 22, 1848. Grant's parents did not attend the wedding. They were upset that their son was marrying into a family that owned slaves.

The proposal also took place at White Haven. We again know the details of this from Julia's own words. Julia was upstairs in her room getting ready for Ulysses to come for dinner. Whether she was playing it fashionably late, running behind schedule or Grant showed up early, she watched him walk up to the front of the house sharply dressed in one of his finest suits. I stood at Julia's bedroom window and saw through the trees. I imagined the whole scene unfolding, as I heard the story told to me for the first time. I had not read this in any book. Pam told me the details while I watched the events unfold in my mind and through my camera. This was yet another moment when history came alive on my journey. Not only did I hear and could relate to the stories of their meeting and courtship, but I was able to stand in the very window that Julia stood in as she watched her future husband walk up to the front of her house to ask for her hand in marriage. These are the stories and the places that continued to make these people so real to me. They walked right off of the oil paintings and into my mind.

After the Grants were married, their first child was born in the house at White Haven. In fact, three of the four Grant children were born there. Mrs. Grant would stay there with the children sometimes when her husband was on a military assignment. When the whole Grant family was staying in the house there, they would spend a significant amount of time together in the family room, just as Julia had done as a young girl. Each of the Grant children were said to have thought that they were their parent's favorite. This says a lot about the Grants and the love they had for and showed each of their children.

The Grants lived in many different locations during his pre-Civil War military career. They had moved back into White Haven after the death of Julia's mother in 1857. Julia wrote that growing up, she had always thought the house "kept itself". Now living there with her husband, children and her father, she took on her mother's role at the house. Her father remained a slave owner, and Julia would now be in charge of slaves that had served her there or been children there when she was growing up.

Julia was always caught between her husband and her father on the issue of slavery. She had grown up with slaves, but had grown to accept her husband's views on emancipation. During the Civil War the Grants purchased White Haven with the idea that they would retire there and raise horses. They never did realize this plan and Julia was said to be heartbroken when they sold the property around 1885 just before Ulysses S. Grant's death.

HARDSCRABBLE

Hardscrabble is the name Grant gave to the cottage that he built for his family in 1856. It was built on Julia's parents' land around the White Haven plantation. Grant built the house out of wood and trees from the land. Park Ranger Karen Maxville gave me a tour of the home. Karen said that Julia wrote that she didn't care for the cabin at all. In her memoirs, Julia calls it "crude and homely." Ulysses S. Grant had retired from the military, and was trying his hand as a farmer to provide for his family.

The log cabin is a four room, two-story structure that was mostly white washed on the inside, which was I learned was to help sanitize the rooms and keep the bugs out. There was a fireplace for warmth and an outdoor kitchen for cooking. The living room and dining room were on the first floor, and the family slept upstairs in a glorified sleeping loft. Julia was not happy with her father who had encouraged her husband to build the house, however, she made the best of things. After a number of military homes, this was the first home the Grants would own together. The house was filled with fine furniture, and other nice items, but it would never compare to the home in which Julia was raised in St.

Louis or at White Haven.

The Grants stay in the Hardscrabble property was short lived. Julia's mother died in January 1857, and less than a year after they moved into the log cabin, they would move out and back into the White Haven house to take care of Julia's father.

Production Note – Keep On Truckin'

The Anheuser-Busch Company bought 281 of the 850 original acres of the Grants' White Haven estate. Ten acres and the main house were given to the National Park Service as a National Historic Site. My contacts at the Grant National Historic Site had secured me access to the Anheuser-Busch property and a private tour of the Grant's log cabin that is on that part of the land. The Anheuser-Busch representative picked me up in the parking lot of the Historic Site. It just seemed easier to pack up my gear on the rolling cart, sit in the back bed of his pick-up truck and drag it behind the truck for the short ride across the street to the Hardscrabble cabin (I took pictures and video this little maneuver…but it didn't make the show). Along the way we passed the Anheuser-Busch family estate (which is magnificent), and the animals and attractions of the Grant's Farm Park. The Hardscrabble house is located on a part of the property with and amazing tall, black gate and fence made primarily of old rifle barrels. There are also two huge elk statues on either side of the gate. The whole experience was yet another unusual set of surroundings and circumstances that added to my adventure.

GALENA, ILLINOIS

The Grants moved to Galena, Illinois in 1860 to join Ulysses' family. His father and brothers owned a leather shop there, and Grant had failed as a farmer and a few other efforts at making a living as a civilian. Galena was a very special place for the Grants. Many significant things in their lives happened here. It is here in Galena that Ulysses S. Grant launched his presidential campaign at the DeSoto Hotel. They regularly attended the Methodist church in town. The hotel and the church are both still standing and in excellent condition. The Grant family pew is still there and marked with a plaque.

They weren't in Galena very long before the Civil War would start, and the military would be Grant's best option again. During the war, Julia and the children lived in Holly Springs, Mississippi at the Antebellum mansion, Walter Place. After the Civil War, Ulysses S. Grant would return to Galena a war hero. Thirteen businessmen in the town got together and bought the Grants this beautiful house to show their appreciation for his service. Mrs. Grant wrote that the house in her "dear, dear Galena" was "furnished with everything good taste could offer."

Landmark Note – Statuesque

There is a statue of First Lady Julia Grant in front of the house in Galena. It is at the edge of the front yard and overlooks the town. It was, at one point, the only statue of a First Lady that existed in the world.

One of the many things we know about Julia Grant, is that she loved to entertain, and this beautiful villa on the hill was the perfect place for the Grants to settle down and relax after the war. They entertained friends and prominent figures of Galena there. The parlor was sizable with high ceilings. Julia and her daughter, Ellen, both played piano, and it is easy to imagine them entertaining dinner guests here before or after dinner. The original armchairs made it that much easier to picture the Grants in their element entertaining their guests. After he announced his run for Presidency, the Grants had an open house for the town to come and offer their support for their adopted war hero and his family.

The Grants' master bedroom along with Julia's dressing room contained some of the most personal artifacts in the house. The Grants' bed is the oldest piece in the house. They brought it with them from White Haven and left it here when they went to the White House. With as much moving and traveling as the Grants did, it's not unreasonable to think they would want something here like this bed to help make them feel at home. Mrs. Grant's lap book is here in the bedroom, as well. This was where she kept her paper, pens, and correspondence. The cover is embossed with "Mrs. U.S. Grant" in gold letters. One of Mrs. Grant's Bibles was on her nightstand, just as if she would be sleeping there and reading from it later that night. Her grandfather was a Methodist minister, so religion was a big part of her upbringing, as it was with most folks in the 1800's.

Her private dressing room was a place of solitude for Julia Grant. A number of her purses and clothes were in this room. Her sewing machine and kit were also in this small but well equipped room. The most remarkable and surprising item I saw in this most private of spaces in the Grants' Galena home, was a pair of Mrs. Grant's size four shoes. They were tiny. They seemed too big for a doll, yet too small for a human. It's always nice to see a room like this to really feel close to one of these First Ladies. It is where she had her alone time. It is where she would sit, meditate, prepare for the day ahead, or reflect on the day that had just passed.

Another thing we know about Julia Grant, is that she love, love, LOVED being the First Lady and living in the White House. Martha Washington compared her life as First Lady to being in prison. Julia Grant said, "life at the White House was a garden spot of orchids and [she wished] it would continue forever". It was reported that she cried on the entire way back to Galena on the train ride out of Washington, D.C. However, after eight years in the White House, the Grants did settle back into their home on the hill in Galena. That period of being settled lasted about two months before the Grants set out on an epic world tour.

President and Mrs. Grant went on a two-year, forty country world tour in 1877. Some of their children joined them on various legs of their tour. The Grants were international celebrities, and because of his war record and their time as President and First Lady, they were treated like royalty. This trip was so significant, that Mrs. Grant takes up about 1/3 of her memoirs writing about it.

They started in England and continued through nearly every country in Europe. They took a U.S. Navy ship through the Mediterranean Sea, and stopped in Egypt and the Holy Land. They traveled through India, China, Burma, Hong Kong and Japan. Many people think this trip was to ease Julia's depression over leaving the White House. Many of the gifts they received, and souvenirs they collected on this amazing trip, were brought back to, and are still kept in the

Galena house.

There are beautiful red vases on the mantel in the parlor given to them by the King of Bulgaria. In the dining room is an impressive bronze dragon urn that stands about 2 ½ to 3 feet tall. The citizens of Yokohama, Japan gave it specifically to Mrs. Grant. There is also a vase that was a gift from the Emperor of Japan. Also here on the mantel in the dining room was what my host and guide in Galena, Jamie Loso, said may have been Mrs. Grant's most prized possession from her travels. Her husband picked leaves in the Holy City and gave them to her. She had framed them herself along with a handwritten and signed note telling the story of the special leaves.

Also, in the dining room are a number of settings of the Grant's White House china. I've mentioned Mrs. Grant's flair and love of entertaining. Not only did Mrs. Grant entertain often, but when she did, she did it right. The Grants were in the White House during the Gilded Era. This was a post-war time of celebration and excess. They employed an Italian chef and served meals that often consisted of twenty-five courses that took over two hours and included six different kinds of wine. One dinner in particular, for Queen Victoria's son Arthur, was a twenty-nine-course meal that cost a reported $1,500. To give you an idea of how much that was, when Ulysses S. Grant was a clerk in his father's store in Galena, his total annual salary was less than $1,000 in 1860.

The Grants visited many friends and diplomatic associates on their trip. Two of the more significant friends that they visited during their travels were Queen Victoria of England and the Emperor of Japan. The Emperor of Japan remained such a good friend; he visited Mrs. Grant in New Your City after President Grant died.

After the Grants returned home to Galena in 1879, they rested for another month or so, and then set out for Mexico and Cuba. The government of Mexico presented them with two beautiful landscape paintings by Jose Valesco, who was very popular at the time. So, the house in Galena was (and still is) full of items that represent the Grants' most memorable journeys and a remarkable life together. The details of the extensive travels of the day are always impressive. It's amazing and daunting to think about taking trips like this in modern times, let alone back in the late 1800's.

Historical Note – Bath Time

The Grants had a beautiful copper bathtub in the washroom next to the kitchen. It was here that I learned the origin of the expression "don't throw the baby out with the bathwater". In the 1800's when clean water, let alone hot water, was a precious commodity -a luxury even – the head of the house (usually the man) would get the first, hottest and freshest bathwater. The next in line (usually the wife) would get the next bath, and the pecking order would continue on down to the youngest (often a baby). When the youngest member of the family was done with his or her bath, the bathwater would be thrown or dumped outside. So, they wouldn't want the servant, slave or whoever was dumping the water to dump the baby out in the yard with it. And there you have it, the origin of "Don't throw the baby out with the bath water".

Travel Note – Dirty Street Rat

The trip that took me through Lexington, KY, Springfield, IL, St. Louis, MO and Galena, IL for Mrs. Lincoln and Mrs. Grant was ambitious. My travels produced ten or more videos that made air, and a ton of other footage and interviews for the archives. I finished up the week in Galena, which is close to Rockford, IL. Rockford is close enough to Beloit, WI that my cousin Rick and his wife Marjean met me at the Rockford airport (where I dropped off my rental car). I was able to spend the weekend with Rick, Marjean, their daughter Heather, her husband Chris and their daughter Zoey in Wisconsin. We went to the Harley Davidson Museum in Milwaukee, cooked out and had a great time. One night while we were playing cards, I said something teasing Zoey (who was about 3 at the time). Zoey turned and very seriously said to me "you're just a DIRTY STREET RAT!" I was told she got it from the Disney movie "Aladdin", and I shouldn't take offense. I was too busy laughing. It was hilarious (Zoey is quite a character). To this day the name remains. I also used Zoey's little plastic Fisher Price desk as a command center to manage all the media files I shot in Galena (see pictures in the center of the book).

SUMMARY

Julia Dent was a privileged girl born into an affluent family. She fell in love with a military man and went against what her father would have preferred and married him. She was raised in a family that owned and believed in slavery. The man she married was anti-slavery. She changed her thinking on the matter. This makes Julia quite unusual for her time. I feel like the fact that she loved living in the White House and her husband being President so much that she cried and cried on her way out of town at the end of his two terms is a bit unusual, too. Even the men, women and families that loved and enjoyed their time there are ready to leave at the end of their terms. The world tour trip they took was so incredible, and even by today's standards still remains remarkable. It was fantastic to see the items from their adventure in their beautiful Galena home. All of this is evidence of an amazing life. However, the true mark of her life is the memoirs she wrote and published. She is the first First Lady to do so. This leaves no questions unanswered for future generations and history hunters like myself. She lets us know exactly what she was thinking and when she was thinking it. Julia Grant was unusual for her time.

Travelogue Food Tip

Galena is a neat little town carved into the mountains of Illinois and the past. There are so many neat little shops, boutiques, restaurants and inns to from which to choose. For a good time and a great burger, go to Dirty Gurt's.

CHAPTER 22

Lucy Hayes

Fremont, Ohio

*L*ucy Hayes was born Lucy Ware Webb on August 28, 1831 in Chillicothe, Ohio. Her parents were Dr. James Webb and Maria Cook Webb. Lucy and Rutherford B. Hayes were married on December 30, 1852. Lucy and Rutherford had eight children together. Lucy Hayes died on June 25, 1889 in Fremont, Ohio at the age of 58.

FREMONT, OHIO

The Hayes's Spiegel Grove Estate is impressive to say the least. The grounds contain the main house and residence, the library and museum (all known as the Rutherford B. Hayes Presidential Center), a very popular bike and toe path, and the final resting place of Lucy and President Hayes. I try not to play favorites with First Ladies. I can't. I enjoy them all so much, each for their own special reasons. However, Lucy will always be one of the really special ones for me. She seemed comfortable in her own skin. She was a beautiful woman. Even her pictures, from the earliest ones that exist of her when she was a young girl, right up to the last known picture of her sitting on the front porch at Spiegel Grove feeding the pigeons, she has the same hairdo and similar style of clothing. When she becomes First Lady, folks in Washington thought and even suggested that she embrace some "big city" flair, but she kept the style in which she was most comfortable (which, by the way, is very nice and conservative. She was a very snappy dresser, and we will get to that a little later in the chapter). She lost children, and mourned them, but she carried on and raised her family and supported her husband. She is the first First Lady to graduate from college. She had causes and philanthropies before it was "cool" or expected from the President's wife. She doesn't drink or serve hard alcohol in the White House, and people still talk and write about her wonderful parties and the fact that she was a perfect hostess. She gets some flack for the no alcohol thing, and is nicknamed "Lemonade Lucy", but not in a mean way or to her face. When I speak about her and this subject, I always say that if you can throw a good party in Washington, D.C. without alcohol, that's saying something! Her White House china is one of the most talked about patterns to this day, and not in a flattering way, but she stuck to her guns and used it. She was unchanged by Washington. Lucy Hayes was a transformative woman as opposed to a transitional woman. She quietly and effectively paved the way for other women who we know and remember better, like Eleanor Roosevelt. Again, before it was "cool" or expected.

Okay, lets get THIS out of the way...the Rutherford B. Hayes Presidential Center at Spiegel Grove in Fremont, OH is credited as having the first Presidential Library in the country. The Garfield folks will tell you that they have the first Presidential Library, and we'll go over that in the next chapter. This is what I have determined in my research, and how I now put it. The Hayes Center has the first "public" Presidential Library and the Garfield folks had the first "private" Presidential Library. As I mentioned earlier in the book, there are a lot (probably over a metric ton) of Presidential and First Lady firsts out there, and everybody likes to claim them. I will also say this about both facilities; they are top notch and represent their first couples very well. Almost everything you need to know about these folks can be learned at each location.

Side Note – Respect

I spoke at the Rutherford B. Hayes Presidential Center on September 20, 2015, and had a fantastic time. I hope to go back to speak again soon. I really do appreciate all the time, effort, information, and access from all of the people at all of the locations. It is important to also remember the people whose lives (the good, bad and the ugly) have been opened up to us. When I return to speak at a place where the President and First Lady are also buried, I stop by for a visit before my speech. It's a time of reflection and meditation for me. I like to "thank them" for sharing their lives and stories with me. As an additional side note, the song "CEMETRY GATES" by The Smiths goes through my head every time I stand at a Presidential gravesite. The specific line "all those people all those lives where are they now" rings out in my mind. I'm not sure why, but it happened during the entire filming of the series and it continues to this day.

When my colleagues at C-SPAN heard I was traveling to Spiegel Grove they all told me what a treat I was in for with the Director, Tom Culbertson. They said he was a wonderful host and a wealth of knowledge. Tom was there when I arrived and promptly explained that he had retired and was putting me in the very capable hands of the new Director, Christie Weininger. Christie is a friend and I've heard her tell this story publicly, so I know I'm not embarrassing her here. She had been on the job for only a few weeks or so. I think we both kind of shrugged, and said "okay, let's do this." My travel schedule only gave me one shot at this, so I really didn't have any other option. I also thought to myself that if I shot a ton of B-roll and worked the edits the right way, I could cover up anything that gave me problems. Well, no edits were necessary. Christie jumped right into Tom's shoes and handled the tour with confidence and accuracy. She is a real pro and I thank her for spending the day with me and completing so many great pieces. Tom ended up being a guest on the live show, because there really is no one who knows more about Lucy Hayes. He's great.

Historical & Travel Note – Count It

Fremont is little town in North Ohio, West of Sandusky, home to Cedar Point Amusement Park (I love roller coasters). I drove there from the Garfield's Lawnfield Estate and National Historic Site in Mentor, Ohio. There are eight U.S. Presidents from Ohio. There are also eight U.S. Presidents from Virginia. However, William Henry Harrison appears on both lists. This is not the only case or issue with a First Lady or President having a birth place that is different than the place or city for which they are known. So, the technicality here lies in where they were born versus from which state they were elected. Of the eight Ohio Presidents, only five have Historic sites and/or museums in Ohio that relate to or tell the story of their First Lady. So, I visited Taft in Cincinnati, McKinley in Canton, Garfield in Mentor, Harding in Marion, and Hayes in Fremont. I covered all of these First Ladies on one long Ohio trip, pinballing across the state. When I was done with my 10 hour day in Fremont, I drove to Indianapolis to cover Caroline Harrison. This was the longest drive of my adventure. This was also one of my most ambitious trips of the entire series.

Rutherford's uncle and guardian, Sardis Birchard built Spiegel Grove between the years of 1859 and 1863. The original home was a two-story, eight room brick structure. Uncle Sardis built the home to share with his nephew, Rutherford, his wife Lucy and their growing family. The Hayes family moved into the house in 1873, and they lived there for two years before they moved out when Rutherford became the Governor of Ohio. The home was expanded in 1881 when they returned from the White House, and again in 1889 to make room for the growing number of grandchildren. A final addition and improvements were made in 1893, but Lucy never lived to see them. It was said that Rutherford never truly enjoyed the house after Lucy died. Uncle Sardis's room remains intact and decorated, as he would have had it, with some of his original items and furniture, in the front center of the house. Lucy and Sardis didn't see eye to eye on many things, but she knew how special he was to her husband and their family, so she made the relationship and cohabitation work.

From his service in the Union Army to his various political positions, Lucy Hayes was a true partner to her husband right from the start. During the Civil War she traveled whenever and wherever she could to be with her husband. She wrote that she had genuine concern for him and his men. She was an excellent seamstress and always took her sewing machine with her to what were usually the winter encampments. One of her sewing machines can be seen right where she kept it – by the window in her bedroom at Spiegel Grove. One story about Lucy and her time during the Civil War is about the mending of a soldier's uniform. If you recall from the chapter on Martha Washington, this was similar to a story I had heard about Mrs. Washington, but was embarrassingly corrected. In Lucy Hayes' case the story was true. A young Private had torn his uniform. Two older soldiers tried to play a joke on their young compatriot, and told him that the woman in the tent up on the hill was there to fix and mend uniforms. So, up the hill he went with his torn jacket in his hand to get it fixed. What he didn't know was that the older men had sent him to the tent of the General's wife, Lucy Hayes. When the Private came back with his mended uniform, the other soldiers were a bit confused. They asked him where he had gone and how he had gotten his uniform repaired. He told the men that he had done as instructed. Mrs. Hayes had mended the man's uniform without question or incident.

Lucy Hayes had a number of causes that were near and dear to her heart. They were causes that she had supported and taken interest in from an early age, but especially after the Civil War when her husband was the Governor of Ohio. She supported veterans and orphans. She took particular interest in children that had become orphans during the Civil War. She saw so much death and loss being so close to the battlefield during the war. She took it upon herself to be the eyes and ears for her husband. She traveled to and visited with veteran's hospitals, mental facilities, and orphanages in a time when women didn't do this. That's what I meant by transformative versus transitional. This is how she blazed the trails for other First Ladies, like Eleanor Roosevelt. Eleanor went "in the field" for her husband, not only because she wanted to, but also because she had to – FDR was in a wheelchair because of polio and it was very convenient for her to do so. But, someone had to be the first, and in this case it was Lucy Hayes.

In the main parlor of the house, there is a painting of Mrs. Hayes tending to a soldier during the Civil War. The painting was done for an orphanage that Lucy supported in Ohio. In the painting, Lucy is wearing a gray dress with a white lace collar and apron as is bending over what appears to be a straw lined bed in some open barn-like structure. The painting is fairly large, in a beautiful gold frame, and encapsulates Lucy's caring nature. It is also in this parlor where people from organizations came to visit Mrs. Hayes and ask for her support. Mr. and Mrs. Hayes also entertained a number of military officers and politicians in this parlor. It is a rather grand room with high ceilings and many books and pieces of art.

Veterans were always welcome and had a special place at Spiegel Grove. Both President Hayes and President McKinley were members of the 23rd OVI in the Civil War. McKinley was a frequent guest at the Hayes's home, as were the surviving members of their unit. The Hayes's hosted many reunions and regular picnics on the grounds of Spiegel Grove for these men and their families.

Another one of my favorite stories about Lucy Hayes and a veteran is from her time in the White House. The soldier was getting an award or involved in some kind of awards ceremony at the White House and he showed up with a badge or patch in the wrong place on his uniform. Some of the folks gathered around made mention of it. As the story goes, Mrs. Hayes didn't bat an eye as she walked over to a dresser or cabinet, opened up a drawer and pulled out a sewing kit. She asked for the soldier's uniform, sat down on the floor and affixed the patch to its proper place. This is the kind of "can do" attitude that seems to follow Lucy throughout her life.

As I mentioned, Lucy Hayes had a nickname. Lemonade Lucy. It's a bit of an unfair nickname, that probably only stuck because of the alliteration. She wasn't the first or the only First Lady to shy away from alcohol or take a vow of temperance. Sarah Polk saw what drinking did to people, and decided that neither she nor her husband would drink in open forums or gatherings. Frances Cleveland had taken a vow of temperance, as well, and much later of course, Betty Ford would go through a very public battle with alcohol. In fact, I hear that President Lincoln was very concerned about the effect alcohol was having on the productivity of people and the good of the country. It has been written that temperance was the next big issue he was going to take on after the Civil War and slavery. Also, it implies that Mrs. Hayes was some kind of booze police going around dumping out people's drinks at parties, which was not the case. In fact, she and President Hayes did serve wine at State Dinners; she had just done away with the whiskey and rum punches. Some people say that Mrs. Hayes restored a bit of dignity back to the White House, dignity that had been lost during the more excessive days of the Grant Administration. Whatever the case, she had taken the vow of temperance as a young woman, perhaps for religious reasons, and it supposedly had nothing to do with politics. In fact, she had people on both sides of the issue upset with her. The people that supported alcohol were upset that she didn't drink or serve hard liquor, and the temperance folks were upset at her for doing things like serving wine at White House functions, and attending events and social gatherings where wine was served. One particular event was held on a riverboat where hard alcohol was being served. When a temperance organization questioned her on attending the event, she said something to the effect that she had merely decided that alcohol didn't have a role in her life, but it wasn't a decision that she was going to impose on other people. I always say if people on both sides of an issue are angry with you (especially in D.C.) then you're probably doing the right thing, or at least on the right track.

Regardless of who was upset with her, she did receive a lot of attention for her stance on drinking alcohol. She also received a lot of gifts of appreciation for her personal temperance. One group even paid for her official White House portrait. Another group called the Women's Christian Working Association put together a set of autograph books for Mrs. Hayes. There were six volumes of famous, influential and important signatures and messages bound in heavy brown leather covers. The group had sent blank pages out to people that had "Illinois State Testimonial" and "Mrs. President Hayes" written at the top of each page, with spaces marked for a person's autograph, town, county and state. "Mrs. James Polk of Polk Place" in Nashville Davidson County, Tennessee signed one page. Samuel Clemmons (Mark Twain) signed a page that read:

"Total abstinence is so excellent a thing that it cannot be carried to too great an extreme. In my passion for it, I even carry it so far as to totally abstain from total abstinence itself."

Samuel Clemmons ("Mark Twain")

Hartford, Conn

Another group gave the Hayes's a set of large, heavy, intricately embroidered floor-to-ceiling curtains, or room dividers, called portieres. They were cream with dark red or maroon flowers, and the Hayes's used them to separate the parlor and library from the President's private study.

Lucy Hayes was a devoted and supportive wife, but she was also a very loving mother. She and President Hayes had eight children together, and five of those children lived to adulthood and gave them many grandchildren. Upstairs is one of the larger bedrooms that belonged to the Hayes's only daughter, Fanny, who was named after Rutherford's sister. Lucy claimed that they didn't spoil or favor any of their children, but the custom furniture set and portrait of Rutherford holding his young daughter say otherwise. Fanny also had a nice doll collection and two huge dollhouses. One of the dollhouses was made by a random Hayes supporter while they were in the White House, the other was built by the White House carpenter. Both are on display in the museum. One of the dolls in Fanny's room was made to look like her mother. The resemblance was uncanny and so real that it was kind of creepy (a similar creepy factor to the Harriet Lane doll at Wheatland).

The Hayes's master bedroom was on the left side on the first floor. It was a special place for many reasons. Lucy wrote in diaries and letters about the special times the family had in their bedroom opening Christmas presents each year after a nice breakfast together. Manning Force Hayes, the last of her eight children was born in this room. The actual bed is still there to this day. Unfortunately, Manning caught a severe case of dysentery and died when he was 18 months old. Lucy had the artwork from a Mellin's Food for Infants and Invalids ad hung up in their bedroom. The baby on the ad reminded her of one of her grandchildren. Little things like this added to the authenticity of the room and the people who once lived there.

The upholstered furniture in the room was bright blue, almost turquoise, velvet. This color was discovered and matched to a swatch of original fabric that was tucked into the framing of a small sofa. This appeared to have been one of Lucy's favorite colors. Much of her furniture in a watercolor painting of one of her rooms in the White House was this color.

This room is also very personal and special, because it is the room in which

Lucy Hayes died. She was sitting in a chair next to the window doing some needlepoint and watching some of the younger children playing tennis in the yard when she suffered a massive stroke. She is said to have just slumped over in her chair. She was moved to the bed and eventually died on June 25, 1889.

Mrs. Hayes was an animal lover. She kept dogs, cats, chickens, goats and cows on the property at Spiegel Grove. Many people who came to visit Lucy at Spiegel Grove were taken out to visit the chicken coop or go on a stroll through the cow fields. One of the last known pictures of Lucy Hayes is of her sitting on the side of the front porch feeding the pigeons. She had holes cut in the steps to give them a place to roost. Many of the family pictures on the front porch included family dogs. It was said that on the day of her funeral all of her cows lined up along the fence and watched her procession roll past.

I mentioned that Lucy had some unusual china made when the Hayeses were in the White House. She had initially wanted ferns or some kind of fern pattern. Theodore Davis was chosen as the artist for the designs. He and Mrs. Hayes discussed the fern prints in the White House conservatory when he had an idea. His idea was to feature different flora and fauna of the United States. Being a fan of the outdoors and animals, Lucy loved the idea and thought it would be a great way to showcase the different flowers and animals of America to visiting dignitaries. When the finished product came in, it was met with mixed reviews, most, of which deemed the design "absurd". Some reporters wrote things like "who would want to eat a lovely meal at the White House and finish with a giant frog or a duck staring up at them?" The china was colorful and well done; it's just that the subject matter was a bit harsh and ornate with lobsters riding waves and bleeding trout or large deer in the woods.

Looking back on the china, it is definitely one of the more memorable patterns of any administration. The Smithsonian keeps a set on display in the National Museum of American History. The museum at the Hayes Presidential Center has a set, as well. They keep it displayed in an original cabinet from the White House. It is a massive piece made of thick, dark wood and looks as though it weighs a great deal. It is a solid piece of furniture. The fun thing about this is that on the display in Fremont, they have a picture from inside the Hayes White House of the cabinet with the china on it. This is so helpful to see cabinet and the china as it was used and where it was used in the White House. It makes for a much more effective museum display, in that it gives you real world reference. I think it's really cool when museums have the photos and the resources to do this, and many of them do. It also makes for a nicer video piece when you can mix the photos in with the artifacts, as they exist in the museum.

President and Mrs. Hayes celebrated their 25th Silver wedding anniversary in the White House on December 30, 1877. The museum in Fremont has a number of gifts and items related to that celebration on display. They have silver platters, plaques, salt and peppershakers, jewelry and all other sorts of mementoes from the celebration. One item that Mrs. Hayes had specially made to remember their anniversary was beautiful cameo brooch. It was oval and had a picture of her husband in the center surrounded by dark velvet, and a silver edge with four diamonds. It was a tasteful and beautiful piece that you would expect from Mrs. Hayes.

The Hayes Center has a fantastic collection of Lucy's dresses on display in their museum. The dresses range from the every day to the special occasion. Arguably, the most recognizable dress Lucy owned was the ruby red velvet dress she wore in her official White House Portrait. It's always great to see the portrait dresses in person. They are even more impressive and elegant than in the paintings. It also serves to make the dress and the woman who wore it come alive. They also have Lucy's wedding dress that she hand made. It is a simple white patterned fabric with gold fringe tassels on each wide opened sleeve. A smooth white bib style collar surrounds the top and kept with Lucy's conservative style and necklines. Some of the fancier dresses she wore to other people's weddings. A dress called "Ashes of Roses" was about as flashy as Lucy got. The satin and lace number had white glass beads and gemstones. She wore this dress to her oldest son Birchard's wedding. She wore a white linen dress with a lace and ruffled bib (very typical of Lucy's style) to her niece's wedding, which took place in the White House. This dress had a darker shawl or coat style wrap as a unique accessory. One dress that showed a bit of her flair, but still kept in line with her non-ostentatious look is a blue velvet gown with intricate patterns in gold and green. This dress also has the lace and ruffles that covered the front of her chest. One of the dresses I found most interesting was worn for a New Year's celebration. It looked to me to be a formal version of her every day dresses, in an almost period version of a dress suit. The outer shell is a tan fabric with intricate patterns, and there is the ever-present lace and ruffles on the chest, but there is an additional button up shirt like layer in between all of that. It is maroon in color (seemingly another of Lucy's favorite colors) and adds to the cuffed accents of the overcoat looking part of the gown. For as simple and conservative as Lucy Hayes was said to have dressed, I found her pieces to be a very intricate pieces of work.

Production Note – Duct...Duct...Goose!

When you watch the video pieces I produced from Spiegel Grove in the live show, you can see that my guide and host, Christie Weininger was wearing a one piece dress with a matching mid-length overcoat. This outfit had no pockets, no belt, and nowhere to hide a mic pack. So, I did what any good producer would do. I busted out my duct tape and made a belt. Christie was a really good sport about it, and I had her take off her coat and hold the tape to her waist as I circled around her a few times. This way, we were able to secure the mic pack in the back and run the cord and clip on mic up the side of her jacket and position it exactly where it needed to be. It's fun improvising in the field like this, but you have to have someone who's willing to roll with you and do what needs to be done to make the shoot happen. Like I said, Christie was a good sport.

SUMMARY

Lucy Hayes was a class act. That's the best way to put it. Her style and beauty exuded confidence and comfort. She didn't let anyone change her. She didn't conform to the criticisms and styles of Washington, D.C. I always say in my live presentations that if you can throw a party in the nation's capital without serving hard alcohol and people still talk about what a great night it was...you're doing something right. I follow that up with the fact that if you spend anytime in elected office or in politics and come out the other side unchanged, as Lucy did...chalk that up as a win as well.

She was modest. At one point she said that she didn't compare to the great women who came before her in the role of First Lady and she was humbled to be in their company. She was the first First Lady with a college degree. She knew loss, and she had seen the tragedies of war first hand. She loved her husband and her children, and didn't let the loss of some ruin her life or the lives of her family and others. She carried on. Most importantly, she had a conscience. She had a heart. She had causes she supported. Lucy Hayes did all of this because she wanted to, not because she had to or was expected to.

Lucy Hayes was unusual for her time, because she made the support of social causes standard operating procedure for modern day First Ladies. I'm not saying that any other First Ladies didn't or don't want to be doing what they are doing or supporting the causes they support. However, imagine if Laura Bush or Michelle Obama had come out and said, "I'm not going to do anything. No causes for me. No reading. No children's health or global women's rights". They would have been destroyed in the press and the court of public opinion. Lucy Hayes did this because in her mind, for her time, it was the right thing to do. She did it before it was something she had to do in her position.

Betty Ford came along much later and took things to the next level by exposing her own personal issues and life events, but she is another inspirational lady for another chapter in another volume. The amazing thing about Lucy Hayes is that I would guess we, as a collective public, probably don't name her if asked to name 10 to 20 First Ladies. Yet, her actions and influence on the role of First Lady are still relevant today over one hundred years after her death.

Travelogue Food Tip

When you are in Fremont, make sure and stop in at Billy's Restaurant and see the "Honey Sisters". Pamela will take your order and Joy will make your food, and they'll do it with a smile and a "You got it, Honey." This is small town charm and diner cuisine at its finest. The last time I was in Fremont, I ate there twice. The first morning I had an omelet the size of small child and the next day I had pancakes bigger than my head. You get more than your money's worth here, and the conversation and atmosphere are priceless. Make sure and tell 'em The First Ladies Man sent you, Honey!

CHAPTER 23

Lucretia Garfield

Mentor, Ohio

*L*ucretia Garfield was born Lucretia Rudolph on April 19, 1832 in Garrettsville, Ohio. Her parents were Zebulon Rudolph and Arabella Mason Rudolph. Lucretia and James Garfield were married on November 11, 1858. Lucretia and James had seven children together. Lucretia Garfield died on March 14, 1918 in Pasadena, California at the age of 85.

MENTOR, OHIO (Pronounced Meh-Nor)

When Congressman James Garfield went to the Republican National Convention in Chicago in 1880 it was to nominate a Presidential candidate, not BE the Presidential candidate. Does this sound familiar? It should. The same thing happened with Franklin Pierce in 1852 at the Democratic National Convention in Baltimore. So, Garfield returned to his wife and five surviving children at their Lawnfield estate in Mentor, Ohio a Presidential candidate for the

Republican Party to conduct the nation's very first front porch campaign.

I met my guide and host, Park Ranger Todd Arrington at the Garfield's home and we started our work in the front hallway. He admitted that this was a strange place to start talking about a front porch campaign, but remember, we're talking about his wife Lucretia's role in all of this not James's. This was where you would most likely find Lucretia during the 1880 campaign. The Garfields had just done some significant renovations to the inside and outside of their Lawnfield home. The last thing Mrs. Garfield expected or wanted to see was seventeen to twenty thousand visitors on her property, but that's what happened.

James Garfield's office was on the second floor, at the top of the steps, and I could easily image the bearded former Civil War General finishing up some notes or a speech and walking down the stairs and right out the front door to speak to his supporters from the front porch. I could also imagine Mrs. Garfield right behind him shutting and locking the door. The massive amount of visitors was destroying the grounds outside and she feared the same would happen if they were to come inside. Who in the world would want tens of thousands of complete strangers to come traipsing through their house anyway, for any reason?

Even more than her house and property, Lucretia Garfield was concerned for the safety of her children. By this time, the Garfields had lost two children (Eliza and Edward), and Lucretia kept a watchful eye over the remaining five. She was very intent on keeping them out of the public eye.

Some people were invited into the house though. In these cases, Mrs. Garfield was a very gracious host, but she still kept a tight leash on the activities and length of the visits. She would serve cold water or lemonade with what were called standing refreshments. They were called that, because the people who came into the house were typically not permitted any further than the front hallway, and there were no chairs provided for anyone sit down and get too comfortable.

The wooden planked front porch ran the length of the house with an overhanging roof and was pretty typical of what you would expect on a Midwestern style house of the day. Pictures don't do justice to what the scene looked like from the porch or inside the house as the Garfields looked out onto a sea of people. I have lived and worked in and around Washington, D.C. for almost my entire life. It's interesting to compare this style of campaign and intrusion into a family's personal life to modern campaigns.

Family was important to the Garfields and Mrs. Garfield was an educated woman who wanted to raise educated children. The living room and parlor were full of books. The family would sit by the fireplace and read on a daily basis. This was a popular activity for the time. Among their favorite authors were Charles Dickens and William Shakespeare.

The Garfield children took dance and music lessons. Their daughter Molly's piano is still in the living room. It was a gift from her parents for her thirteenth birthday. Similar to Harriet Lane's piano and music book at Wheatland, this piano spoke to me. It made the Garfields and their children very real. Molly was a solid piano player and she enjoyed practicing. It only makes sense that she would be rewarded on a significant birthday like becoming a teenager with such a grand and well-deserved present. I am a drummer, and I got similar musical gifts for things like good grades or milestone birthdays and Christmases. I could very much relate to this artifact and the story that went along with it.

The fireplace mantel in the dining room was framed with painted ceramic tiles. There were flowers, plants, birds, bees and other animals all hand painted in what I was told to be a family project. Lucretia had painted the four corner tiles, a family friend had painted another, and the children painted the rest. This was another project that made the entire Garfield family come alive, and it made Lucretia a real mom in my eyes, and not just a President's wife.

James Garfield once said of his wife Lucretia that she had "faultless taste." You can see this in her selections of color patterns and furniture. Mrs. Garfield was known to have chosen her wallpaper and color schemes very carefully. Park Ranger Mary Lintern showed me around the interior of the house, and highlighted specific items that showcased Mrs. Garfield's artistic side. The china that the Garfields brought with them to the White House was the best from home. They didn't order or commission special White House china. The collection at Lawnfield is as extensive and as complete as any I have seen at all of the National Historic Sites, museums or locations during all of my travels. They have dinner plates, side plates, bowls, dessert plates, serving platters; soup tureens, gravy boats, cups and saucers, and they have more than one of each. Mary was all too happy to put on some white gloves and pull some out of the built-in china cabinets for me to get a closer look. The Garfield china is a Havelin Limoge patterned with a single gold "G" at the top center. The pieces are bordered with a thin gold edge around a pale pink strip with more intricate gold filigree as an inner border. The china was used for every day dining while they lived there in Mentor.

There are also eleven plates on special shelves above the dining room mantel. The plates had various pastel colored borders, with flowers painted in the center. They are believed to have all been painted by Mrs. Garfield. China painting was very popular during this time, and they were all beautifully designed and painted.

The centerpiece on the dining room table was a beautiful award winning sculpture that Lucretia Garfield purchased at the Centennial celebration in Philadelphia called the "Barge of Venus". Mrs. Garfield reportedly loved all of the exhibitions at the celebration and was particularly fond of the new science and technology displays.

The dining room was, of course, a place to eat, but it was also an opportunity for Lucretia and her husband to teach their children. They often played learning games, read aloud to each other or recited poetry. They even had fun quizzes and tested each other's knowledge during dinnertime. Lucretia said that education was the "key to success".

The bedrooms upstairs are all of good size, and as well decorated and furnished as the rest of the house. There were lots of light blues, soft purples and other pastels in the upstairs rooms. This creates a very soothing atmosphere that mixed well with the medium toned wood of the doors, frames, windowsills and other accents in the house. In Mr. and Mrs. Garfield's bedroom hangs a portrait of each of the two children they lost at very young ages. Eliza is painted with her hair done just right. She looks like a little toy doll. Edward is wearing a proper Sunday hat and looks like a perfect little gentleman. It's difficult to hear all of these stories about how many children were lost in these early times before medical advancements.

Production Note – And He Walked On Down The Hall

It always surprises me in these homes that for as open and sizeable as the rooms are, the hallways are often narrow and tight. I always had to keep a watchful eye over my gear and trail of cables and wires. These houses are full of precious and irreplaceable artifacts, and I didn't want to be the guy they told bad stories about after I left.

After President Garfield's assassination in 1881, Lucretia returns home with her children and Lawnfield was a different place for her mentally. However, she also changed it physically. She moved the kitchen to the back of the house, and opened the center of the house up to be a reception area. She stopped using the downstairs summer bedroom, and slept almost exclusively upstairs. The biggest change was the addition of a back wing with the second floor dedicated as the president Garfield Memorial Library.

When James Garfield was a Congressman, and living in Washington away from his wife and children, there were some documented incidents of infidelity. The Garfields worked past them and stayed together. Mrs. Garfield was worried about what her children would hear later in life about their father, and wanted to preserve his memory and accomplishments in a way that highlighted his career and the family they had created together. The library seemed like the best way for her to do that.

As I walked up the steps in the back of the house to the second floor, Ranger Arrington stopped me on what he called the Memorial Landing. It is dominated by a life size painting of Major General James Garfield from his time in the Civil War. Caroline Ransom painted it in 1863. It is an impressive way to greet visitors to the library. When Mrs. Garfield first built the library it was to preserve the work and memory of her husband for herself and her children. Mrs. Garfield spent a lot of time in the library. She kept a writing desk in the main room. On that desk is a letter written by Mrs. Garfield on her personal stationary marked with a ¼ inch black border. She used this stationary for the rest of her life to signify the mourning of her husband. Another interesting personal item in this room was Mrs. Garfield's "spider table" as they call it at Lawnfield. The small end table has a mother of pearl inlay border and spider web motif with a little spider and fly. Spider webs were considered to be good luck in the Victorian Era, and it's not the only place in the house where you see this design represented.

The library is wall to wall with built in bookcases and shelves full of books from President Garfield's collection and a number of gifts and tribute items Lucretia and the Garfield family received after his death. Among her favorite pieces was a pressed stone mosaic from an Italian admirer. It had a profile of President Garfield surrounded by colorful flowers all under glass in a beautifully intricate and ornate black frame. Another significant piece in the library's collection is an impressive larger than life bust of President Garfield carved in 1883.

Author's Note – Busted!

I grow a beard every winter. It's not for any playoffs or sporting event and it's not for any awareness or cause. I have more hair on my face than on top of my head, so I work with what God gave me…or left me with. Typically, I begin the process in September or October and it fills in nicely by the time the really cold weather sets in. By the time I got to the wives of he bearded Presidents (Lincoln, Grant, Hayes, Garfield, B. Harrison) my beard was thick and in full on Civil War style. I looked like a descendent of Hayes or Garfield. So, I got my picture taken with any and all busts or paintings I could at each location (thank you to all the people at all of the places that played along with this nonsense). The picture of me with the James A. Garfield bust turned out so well, I'm going to have my friend Michelle Barker-Finn (Toad Creek Clay) make a FIRST LADIES MAN bust for me to put in the house. Why not? Lincoln had one when he was living in Springfield. Friends who know me and visit will get the joke, all others who don't? Well, that's their problem.

The most impressive thing, in my humble opinion was what Mrs. Garfield called the "Memory Room," but what I call the vault. It is a fortified fireproof room with a bank style vault door that held all of the President's official papers and documents. Mrs. Garfield kept a desk in there to sit and read her husband's papers. Queen Victoria of England sent an elegant wreath of white flowers and greenery that was put on Garfield's casket as he lay in state at the U.S. Capitol in Washington, D.C. This wreath is now in a black-framed glass case and is kept on a top shelf in the vault. Now that it's open to the public, this Memorial Library keeps President Garfield's memory alive for today and for future generations.

This space in the house was also used to host a special wedding. Two of the Garfield's children (Mollie and Harry) got married in a double ceremony in the library on June 14, 1888. Close family and friends, including some of President and Lucy Hayes's children, attended the wedding.

***

Historical Note – Everybody Wins!

This is the first Memorial Presidential Library that was originally intended for private or family use. It is this technicality that is the sticking point between the Hayes and Garfield Libraries as to who had the first official Presidential Library in the country. It is my position that due to the nature of their construction dates, intentional uses and availability to the public that Garfield had the first Memorial Presidential Library and Hayes had the first Public Presidential Library. In my version, everybody wins and both Hayes and Garfield are first. See how easy that was?

***

Even more significant than the changes Lucretia Garfield made to their home in Mentor, may be the one room she did not change. Mrs. Garfield called the President's private office his "snuggery". This is the room at the top of the main steps that I spoke about during the front porch campaign. It remains today as it did the last time Garfield walked out of the front of Lawnfield for his inauguration in 1881. It is a surprisingly small room with a desk, books and bookshelves and a fireplace. It is mostly the same medium toned wood that runs throughout the house. The only thing that Lucretia changed in this room was she had "IN

MEMORIUM" carved in the wood mantel over the fireplace. This is the title of the Alfred Lord Tennyson poem that was near and dear to James and Lucretia's heart.

The Garfield's daughter Eliza, who they called "Trot" died in 1863 when she was only two or three. James Garfield was a Congressman in Washington, D.C. at the time. The death of Trot was hard on Mr. and Mrs. Garfield. I'm sure being away from each other didn't make it any easier. However, the tragedy brought James and Lucretia closer together than they had ever been. James wrote an impassioned letter to his wife from Washington. In the letter he told his wife that the Tennyson poem had taken a special meaning for him and had helped him grieve the loss of their young daughter. It had given him great comfort, and he encouraged her to read it and seek that same comfort. From that point on they shared the poem together as their favorite.

SUMMARY

Lucretia Garfield is another woman who didn't have her eye on the White House from the beginning. She stepped up and moved herself and her family into the role to support her husband. Sadly, her husband is assassinated less than a year into office. So, we never really get to find out what kind of First Lady Mrs. Garfield would have been. We do know, however, what kind of wife and mother she was. The way she protected her children from one of the most personally invasive campaigns in our history is remarkable. Her home and property were invaded by as many as 20,000 people during the first front porch campaign; a campaign that she never expected to happen. After her husband's death she goes out of her way to preserve her husband's legacy for herself, her children and eventually her country. She was a highly intelligent woman who embraced science and technology. She was artistic and enjoyed crafts and home improvement. She created the first Memorial Presidential Library. It's a shame she didn't get the chance to show us more of what she could do. Lucretia Garfield was indeed unusual for her time.

Travelogue Food Note

When in Mentor, Ohio save room for a meal at Melt Bar & Grilled. This is a hip bar that serves specialty grilled cheese sandwiches and craft beers. The décor is plastic holiday lawn ornaments and alternative music concert posters. I was surprised and amused to see a poster from a show that my old band WHO IS GOD? played in D.C. with The Rollins Band, Helmet and Sausage. I quickly snapped a shot of the poster and sent it around to all of the guys with whom I am still in touch. They loved it! The heavily tattooed and punk rock looking staff is super friendly and very willing to help you sort your way through the extensive menu. They have a notorious food challenge here that has been featured on Travel Channel's "Man vs. Food." If you can "defeat The Monster" you will be "immortalized in the Melt Challenge Hall of Fame" (and you get a t-shirt and a shot glass). The Monster is made of 13 different cheeses on three slices of bread with slaw and fries. It weighs in at over 5 lbs. So, I had fasted all day in preparation for my visit. I asked the bartender if anyone ever tried the challenge. She said that people tried all the time ("mostly drunk frat guys"), but in the 8 or 9 months that she had been working there she had never seen anyone do it. She recommended a sandwich called "The Dude Abides", and I wisely went with her recommendation. It was a delicious creation that consisted of homemade meatballs, fried mozzarella wedges, basil marinara, roasted garlic, with provolone and Romano cheeses. The side of fries and slaw that came with it just sat on my plate and silently mocked me for thinking I had a shot at defeating the Monster. I bought a t-shirt. I will go back.

CHAPTER 24

Ellen Arthur

Washington, D.C.

$\mathcal{E}$llen Arthur was born Ellen Lewis Herndon on August 30, 1837 in Culpepper County, Virginia. Her parents were Captain William Lewis Herndon and Frances Elizabeth Hansborough Hernsdon. Ellen and Chester Arthur were married on October 25, 1859. Ellen and Chester had three children together. Ellen Arthur died on January 19, 1880 in New York, New York at the age of 42.

WASHINGTON, D.C.

Ellen Arthur – or Nell as friends and family knew her – never lived to see Chester Arthur become President. Ellen Arthur died while her husband was the Chairman of the New York State Republican Executive Committee. She didn't even live to see him as Garfield's Vice President. Most folks were probably not expecting Arthur to become President, and certainly not less than a year after be-

245

ing elected Vice President. But, an assassination will do that. Washington, D.C. was once again without a First Lady.

President Arthur's sister, Mary Arthur McElroy was married and lived with her husband and family in Albany, New York. President Arthur was surprisingly adept at hosting a social function without his wife. He never named his sister as an official White House hostess, but she did rent an apartment in Washington and stayed there for a majority of the social season to help her brother.

Most of Ellen and Chester's life together was in New York City, and there is only a small plaque on a dilapidated brownstone at 123 Lexington Avenue near East 28th Street to commemorate its historical significance. There is nothing left of Ellen's birth home in Culpeper County, Virginia. That leaves Washington, D.C. and the Church of the Presidents. This location is more than appropriate for what little we do know about Mrs. Arthur. She was very active in the Church of the Heavenly Rest in New York City on Fifth Ave and 90th. Ellen supposedly had a beautiful voice and sang in the choir at their New York and Washington, D.C. churches.

Production Note – Best Dressed

When I went to the Benjamin Harrison House in Indianapolis, IN, they had a dress on display in their 3rd floor museum that belonged to Mary Arthur McElroy. The dress was part of a special exhibit that the Harrison folks had put together of various First Lady's and White House hostess's dresses, and I just happened to be there at the right time to see it. It was on loan from the National First Ladies' Library in Canton, OH. Mary's dress was a conservative yet elegant two-piece teal green ribbed silk day dress. It had a subtle pattern and silver threaded embroidered fringe around the hem. I captured video of the dress for archival purposes, but the Arthur show had already aired. It was still very cool to put an artifact (a dress no less) and a size and shape to the woman who performed the hostessing duties in an otherwise womanless administration. I will have more on the Harrison House and the third floor museum in the Caroline Harrison chapter.

My afternoon at the Church of the Presidents started out with something very special. I loaded up my truck at C-SPAN and drove over to St. John's Episcopal Church at 1525 H Street NW, Washington, D.C. to capture interior and exterior footage for the Ellen Arthur portion of the series. This church is known as the Church of the Presidents, because every sitting President of the United States has attended services here, dating back to James Madison. The church is an historic Greek revival building designed by Benjamin Henry Latrobe (the architect who designed the U.S. Capitol Building). It sits conveniently at Lafayette Square, across from the White House.

What I didn't know – but which makes complete sense – is that there is a special door on the side that is reserved for the President and his family. Because of my load of gear, I was instructed to use this door (I took a picture of myself going through it, of course). This was just another special little "privilege" that was extended to me in my travels. I'm sure other non-Presidential citizens go through this door, but not anyone I know.

Ellen and President Arthur both had ties to this famous Washington, D.C. church. As an only child, Ellen and her widowed mother attended the church, having moved to D.C. after the death of Ellen's father, an honored Naval officer. Some accounts even have her singing in the choir there. It is also said that young Ellen and her mother would've known Dolley Madison (drink) from worshiping there together.

President Arthur's ties to the church went beyond being a President and attending services there once in a while. He was apparently quite an active congregant. President Arthur had a stained glass window designed in his late wife's memory by his good friend Louis Comfort Tiffany. The window is still in its original place in the church today. It is made up of two large horizontal rectangular panels. At the bottom of the lower panel it reads "To The Glory Of God And The Memory Of Ellen Herndon Arthur Entered Into Life January 19, 1880".

Each pane depicts an empty tomb scene that is symbolic of the resurrection of Jesus Christ. The upper panel represents an account in the book of Mark. There are three women who have visited the tomb at dawn to be greeted by a man in white claiming to be Jesus. The lower panel is from a version that is told in the book of John. Mary Magdalene is shown at the tomb with her red hair. She is greeted at the empty tomb by two angels in white. The window is on the south wall of the sanctuary, directly across from the honorary "President's pew". This made it so President Arthur (and all Presidents who would follow) could sit in his pew and gaze across the room at the window. As I stood there drifting back in time to the early 1880's I imagined Arthur sitting in his pew and looking over his right should to see the choir loft and stopping for an extra moment to look at the window as the voices from above would also, no doubt, remind him of his wife.

President Arthur had chosen a bedroom on the North side of the White House. This is the side that faces the South side of the church, which is the side of the church where his wife's window was hung. Today, the President's upstairs dining room is found in what had been President Arthur's bedroom. Arthur is one of the few Presidents who chose a bedroom on the North side of the house. He also made arrangements with the church to keep the window lit from the inside. We have to wonder if this was intentional so he could see his wife's window from his White House bedroom window.

Production Note – Dancing In The Street

Similar to my experience at the Octagon House for the Dolley Madison show, I had to stand in the middle of the street and avoid traffic to get the shots I needed for the outside of the building. It is difficult to get usable footage outside, in public, during the day, in a major city. You want to avoid close ups of people's faces to keep them fairly anonymous. A shot can't start with someone walking in the middle of your shot. The same goes for cars, and a big truck will just plain ruin your shot. You don't always have to have audio (what TV people call "nat sound" – sound that is going on in life and the real world around you) on b-roll like this, but it's nice to have some sound on there, otherwise it sounds artificial, muted. So, we have to try to have sound, but minimize the distracting audio that will take away from what you want the viewer to notice. Construction noise and work crews can completely destroy an outdoor shoot like this. I have a personal preference for getting shots no less than 30 seconds. This is to give you plenty of "pad" at the beginning and end of your shot when you sit down to edit with your footage.

SUMMARY

The Arthur Administration has been compared to the Jackson Administration, because of the absence of First Ladies. Both Presidents lost their wives just before they became President. Ellen Arthur didn't even see her husband become Vice President. By all accounts she was well liked, and a savvy entertainer. She was a beautiful woman with a lovely singing voice that was showcased in the various churches she attended throughout her short life. These are the kinds of Presidential wives that really make you wonder what kind of First Ladies they would have been. She is the only First Lady with a stained glass window dedicated to her memory in the historic Church of the Presidents. The timing of her death and the dedication of the window, combined with the rare location of President Arthur's bedroom in the White House, made Ellen "Nell" Arthur unusual for her time, even among other First Ladies.

Travelogue Food Tip

DC, like any major city, is full of amazing restaurants. Over the past five years or so, it seems that they are getting even better and new places are popping up over night. I like to go out to eat, and enjoy trying new places. This does not mean I have forgotten about some of my old favorites. I always (especially in the summer) go to Perry's on Columbia Road in Adams Morgan. They have one of the best rooftop dining experiences in DC, the menu is consistently imaginative and delicious, and the sushi there is some of the best I've ever had. You just can't go wrong at Perry's.

CHAPTER 25

Frances Cleveland

Washington, D.C. – Baltimore, Maryland – Deer Park, Maryland

*F*rances Cleveland was born Frances Folsom on July 21, 1864 in Buffalo, New York. Her parents were Oscar Folsom and Emma Harmon Folsom. Frances and Grover were married in the White House on June 2, 1886. Frances and Grover had five children together. Frances Cleveland died on October 27, 1947 in Baltimore, Maryland at the age of 83.

WASHINGTON, D.C.

Grover Cleveland was the second of only two men to be elected President of the United States of America as a bachelor. Unlike President James Buchanan, Cleveland did not stay that way for long. He married a much younger Frances Folsom in a small White House ceremony just over a year after he took office. He is the only President, and thus, Frances the only First Lady, to be married in the White House. Frances Cleveland has the unique and distinct honor of being the youngest First Lady in history, too. She may always have that title. When Grover married Frances, he was 49 and she was 21. It is unlikely that even if another single man is elected as President that he will marry a woman nearly thirty years his junior, but hey…you never know, right? Before President Cleveland married Frances, there was Rose.

Rose Cleveland was the President's youngest sister. She was a teacher and writer who lived in New York, and she agreed to help her brother out by hostessing during the first year of his first term. She even stood next to him as he was inaugurated. Surprisingly, Rose found her time in the White House to be less than interesting. She was a highly educated woman who spoke eight languages, and said that she had little patience for the small talk at Washington social gatherings. Some guests said that Rose was "grim" and "terrifying". Most of what we know from Rose's accounts was that she was just bored, often passing the time in reception lines by conjugating Greek verbs in her head. When her brother married Frances in 1886, Rose was more than happy to return to her academic life.

When he took office, President Cleveland was asked about marriage and whether or not there was any special lady in his life. He said something like his future wife had not graduated college yet, and the press laughed. Everyone would soon know, that the President wasn't kidding. As it turns out, Grover Cleveland had been making secret visits and even sending flowers to a young college student in New Jersey named Frances Folsom. The two had known each other long before he was elected President.

Grover Cleveland and Frances's father, Oscar Folsom, were law partners. Cleveland gave the Folsoms a baby carriage for Frances when she was born. Amazingly enough, Frances first knew her future husband as "Uncle Cleve" when she was a young girl. When Frances's father died, he left the bachelor Grover Cleveland in charge of the family's finances and well being. In fact, when Frances and her mother would visit or Grover would spend time with the Folsom family, people most likely thought he was courting Frances's mother. This is similar to what the public thought when President Tyler was courting Julia Gardiner. Julia Tyler had, at the time, been the youngest First Lady, at age 23, before President Cleveland married Frances. I am guessing that when Oscar Folsom told his friend Grover to take care of his family after he was gone, he didn't mean for Cleveland to marry his daughter. But, again, you never know, right?

The White House has seen many weddings over the years. The first White House wedding took place in 1820 when the Monroe's youngest daughter Maria got married there. Maria Monroe married her cousin Samuel L. Gouverneur. Franklin Delano Roosevelt and Eleanor Roosevelt Roosevelt were 6th cousins. So, maybe the whole Uncle Cleve thing isn't so strange after all, but the Roosevelt story is for "Unusual For Their Time Vol 2" so, stay tuned. Meanwhile, back in the Cleveland White House, there was a wedding to put on.

Frances Cleveland was the Jacqueline Kennedy of her time. She was young and attractive and the public couldn't get enough of her. Women emulated and copied her hairstyles and clothes, and men of the day were, no doubt, very envious of the President with his young trophy wife.

Because Frances was so much younger than her husband, it is no surprise that Grover Cleveland died well before she did. Frances even remarried five years after President Cleveland's death. It is for this reason that we don't really have a house to "visit" Frances Cleveland to learn about her life. And while we may not have a house or home for Mrs. Cleveland, we do have one of the greatest museums and institutions in the world. Mrs. Frances Cleveland was the first First Lady to get me what was essentially a back stage pass to the Smithsonian Institution's National Museum of American History. For a guy who grew up around Washington, D.C., this was like getting the Golden Ticket to Willy Wonka's Chocolate Factory.

My contact at the museum for Frances Cleveland and throughout the rest of the series was Lisa Kathleen Graddy. She and her team are the best of the best, I mean come on – it's the Smithsonian we're talking about here. They were a fun and knowledgeable group of people with whom to spend time. We worked together to tell the stories of some of the First Ladies by accessing some of the most rare and valuable artifacts in one of the world's greatest collections. Graddy brought me into special elevators, down back hallways and through touchpad-coded doors, into the Political History Storage Room. On my way down the halls and past the offices, I saw some of the most amazing things, posted on walls and scattered across people's desks and workstations. It really is a historian's wonderland.

Behind the coded and locked doors of the storage room were cabinets and closets and drawers and work areas used by the Smithsonian staff to work on all kinds of projects (including the backroom "Indiana Jones" segments of discovery we recorded together). These are some of the special videos that made the series so much fun. It really gave the shows that "ah ha" moment of discovery and special access. The artifacts and items in this room were there for any number of reasons. Some of the things in here were just "resting". It takes a lot out of an item to keep it on display or lend it out to another museum for a traveling exhibit. These items can be up to a couple hundred years old (or older) and even the air and light of a room can deteriorate an artifact at an alarming rate. Some of the things in this room are there because they are too delicate to ever be out on display, but too valuable to go anywhere else. Other items kept in this storage room are there to be refurbished or reconstructed. It was a dream come true to get this behind the scenes tour and access to a world-renowned facility like the Smithsonian Institution.

Okay, okay…back to the wedding. The centerpiece of any wedding, especially when you're talking about the First Ladies, is her wedding dress. In this and every other department, the folks at the National Museum of American History did not disappoint. They have had Frances Cleveland's wedding dress on display before, but when I was there it was wrapped up and stored in multiple boxes. They had no problem taking it out of the boxes for me.

Mrs. Cleveland's wedding dress was beautiful and in remarkable condition. It was mostly white satin, with a sturdy bodice and long flowing train. It had a long sleeved gown with matching white satin chest insert and collar. There was a sheer white almost veil quality wrap that goes around the shoulders to soften the overall look of the gown. There was also an amazing lace underside to the gown that wouldn't even be seen while the gown was worn. The attention to detail in every part of this wedding dress was astounding.

Also in the wedding collection were souvenirs from the Cleveland wedding with pictures of the couple on them. Items like this with images of the Clevelands on them would be enjoyed by the public and kept the Cleveland's relevant, as pop culture figures, for at least the next 12 years. The country's President was marrying a beautiful young bride, and the public considered her a celebrity. There was even a song written about the Cleveland wedding. It was called "The Cleveland Wedding March". The Smithsonian of course, has an original copy of the published sheet music. Everyone wanted his or her own piece of the couple's special day.

One of the more remarkable artifacts, in a drawer full of artifacts from the Cleveland's wedding, was an original cake box. It was a small box covered in white satin about the size of a harmonica box (if you know what the size of a regular sized harmonica is). The little boxes originally had a piece of wedding cake wrapped in lace inside. Each guest was given a piece as a wedding memento. Grover and Frances Cleveland took the time to sign a card on each of the cake boxes for their guests. It's fun to imagine The President and soon to be First Lady sitting up late in the White House the night before the wedding signing cake box cards. And there it was, the moment when Frances Cleveland became "human" to me. That signature in black ink on the cake box card, conjured an image of Frances sitting at a table, with one stack of blank cards and one stack of signed cards. I could see President Cleveland signing a card and sliding it across the table to Frances. I can even embellish the scene in my mind with flirty comments, a few giggles and a kiss or two here and there. It's real, it's human, and many of us have done something similar. This particular cake box in the storage room at the museum was originally given to the man that married Grover and Frances Cleveland. He was a minister named Byron Sunderland, of the First Presbyterian Church of Washington, D.C.

Frances Cleveland had the unique status of also being the first, and only, First Lady to serve two non-consecutive terms in the White House. A four-year Benjamin Harrison Presidency interrupted Cleveland's two-terms as President. It is reported that as she left in March 1889, Mrs. Cleveland told members of the White House staff to take care of the place, because she would be back in four years. As it turns out, she was right.

When Grover Cleveland ran for President a second time against Benjamin Harrison in 1893, Frances Cleveland was a huge asset to his campaign. She had been such a popular First Lady; they used her likeability to their advantage during the campaign. There were posters of Grover Cleveland, of course, but there were also posters of Frances Cleveland. It would seem that the country not only thought they were voting for a President, but that they were voting for a First Lady, as well. In the drawer full of campaign items were buttons and small painted portraits of Frances on glass, banners, playing cards, and even painted souvenir plates. The Merrick Thread Company even used the Clevelands in an ad campaign. There is a small poster in the collection with Grover Cleveland on the left and Frances Cleveland on the right and it states, "binding the country and the First Couple together".

While the Clevelands were between Presidencies, Frances gave birth to their first of five children, Ruth Cleveland. There is a lot of speculation and opinion that the Baby Ruth candy bar was named after the Cleveland's daughter. I can't find significant proof that this is accurate.

Historical Note – Like Taking Candy From A Baby

The Curtiss Candy Company was based in Chicago. The company's offices and factory were on the same street as Wrigley Field. Babe Ruth was all the rage in 1921 when the company renamed its Kandy Kake bar the Baby Ruth. Ruth Cleveland was born in 1891 and died in 1904. It seems unlikely that the company would name their most popular candy bar after a President's daughter who had been dead for at least 16 years with no ties to Chicago. It is believed that the company claimed to have named it after President and Mrs. Cleveland's daughter to avoid having to pay the baseball player, Babe Ruth.

While the candy bar may not have been around when Ruth was born, the public's fascination with the First Lady and her growing family was alive and well. In fact, baby Ruth had a political counterpart. Benjamin Harrison had a grandson about the same age at the time, and a song was written about the two children called "Baby Ruth and Baby McGee". The lyrics printed reveal the story of two babies wondering who will be the next child in the White House. The front page of the music has two cherubic looking babies under arcs of lucky horseshoes with words by George Cooper and music by Adam Geibel.

The Clevelands had a second daughter while they were in the White House during their second term. Her name was Esther, and this new Cleveland baby only fueled the public fascination with their children. In the Smithsonian, a large cardboard box was pulled down off of a high shelf in a cabinet, and I was told that I hadn't seen anything yet. As Graddy pulled back the tissue paper on a life sized 3-foot baby doll, I gasped as she sat the doll up in the box and one eye opened and then the other, but only ¾ of the way. ANOTHER CREEPY DOLL! The doll belonged to Esther, and it was among a number of artifacts from the children in the collection. The children were so popular that President and Mrs. Cleveland feared for their safety.

The American people have always had a strange relationship with their Presidents and First Ladies. We elect them. They essentially work for us. We "hire" them. However, they become celebrities. We sometimes feel as though they are property that belong to us and forget that they are human beings. Over the years, and especially during the 1700's and 1800's, when the White House was fully accessible to the public, people used to take all kinds of things from the White House as souvenirs. They would take silverware, plates, even going to such extremes as to tear off pieces of curtains and carpet, to take home with them after a visit. The sense of entitlement and familiarity with the Presidential family was beginning to carry over to the President and First Lady's children, as well. When the Cleveland children were in the yard with their nanny, people walked up to them and tried to pick them up, and play with them. They wanted to have their pictures taken with them, and Frances Cleveland started to fear for her children's safety. With this in mind, the Cleveland's bought a second home in Washington, D.C. and only stayed in the White House during the social season. The public viewed this as rude and snobbish behavior, but the primary reason was for the privacy and protection of their children.

As I mentioned at the beginning of the chapter, Frances Cleveland was extremely popular and many women in Washington and all over the country were imitating her style. The National Museum of American History has some wonderful pieces of her clothing that exemplify her personal style. I set up my lights and camera in front of a large horizontal cabinet so we could just flip through and pull out different pieces to showcase Frances Cleveland's flair.

They have a broad spectrum of clothing that Mrs. Cleveland would have used at different events and during different times of the day. It was also pointed out that many of the pieces could still be considered fashionable today. Mrs. Cleveland had ornate bolero jackets, and lovely evening bodices with intricate lace and beadwork. She had stylish vests with matching collars and an evening gown with glimmering beaded butterflies that were fixed to the shoulders. One article was written about this gown said that "the butterflies appeared as if the would alight from her very shoulders".

The reception dresses and gowns of the 1890's had sleeves and large poofy shoulders. They were often referred to as a "leg of mutton" style shoulder. One of Mrs. Cleveland's dresses in the collection was originally in this leg of mutton style but looks a bit different today. It is a very special dress that belonged to Mrs. Cleveland during her husband's second term as President. However, family members modified the dress over the years. The dress that started out as Mrs. Cleveland's 1893 Inaugural gown turned into a wedding dress that was used by a number of her grandchildren. It is a beautiful white satin floor length gown. The various granddaughters who used the dress over the years changed the top bodice piece to be more fashionable with the times. This had to be a very special heirloom to each of the women who wore it.

BALTIMORE, MARYLAND

One of the many amazing things about this journey, that also helped to humanize these women for me, was to meet and talk with members of their families. This was especially nice when the family member knew and remembered their First Lady relation. With help from the folks at Grover Cleveland's birthplace home, I was able to find one of Frances Cleveland's granddaughters. I was told that Ann Cleveland Robertson was in her 80's, lived in Baltimore, Maryland, and was willing to do a phone interview with us for the live show about her grandmother. So, I called Mrs. Ann Robertson to have a chat with her about her grandmother, First Lady Frances Cleveland.

Mrs. Robertson is a delightful lady who definitely inherited what she told me was her grandmother's good humor, the ability to laugh at herself and a warm, loving nature. She has so many wonderful stories about "Granny", and is an excellent storyteller with an infectious laugh. Mrs. Robertson was in her twenties when her grandmother died. The only sad story she shared with me was about the day her grandmother died.

Mrs. Robertson's parents were divorced, and she actually spent a lot of time with her grandmother. She spent many of her summers in New Hampshire at Frances Cleveland's summer home. Mrs. Robertson and her grandmother were very close. In October 1947, Mrs. Robertson's father (Frances Cleveland's son) was turning 50. Frances Cleveland was in Baltimore for his birthday party. Mrs. Robertson was in Tennessee working after college and living with her mother. Since she was not at her father's house in Baltimore, her grandmother was staying in her room. So, when Frances Cleveland died in Baltimore on October 27, 1947 it was in her granddaughter, Ann Cleveland Robertson's bed. To this day, she told me, she misses her "Granny" dearly, and regrets not being there when she died. It's one thing to read in a book that Frances Cleveland died in Baltimore on October 27, 1947. It's quite another story to hear it told from her granddaughter who still thinks about her and the positive influence her First Lady Grandmother had on her life.

All of the other stories Mrs. Robertson told were full of laughter, good times and pleasant memories. One of her favorites was the time she got a playful scolding from her grandmother for skipping a regular family event to hang out with some of her friends. Ann's family would get together in New Hampshire every Sunday night during the summers and sing hymns with their friends the Finleys. Mrs. Finley was Ann's Godmother and a close friend of Frances Cleveland. Ann had decided to skip this particular Sunday night and go bowling with some friends. The next day Frances Cleveland got a call from Mrs. Finley asking where Ann had been the night before, as she wasn't at their regular get together. So, Ann got called into Granny's office to explain herself. As Mrs. Robertson tells the story, her grandmother scolded her with a smirk and assured her granddaughter that she would be at the next sing a long. Apparently, though a kind and nice woman, Mrs. Finley was fairly strict and religious. So, to keep in good standing with her close friend, Mrs. Cleveland wanted to make sure that Ann wouldn't miss another Sunday night at the Finleys.

Another charming story revolves around Frances Cleveland and a life long pledge of temperance. Similar to Lucy Hayes and Sarah Polk, Mrs. Cleveland was not a fan of alcohol. She served it in the White House, but didn't partake of it herself. Later in life, Mrs. Robertson recalled that, Frances Cleveland was taking medicine for her heart, and that this medication had alcohol in it. She said she thought it was straight up whiskey. This one particular morning, she had stopped by to visit with her grandmother (as she often did), and Granny was on the porch off of her bedroom having her breakfast. When Ann got there, Mrs. Cleveland had already taken her heart medicine and was a bit looped. She said the two of them sat there laughing about how Mrs. Cleveland had gone her entire life without drinking, and now she had to for her health. It's one of the things that Ann Cleveland Robertson said she loved most about her grandmother. "Granny didn't like the whiskey", Ann assured me, but she enjoyed a good laugh even at her own expense.

DEER PARK, MARYLAND

We know that Frances and Grover Cleveland were married in a small ceremony in the White House. We know that they were the only couple to do so. We know that Frances Cleveland was and remains the youngest woman ever to be First Lady. We also know that the Clevelands traveled to a mountain resort in Deer Park, Maryland for their honeymoon. They stayed in a cottage there. They got there by train, passing through Cumberland, Maryland (which was a large hub at the time), and took a carriage from Oakland out to the resort.

I didn't have time to travel to the Deer Park honeymoon destination for the series. However, I do go to Deep Creek Lake, Maryland quite often. The lake is about 15 miles from Deer Park. In fact, I had always heard about Deer Park growing up. My parents used to go there for nice dinners without the kids (my brother, Jeremy and me). So, I recently rode my bicycle out to the location one beautiful summer day right around the time of year that the Clevelands would have been there after their wedding on June 2, 1886. There are roadside plaques that tell the story of their visit. There is an open lot where the resort used to be, and some the cottages have been rebuilt and are now privately owned. I wasn't able to connect with the owner of the honeymoon cottage on this particular trip.

However, I have his contact information and will be setting up another visit soon.

I checked in with the Garrett County Historical Museum, and its President, Bob Boal, hand drew a map of the layout (both now and when the Clevelands visited in 1886). Bob also encouraged me to go over to the Museum's new building to see the actual coach that brought the Clevelands from the train station to the resort. Railroads were big business back then, and some of the industry magnates lived out in Western Maryland or had substantial vacation estates out in these mountains.

SUMMARY

The fact that a 21-year-old Frances Folsom captured the heart and married the President of the United States to become the youngest First Lady in American history makes Frances Cleveland unusual for her time. The fact that she does a more than competent job at it and has the confidence to tell members of the White House staff that she will return goes above and beyond unusual and remarkable. Frances Cleveland inspired a nation of voters and a generation of women with her image and style. She was an educated woman who continued to support education for women and the elevation of their status in society. She was a protective mother, and by personal accounts from one of her granddaughters, a warm and loving woman that had a great sense of humor and no problem laughing at herself. In all the stories I was told, Frances Cleveland was wonderfully supportive and helped her husband's career just by being his wife.

Travelogue Food Tip

Ever since I was a kid going to Deep Creek Lake, the Cornish Manor restaurant in Deer Park has been a well known and excellent place to eat. My parents never took my brother and me there, and I don't blame them [too nice and too expensive for a couple of knucklehead kids – they were wise too take us to Wynlynn's Pizza Parlor and let us waste our allowance on Donkey Kong]. They saved the Cornish Manor for Anniversaries and other special occasions. However, I have eaten there as an adult, and even though the owners and management have changed throughout the years, they always keep up the standard of excellence there. This is a great place to have a really nice meal and feel close to the Presidential newlyweds if you find yourself up in that neck of the woods.

CHAPTER 26
Caroline Harrison

Indianapolis, Indiana

aroline Harrison was born Caroline Lavinia Scott on October 1, 1832 in Oxford, Ohio. Her parents were John Witherspoon Scott and Mary Potts Neal Scott. Caroline and Benjamin were married on October 20, 1853. Caroline and Benjamin had two children together (a third was stillborn and un-named). Caroline Harrison died on October 25, 1892 in Washington, D.C. at the age of 83.

INDIANAPOLIS, INDIANA

I consider myself to be a fairly well traveled individual. I know plenty of people who have been to more places than I have, but I also know plenty of people who enjoy staying put and don't get out much. It is fair to say that I am not the stay-at-home type. I always like work that takes me places. Especially if it's somewhere I've never been before. I had never been to Indiana before. It was a long drive from Spiegel Grove in Fremont, Ohio to my hotel in downtown Indianapolis. Standing at almost 300 feet, the Indiana State Soldiers and Sailors Monument at Monument Circle welcomed me to town. The first thing I noticed was how active and clean and friendly the city was. It was late (after 11pm) on a weeknight, and there were a lot of people walking around the city, or just hanging out at the center of town.

I'd been in the car for about 4 hours after a 10-hour day at the Hayes Center in Fremont. I had to check into my room and get the video cards uploading the Lucy Hayes material from that day's shoot to my hard drive. I had filled up all my video cards and would definitely need them the next day for Caroline Harrison. I started transferring and managing the video files, and decided to get some fresh air and a bite to eat, and see a little bit of the city before I went to sleep.

Travel Note – Get Out A Little

A long time ago when I first began to travel for work I decided, that I would not live my professional life from the inside of a hotel room. Sure, life on the road is tough. The hours are long. You're sleeping in a different bed every (or every other) night. But, I think of it this way, I am being paid to explore places I might never see again. I must take full advantage of these opportunities, (as long as the work is done and done well) and explore as much of these places as possible.

As I walked around Monument Circle and checked out my surroundings, I was quickly reminded of why I enjoy the Midwest so much. The people are genuinely friendly. There is a light overall mood or vibe in the air. Midwest cities typically have so much culture, history and opportunity to offer along with that cool vibe. I was happy to discover Indianapolis was that way. I stopped in a sports bar that had a few games on, and they were serving a late night bar menu (access to decent late night food is essential for a city to make my favorable list). I ordered some chicken wings and a Caesar salad. The bartender was very friendly, and gave me a few tips on where to go, what to see and listed off a few restaurants for dinner options for the next night. Having gotten my fresh air, food and information, I headed back to the room to check on my files and go to bed.

Production Note – Up All Night

I rarely slept through the night in situations where I was uploading files or managing my media. And that media management was necessary almost every night of my journey chasing after these First Ladies. It certainly was every night after a full day of shooting, as I needed to store my footage from the day, and clear my cards for the next day and Lady on the agenda. I always feared a power outage or some other glitch or hiccup would render me stuck in a really bad position for the following day. The production and travel schedule, and the gear and resources didn't allow for many interruptions and certainly did not allow for major mistakes. You see, even after a full 10-hour day of hauling gear and recording interviews and b-roll, once back at the hotel, the second part of my day was only just beginning. Truth be told, very early on during one of my first trips (I honestly don't remember which one), I got to my hotel, hooked everything up, plugged everything in (or so I thought), and initiated my whole media management process, and then, I went to bed. I woke up in the middle of the night and groggily walked over to the desk to check on my multiple batteries that were charging, my laptop and hard drive that were whirring away, downloading my work from the camera and cards only to find that the laptop was dark and silent. After the initial confusion cleared, panic set in at some ungodly hour of the morning. I thought my laptop was broken and I had lost all my footage from the day before. It turned out that I simply hadn't plugged my computer in, and it had run out of power after a few hours of working with the files. So, I had to plug everything back in, double check all connections and start the process where it had left off. This isn't as easy as it sounds, because I had to double check that files weren't missing or being dropped or duplicated – basically I had to babysit the whole operation to make sure I was getting everything where it needed to be. When I was fairly certain that everything was back on track, I caught a couple of hours of sleep. When I woke up, I discovered that in my re-connecting of the laptop I had bumped or unsettled one of the batteries in its charger and had to start that (very slow) process over again. It was essential that each day I had clean and empty video cards, and fully charges batteries.

No ifs, ands or buts. This was the first and last time I made either of these mistakes. It was also the end of sleeping with both eyes closed.

The next morning started early in Indianapolis, as I drove an easy commute of about 15 minutes to the Benjamin Harrison Presidential Site to meet President and CEO, Phyllis Geeslin. Phyllis has been at the site for some time, and spoke very highly of C-SPAN from past projects, and was looking forward to our day together. After she greeted me she explained that because of meetings I would be spending the morning with curator, Jennifer Capps. Jennifer would show me specific artifacts in the third floor museum, and Phyllis would give me a tour of the house and grounds in the afternoon. This plan worked out perfectly.

Jennifer and I began to set up on the third floor (we had started out meeting in the basement offices). This posed a bit of an issue. How were we going to get all my gear up narrow winding steps to the third floor, which had been converted, into a museum and storage space? My new friends had a solution. Much to my relief and surprise, they had a little elevator. When I say little, I mean little, but in a few trips, it did the trick, and my back is forever grateful for that little hidden elevator. So, we got everything upstairs, set up and began recording.

Caroline Harrison was in charge of a significant renovation during her time in the White House. She had gone to Congress and petitioned them for a significant amount of money to redecorate and make the improvements she felt necessary. When she had completed her renovations, White House photographer at the time, Frances Johnson gave Mrs. Harrison a photo album that documented her work.

The Harrison house collection has a number of cloth swatches from the renovations. There are light and dark pieces, smooth and patterned pieces, velvet and silk pieces all from various rooms in the Harrison White House. There is a marvelous golden orange swatch from the East Room, and a simple pale green fabric from the Harrison's bedroom. Did your parents ever reupholster or redecorate your house as a kid? Maybe you've done it to your own house, or been to a fabric store to make some new curtains. This is exactly the feeling I got when

I saw all of these fabric swatches. And yup! You guessed it! Mrs. Harrison just became human. I could get a clear image of the woman I had seen all the oil paintings and books. She had just stepped out of the pages of history and sat down on a couch in the White House with a rainbow of colored fabrics and a mountain of decisions to make about the color schemes and interior design ideas for one of the most well known houses in the world. This was pretty amazing to me.

Mrs. Harrison loved to entertain, and was thought to be an excellent hostess. This was well represented in all of the party, dinner, delegation, celebration and event souvenirs that were kept and preserved by the Harrisons. There were ribbons of red, white and blue, purple, pink, yellow, all with prints of eagles or the executive mansion itself with names and dates elegantly printed on them. There were items from events that occurred during practically all four years the Harrisons were in the White House.

Another amazing resource from Mrs. Harrison's life in the White House was her White House diaries. This was her stories and her experiences in her own words. These diaries are extremely fragile and are not often on display. It was very special to have had them out and carefully looked through for these video pieces. The one that was shown to me was from 1889-1891, and all written in Caroline Harrison's handwriting. She wrote about many of the events for which they had the mementoes I just wrote about, as well as many others.

She wrote very specifically about the Pan-American Conference and the centennial celebration of George Washington's first inauguration. There were seating charts and menus from these events, as well. She even wrote about the seven and a half hour parade that took place in Washington's honor. There were also things in the diary that would seem mundane at the time, but extremely interesting now some 125 years later. She wrote about the weather, and her feelings on daily events and news.

She also shared her thoughts on issues and subjects of philanthropic interest to her. She was very involved with veterans, soldiers, orphans and people that suffered from both physical and mental illnesses. She visited institutions and asylums, and frequently wrote about her experiences there. She mentioned going to Arlington National Cemetery to decorate soldiers' graves. Her artistic ability comes out in an entry about crafting floral arrangements.

One of the personal things she wrote about was the christening of one of their grandchildren in the Blue Room. After reading and hearing about this event, I was shown the family's christening set that still had water believed to be from the River Jordan in Northern Israel inside. Caroline's sister was said to have collected it for the family during a trip to the Holy Land.

At this point I had to stop the camera and ask if I could put on a white cloth curator's glove and hold water that was over 125 years old from the same river that is believed to be the baptism site of Jesus Christ. Believe what you want to believe, anyway you slice it, if this is even close to being true, that's a cool thing to see and hold first hand. The set was a stainless steel canister that held glass vials of blessed holy water that was all stored in a plain, but beautiful wooden box.

Mrs. Harrison also wrote about the first White House Christmas tree and a pair of opera glasses she received as a Christmas gift. The Harrisons are credited with having the first decorated Christmas tree in the White House. Christmas tree decorating hasn't been around since the beginning of time, and the Harrisons had a family tree on the second floor, that was not open or available for the public to see. The practice of having a public Christmas tree on display came much later, and we'll get to that in the Hoover Administration chapter in Volume 2. However, having the opera glasses on hand to see and hold after reading about them in Mrs. Harrison's own words, written by her own hand was something special, too.

When Mrs. Harrison moved into the White House in March 1889, she was very interested in how the place worked and operated. One of the first things she did was to go down the basement and start looking around. One of the most significant things she discovered was past administrations' china. She found sets, partial sets, individual pieces, all packed up or spread about in disarray. She took it upon herself to begin to categorize the pieces. She asked White House staff to identify which patterns belonged to which administrations. The very idea of a White House china display began with Caroline Harrison.

In 1891, Mrs. Harrison decided to pick out her own china pattern. There was never a full set ordered or made, but a significant amount of various plates and tea services were created. Mrs. Harrison just avoided the specialty platters, gravy boats and serving trays. She had wanted to keep all manufacturing and design in America, but found it impossible to get a reliable porcelain company in the States. So, the blanks were made in France, and the design was done domestically. She picked a design similar to the Lincoln china with sculpted edge and an eagle emblem. Her main border colors were a darkish royal blue with gold painted corn and goldenrod, which she felt represented the crops of America. Smaller plates and other tea services were all white with the gold painted patterns.

—————————————

Historical Note – Chinatown

Prior to the Harrisons' arrival in the White House, much of the White House china was taken by the outbound first family, and it was either thrown out, broken, boxed up in the basement or sold at auction, if in good enough condition. This is why so much White House china exists in private collections to this day. You'll remember from the Monroe chapter that the folks at Ash Lawn-Highland had to obtain much of their collection on EBay and at public auctions to fill their china cabinets and dining room table.

—————————————

As I mentioned, the third floor of the Benjamin Harrison home had been partially converted into a small museum. When I was there they had a number of dresses on loan from the First Ladies Library in Canton, Ohio. While most of these dresses were from women other than Caroline Harrison, it added to the atmosphere of the room, and they were very interesting to see and study. The rest of the room was surrounded by cases and displays filled with Harrison artifacts and belongings. There were hats, shoes, purses, painted fans, and souvenirs from trips. All of the items here that belonged to Mrs. Harrison gave me a real sense of her style and fashion. She was a very classy lady who kept up with the fashions and times of the day, but did so in a very age appropriate way. She had a classic style of elegance without seeming snooty or out of touch. She was a sort of stylish mother figure. The most significant piece, or pieces I should say, was a jewelry set that was owned by Benjamin Harrison's grandmother and wife of the 9th President of the United States, Anna Harrison. Yes, William Henry Harrison was Benjamin Harrison's grandfather. They are the only Grandfather and Grandson Presidential relation in the history of our country. This jewelry set came to the Benjamin Harrison house through the family, so it only makes sense that Caroline Harrison would have had the opportunity and occasion to wear this family heirloom. It was an interesting and strangely appropriate way to link the two women and the two administrations together. It reminded me of my mom's jewelry box with things in it that had belonged to her mother, my Nana.

After completing our work together in the upstairs museum, it was time to get set up with Phyllis downstairs and take a tour of the house. We started in the place that made the most sense. The front porch.

Benjamin Harrison led a very popular and ultimately successful front porch campaign. It was so successful and so many people showed up (an estimated 300,000 or more) that some speeches and events had to be moved downtown. Wherever the event was held, Caroline Harrison was next to or not far from her husband's side. The majority of the speeches and events were from the front porch of the Harrison's house. Mrs. Harrison was always prepared to invite guests into the house for handshakes, meetings, refreshments, or a tour of their home. I should mention here that as soon as I walked into the Harrison's home I was taken back in time. There is little to no evidence of the modern world. This is another fine example of a President and First Lady's home that looks as if they might walk through the front door at any moment.

One of Mrs. Harrison's favorite rooms in the house was the dining room. The room was decorated with many of Caroline's original paintings. She was a very accomplished artist. She liked to paint birds and flowers and other subjects of nature. Mrs. Harrison also enjoyed china painting, which was very popular at the time. There were wonderful examples of this in the dining room. The furniture in here gave the same feeling of elegance without being over the top that Mrs. Harrison had in her clothing and accessories. One group that was particularly important to President and Mrs. Harrison was the African American community. They were greeted during the front porch campaign, and invited into the Harrison house just like any other group of people. They met with both Benjamin and Caroline Harrison, and were shown the same hospitality as any other group of voters. This is important to note, when you think that this was in 1888.

The front parlor is equally as impressive as the dining room and the rest of the house. This room has one very special item that relates to Caroline Harrison, though. When the Harrisons first moved into the White House, Mrs. Harrison didn't have a piano there with her. Her oldest son, Russell bought his mother a piano. Caroline used to love to play, and she even played in her church back in Indianapolis. Caroline Harrison never came back from Washington, D.C. She died in a coma from tuberculosis 1892. Her piano, however, did come home. Benjamin Harrison put it in the front parlor, which is where it remains today. President Harrison remarried a few years after his sweet "Carrie" was gone, and his new wife (Caroline's cousin and former secretary) redecorated the house. Benjamin Harrison died in 1901, and his second wife, Mary Lord Dimmick sold the house in Indianapolis in 1937, and moved to New York. Mary sold the house to a foundation that pulled all of Mrs. Harrison's furniture out of storage and restored the house to its original glory, back when Caroline and Benjamin shared it together, as husband and wife.

Historical Note – Death In The White House

Caroline Harrison is the second First Lady to die in the White House. Letitia Tyler was the first First Lady to die in the White House and the third (and hopefully final) will come in Volume 2.

An example of the partnership President and Mrs. Harrison shared can be seen in the President's private office behind the family parlor. It was, as you would imagine, filled with books, documents and mementos that reflect a successful political career. The room was appointed with comfortable chairs and a large wooden desk that served as the centerpiece for the room. However, this office had something you might not expect to find. Caroline Harrison kept a desk in here, as well. This showed me a closeness that extended past the formal, and past the usual. Mr. and Mrs. Harrison needed each other. She was the even greater woman behind the great man. It reminded me of, then General, George Washington needing Martha at his side during the winter encampments of the Revolutionary War. Support was something that in one form or another most of the men who became President needed from their wives. And in one-way or another, they each gave it. Carrie was never far from Benjamin when they lived together in this house, and this beautifully feminine desk was proof of that.

Phyllis and I made our way upstairs to get a look at the bedrooms and family living quarters. Caroline Harrison was 57 when her husband was elected President. She was a bit older than her predecessor (Frances Cleveland being 21 when she became First Lady), so grandchildren were a huge part of the Harrison White House, and their lives at home in Indianapolis. One of my favorite things about Caroline Harrison is that she had a horse named John and a goat named Whiskers. This was just another humanizing factoid. One day the Harrisons decided to take a grandchild or two on a stroll on the grounds of the White House. They hauled out a little cart and hooked it to Whiskers the goat (why not, right? Seems like a perfectly normal thing to do). Well, something must have spooked Whiskers, because he took off down Pennsylvania Avenue with the Presidential grandchildren bouncing up and down in the cart. Witnesses said President Harrison chased after Whiskers and his grandchildren. The thought of this scene still makes me laugh, every time I hear or think about it. I mean, come on…a runaway goat cart? That's right out of the Little Rascals.

The upstairs rooms well represented the children and grandchildren of the Harrisons. Their daughter Mary had a sizable front room with wonderful thick hardwood furniture. You could tell that their children were well taken care of, but not spoiled. It's interesting to see that the daughters in these Presidential families almost always get a little extra when it came to their rooms and private spaces.

There was also a special nursery for grandchildren next to the other rooms on the second floor. Again, grandchildren were a focal point of Caroline Harrison's life. They were christened in the White House, had birthday parties in the White House and the home in Indianapolis was no exception. The grandchildren's room at the Harrison's home was well appointed and more than comfortable to host any of the grandchildren at any time and for any length of stay.

Mrs. Harrison's master bedroom suite and sitting room are both something special in this home. As is the case with many of these women, you can really get a sense of their character in these private places. The floors are dark wood, and other parts of the room were accented with the same wood. There is a beautiful floor length mirror that is easy to picture Mrs. Harrison using to get ready for her day or a special event. The curtains are a long flowing pale gold, which worked very well with the green, brown, cream and white floral patterns of the wallpaper. This room was fashionably decorated and full of things that were important to Caroline.

We know music was very important to Mrs. Harrison, and there is a smaller piano here in the room. She played piano in her church and could've easily practiced before each Sunday performance here in her sitting room. She also had a fan on display that was given to her by President and Mrs. Grant's daughter-in-law. It is a beautiful feathered black, white and gray fan that she kept in a matching wood and glass display case.

Caroline Harrison has been described as a confident woman with a purpose who served her country and community well. She often entertained her lady friends and had tea here in her sitting room. She was part of a literary club, and enjoyed Dickens and Shakespeare. She was active in the local orphan's asylum in town, and visited weekly with clothes and food. She could have been seated with many other board members of these groups and discussed a variety of pressing issues of the day.

Mrs. Harrison was also very artistic and craft minded. Here in the room was her black Singer sewing machine. She enjoyed all kinds of piecework like embroidery and beading. She also kept a display easel here in her sitting room. She frequently painted, and you can imagine any one of her latest pieces on display for friends and visitors to admire. It was pointed out that this room had a wonderful view of her flowers and garden out in the yard. This is where she could have easily gotten inspiration for some of her paintings and artwork.

Since we were talking about her gardens, it only made sense to take another look outside and walk around the yard. Mrs. Harrison kept a beautiful garden when she lived in their Indianapolis home. She loved flowers, and the birds and insects that they attracted. Caroline kept more than flowers in her garden, and the strawberry vines that exist today are believed to have grown from the same vines that she kept here back in the late 1800's. The day that I visited had turned remarkably sunny, and it was a nice way to finish up my trip to Mrs. Harrison's home.

SUMMARY

Caroline Harrison was a caring and community-minded woman. She was a good role model to women across the nation and loved her family very much. She was the first President-General of the Daughters of the American Revolution. She delivered the first public speech written by a First Lady. Caroline Harrison also had electric lights installed in the White House during her time there (although she was apparently afraid to touch the switches that turned them on). Even though she never saw it completed, we have her to thank for inspiring the White House china collection that now spans almost every Presidential administration of the United States. This is huge, because china is one of the first things we think of when we think of First Ladies. She was very artistic, and a fairly prolific painter. She continued trends and activities that were started by First Ladies who came before her, like Dolley Madison, Harriet Lane and Lucy Hayes, while blazing new trails with women's groups like the Daughters of the American Revolution. Caroline Harrison was also a strong political partner and asset to her husband, and he knew it. For all these reasons and more, Caroline Harrison was unusual for her time.

Travelogue Food Tip

The hippest part of town with the best restaurants is on and around Massachusetts Avenue. If the weather cooperates, I recommend walking around town and making your way to this part of the city. There are sidewalk cafes and neat shops all up and down both sides of the street. I decided to take my bartender's advice from the night before and go to Forty Five Degrees. It was one of the best food decisions I made during the entire adventure. Forty Five Degrees is a modern Asian fusion joint that specializes in sushi. The décor was super chic without being uncomfortable or stuffy. They played great music, and had flat screen monitors up all around. The night I was there, they had "16 Candles" playing. I was taken a bit by surprise when 8 to 10 women six feet and taller came strolling in wearing athletic flip-flops and warm up suits. My waiter told me they were members of the WNBA's Indiana Fever (which didn't come as a surprise to me). He told me that a lot of sports figures and local celebrities hung out and ate there. I had sweet Thai chili calamari to start off with that was amazing. For my main course, I had two specialty sushi rolls – the Forty Five Degree Roll and the Playboy roll. I recommend them both, but the Playboy roll is a must. It comes to your table on fire and wrapped in foil. I give the roll two thumbs up for taste and presentation.

CHAPTER 27
Ida McKinley

Canton, Ohio

*I*da McKinley was born Ida Saxton on June 8, 1847 in Canton, Ohio. Her parents were James A. Saxton and Katherine Dewalt Saxton. Ida and William were married on January 25, 1871. Ida and William had two daughters together (one died at the age of four the other died after only four months). Ida McKinley died on may 26, 1907 in Canton, Ohio at the age of 59.

Author's Note – 12-12-15

I am currently on a plane writing the chapter for Ida McKinley. She is the last woman of Volume One. She was the last woman to be covered in season one of the C-SPAN series "FIRST LADIES: Influence and Image", and the last First Lady of the 19th Century. All of these facts are no strange coincidence. They are a bit of a surprise to me, though, in that I didn't design or premeditate the project in this form. It does, though, make complete sense. I am writing about this woman, Ida McKinley, with a view to which I have grown so accustomed. 35,000 feet above the ground, looking out of a plane window. I am headed out of town on a pilgrimage of my own. One that – like this project – would've made my mom smile. It is a strangely romantic way to complete this leg of the journey.

CANTON, OHIO

Speaking of journeys, as a young woman, Ida Saxton had quite the journey of her own. She and her sister, Mary, were sent on a six-month (some sources say eight months) European vacation when Ida was 21 years old. This was not uncommon for young women of privilege to do. Ida Saxton was the daughter of James Saxton. Her father was a well known and respected banker in Canton. He was also the third wealthiest man in town. She and her brother and sister were educated in the finest schools in Canton, Cleveland, and New York. Ida and her sister even attended the Brooke Academy in Media, Pennsylvania for finishing school. Her early life and her European travels are well represented in the parlor of the Saxton McKinley house in Canton. It is called the Saxton McKinley House, because it is the house that Ida is born and raised in, but it is also the house the she and William McKinley would live in; eventually converting the top floor into their living space and offices. Before she met and married William McKinley, Ida lived there with her mother, her father, her brother and sister and her grandmother. The Executive Director, Patricia Krider was kind enough to spend the day with me here at the house.

The parlor is beautifully decorated with original pieces, and reconstructed from a black and white photo donated by a family descendant.

Production Note - A Picture Is Worth A Thousand Words

At the risk of being redundant – AGAIN– photos like these are absolutely invaluable and amazing. It gives your mind's eye a reference point for accuracy that far surpasses just a room with old stuff in it. You can see the room in the picture, as it was when the people lived and occupied the space, and then you can look up and compare the remarkable recreation.

In addition to the remarkable furniture and décor of the room, there are wonderful family pictures and paintings. There is a marvelous picture, believed to be the earliest, of Ida and her two siblings. There are also large portraits of her parents that complete the family representation in the home. Ida was very musical, as were most educated women of her day, and there is a piano in the parlor that she would have, no doubt, used to entertain her whole family as they might have sat in the evenings and read by the fire. I was told that Ida McKinley was the first First Lady to provide musical entertainment after State Dinners in the White House. This early education and musical ability were obvious inspirations for this activity.

In the letters that Ida wrote and sent home to her family from Europe, she spoke of music boxes. The many stores and musical boxes she saw on her trip fascinated her. She wrote about their quality and looking for just the right one. She finally found one to her liking in Geneva, Switzerland, and bought it as a gift for her mother. Not only do they have the music box on display in the parlor in Canton, but also is still plays. It is about the size of a typewriter and is beautifully crafted.

I mentioned that Ida's father was a very successful banker. He was also a very unusual father with unconventional methods for his children's upbringing, especially when it came to his daughters. He wanted to raise his daughters with the life skills to live independently without the help or need of a man. Keep in mind this is the mid 1800's we're talking about here. He wanted Ida to "be able to support herself if trouble [came] her way". He gave her a job in his Stark County Bank, so she could learn to have and manage her own money. She started as a teller, and moved her way up to manager. These skills came in handy on their European adventure. When Ida felt their chaperone wasn't managing the funds for the trip properly, she stepped in and became the self-appointed accountant for the trip. It was in her father's bank that she first sees and meets a young Civil War veteran and lawyer named William McKinley, Jr. After she returned from Europe, their relationship truly began to develop.

Unfortunately, Ida McKinley didn't get to enjoy good health or continue an adventurous life much past her 20's. She remained active and involved in her husband's career, but she was considered a semi-invalid for most of her adult life. She and her husband had two daughters together. Katherine was born in 1871 and died in 1875 from Typhoid Fever. Their second daughter, also named Ida, was very frail and died four months after she was born. Mrs. McKinley never fully recovered, either mentally or physically, from these loses. Some books tell you she had epilepsy and others will tell you it was more of a mental depression, confusion and hysteria. She was prone to seizures, and her outbreaks were common. If you were a dinner guest of the McKinleys, you could have very easily witnessed a nonchalant President McKinley drape a large dinner napkin or cloth over his wife's face to cover one of her seizures, and continue speaking as if nothing were happening. Then, as calmly as he put the cloth over her head, he would take it off when the episode was over. Some people I tell this story to find it harsh or cruel. I always explain that I think just the opposite.

Ida McKinley wanted to be a part of her husband's professional and political life. He wanted her to be involved, too. Many women before and since Ida McKinley have taken lesser roles as First Lady because of similar conditions or illnesses. She refused to have a relative stand in for her as hostess. She didn't want to take a back seat. She wanted to be in the room and in the action. While the McKinleys were in the White House, protocol for state dinners and receptions was revised. Typically, the wife of the visiting guest would sit next to the President. In the McKinley White House, Mrs. McKinley sat next to her husband, so he could assist her if a seizure occurred. It was even written in Harper's Bazaar that her involvement as First Lady was "an inspiration to all woman who for one reason or another are hindered from playing a brilliant individual role in life". I believe this speaks very highly of both of them. So, I see the whole napkin thing, as a way for President McKinley to have his wife with him (where she wanted to be), and not be stared at or become a spectacle during a momentary display of erratic behavior. I see this as a loving husband protecting his wife.

Wherever Ida and William lived they set up a living space with a parlor or sitting area just outside McKinley's office. They did this in Columbus when he was Governor, in Washington, D.C. when he was a Congressman and President, and the Saxton McKinley House in Canton was no exception. Ida McKinley would sit just outside her husband's office and greet his guests and appointments. McKinley would show visitors into his office and intentionally leave his door cracked open. The purpose of this was so that Ida could listen in on all of his meetings. After each meeting, McKinley would ask for his wife's take on the exchange. She was one of his closest confidants.

The office in the Saxton McKinley house is as it was in the days when Ida and William lived there. They converted what had been the third floor ballroom of the home Ida grew up in, to a third floor apartment. The office was one of the largest rooms on the floor. It was filled floor to ceiling with books housed in built-in bookshelves, and the focal point of the room was a massive desk. This room, too, was re-created from an old black and white photo from when the McKinleys lived there. The accuracy, attention to detail and pieces of original furniture made me feel as if I were stepping into the room for a meeting with President McKinley myself. It was really interesting to walk past the spot with my camera where Mrs. McKinley would have been sitting, and imagine the door being cracked just enough for her to hear the conversation.

The largest part of the third floor of the house has been converted into a museum with beautiful cases of glass and wood to tell the story of Ida and President McKinley's life. It is here that I learned about Ida McKinley the campaign asset. William McKinley was the last veteran of the Civil War to be elected President, and as a veteran, he attracted the masses. President McKinley ran a very success-ful front porch campaign while living with his wife in Canton. Many of the glass cases on the left side of the room contain campaign memorabilia from the 1896 Presidential election.

The general public knew something of Ida's poor health, and McKinley's opponent, William Jennings Bryan and his team, tried to use that against him. McKinley's team was on top of things, and got out in front of things by publish-ing an Ida McKinley bio pamphlet (the first of its kind on a candidate's wife). This piece tells the story of an active, vivacious and highly educated woman. The booklet is slightly smaller than a typical sheet of today's printer paper, and a rare item to have been written about a woman in those days. It is an excellent addition to the campaign collection in Canton. They have the typical things you would expect to find in a campaign memorabilia exhibit, like ribbons, buttons, pictures and posters. They also have unusual items like a silver spoon with Mrs. McKinley's picture on one side at the end of the handle, and the White House on the other. It would seem that the McKinley campaign went all out when it came to Ida McKinley swag, and presenting a positive and involved woman behind the Presidential candidate.

This carried over to the front porch campaign, as well. Mrs. McKinley would always be seated next to her husband, as he spoke to the masses in front of their Canton home. Having her seated in a chair meant that people had to approach her, and she wouldn't have to stand for long periods of time. In addition to being seated, Mrs. McKinley would often be holding something. She would have a bouquet of flowers or a fan, anything to avoid having to shake hands or engage in physical contact with strangers. This approach to Mrs. McKinley's public ap-pearances gave her a quiet image of elegance while also showing her support for her husband's political ambitions.

WILLIAM MCKINLEY PRESIDENTIAL LIBRARY AND MUSEUM

I completed my work at the Saxton McKinley House with Pat, and headed across town to meet Curator, Kim Kenny, at the William McKinley Presidential Library and Museum. It was about 15 minutes from where I had been working for the first half of the day. Kim was anxious to show me around the back rooms, closets and storage lockers of their massive facility. And I was excited to see them based on our initial phone conversation, when we set up my visit. Their collection sounded fantastic, and included many things I hadn't yet seen in my travels. The building is also a museum for the city of Canton. Kim and I lugged my gear from one end of that museum to the other. We went through coded doors, padlocked garages, bolted doors and clasped drawers to see everything we could see that belonged to or had something to do with Ida McKinley.

Production Note – Cartless In Ohio

My metal cart with wheels never made it to Ohio. Canton was the first stop on this particular whirlwind trip. This cart is a big part of how I was able to make things happen. If you can't carry the gear efficiently, and you are slowed down by multiple trips back and forth from the car or up and down flights and floors, production can be slowed to a turtle's pace or be stopped in its tracks altogether. The airline that lost the cart did everything they could to get it to me. The problem was, that everything they did was the wrong thing to do. In their defense, I didn't stay in one place very long. It seems my pace was too quick for even a major airline. However, they got information, times, dates and places wrong, that in my opinion, made all the difference in whether or not I got my cart. When I got back from this leg of my journey, my cart was waiting for me at my desk at C-SPAN. Which was nice…for my next trip. But it made for a long embattled voyage through Ohio. Man, I could've really used my cart on that trip.

Mrs. McKinley was known for her knitted slippers. They came in all sizes; she predominantly used blue, gray or ivory yarn, they often had matching ribbon ties, and it is believed she made over 4,000 pairs. One of the unique things about them was their genuine leather sole. She made most of her slippers for veterans and children, particularly orphans. Mrs. McKinley would also donate her slippers to auctions and charities that benefited veterans, orphans and children. Remember, she wasn't in the best of health, so she couldn't always visit these institutions or make speeches at public events for them. She felt this was her way of getting involved and contributing.

The McKinley Museum has a number of Mrs. McKinley's slippers in all shapes, sizes and colors. They also have one of her sewing bags and a set of her crocheting needles. The sewing bag was light blue satin, which was one of her favorite colors, and could be pulled closed with a drawstring. This particular sewing bag had a picture of her husband stitched into it. Mrs. McKinley often kept or put President McKinley's picture on her personal accessories and belongings. I was fortunate enough to get to Canton right after one of Ida McKinley's billfolds was donated to the museum. The billfold was also light blue in color and had a picture of her husband sewn into it. This item had never been on display, and only been recently seen by the museum staff, and now me.

Some speculate she developed a bit of an obsession with her husband and his safety after losing their only two children. No matter what the case, these slippers and her husband were both very important to her. It was something special to see items that represented the slippers and their process so clearly and completely. To see her husband so vividly characterized there as well was also quite remarkable.

Throughout the series, one of the techniques in filming that really seemed to work and fit in well with the rest of the show, was the "walk and talk" interview that took the viewer through doors, down hallways and into rooms. This gave the folks watching at home a sense of being there with me. It seemed as though we were discovering things together, and we were. The material I captured here at the McKinley Museum was among the best of this style of shooting. Kim was great at opening doors, punching in codes, working padlocks, opening drawers and pulling out artifacts, all while talking her way through it. I have done a lot of TV over the years, and I promise you this is much harder than it looks. She did it well and she did it on the spot; having never worked with each other before, the end result was extremely effective. Some of the best examples of our work together were opening a large storage closet secured with a padlock, and walking down a narrow corridor to open some long shallow drawers that held some very special items.

When President McKinley was shot, it is written that one of the first things he said was, "my wife, be careful how you tell her. Oh, be careful!" Ida had been concerned about her husband's safety since losing her daughters and had even predicted or had premonitions of her husband's death. So, when anarchist Leon F. Czolgosz shot President McKinley at a public event in in Buffalo, New York on September 6, 1901, people close to the President were very concerned about how Mrs. McKinley would take the news. She was upset, of course, but everyone was very surprised at how well she kept her composure, and stayed at her husband's side until he died just eight days later on September 14th. She put on a brave face for the funeral, and then went into six years of morning, became a recluse and mostly, she stayed at home.

In the long shallow drawers in the closet behind the padlocked door, were a number of things that symbolized Ida McKinley's loss of her husband. There are many condolence letters, and cards in the collection. They also have a few appreciation cards that Mrs. McKinley would have sent. They were black bordered with a note from Mrs. McKinley, but they were unsigned. She received so many notes and letters from people that to send a signed appreciation card for everyone was just impossible. However, there are responses and signed letters that went out to family members and close friends. These were noted and kept track of in a black leather bound notebook. The interesting thing here (beyond the significance of what it was) is that Mrs. McKinley and her secretary made notes and dates in the upper corners of many of the pages to keep track of when and to whom responses were sent out. I think these items and seeing the handwriting, not only of Mrs. McKinley, but the family, friends and general public, humanized all of them. These artifacts brought to life a time surrounding McKinley's assassination more than anything I had read in a book. Again, these were real people who loved, lived and lost. Everyone has experienced death in their lives, and depending on how close that experience is, you know about books, letters, cards and notes of appreciation.

Not all of the letters, writings and items in these drawers were sad. In fact, some were from what were arguably the happiest times in Ida McKinley's life. There are a number of letters that she wrote back to her parents from her trip to Europe. She wrote about being in Scotland and seeing the people and places that Robert Burns wrote about in his poems and lyrics. Ida wrote that his work took on so much more meaning to her now having been there (I could relate). Before Ida was married, she was a Sunday school teacher, and they have one of her personal hymnals, which she would have carried with her to church. The museum also has Ida and William's marriage license. Of course, William's signature is the only one on it, and the only one required by law at the time, but it is the license that lists them both. So, it was nice to get the balance of happiness in there to help tell the whole story of Ida's life.

One thing Ida was known for (other than her slippers) was her fashion. She was reported to have spent over ten thousand dollars of her own money on dresses while in the White House. She had a considerable inheritance from her parents, and she didn't have the physical ability to travel far or often, so, for a semi-invalid First Lady, a fantastic wardrobe makes complete sense, especially given her proclivity to attend public events with her husband. The William McKinley Presidential Library and Museum has no shortage of Mrs. McKinley's dresses. She favored the colors blue and ivory, and wore the high collars and leg of mutton sleeves that were all the rage of her day. There is shelf after shelf (from floor to ceiling) stacked with large gray museum storage boxes filled with her dresses. Every dress was as beautiful and magnificent as the one before it. I was shown dresses that had been on display, dresses that had never been on display, dresses that were being repaired from being on display and dresses that were being reconditioned so they could go out on display for the first time. I learned that in many cases, these dresses were destroying themselves over time. The heavy glass beads and sharp, mirrored pieces that some of these dresses incorporated were cutting through the thread that held them to the dress. Even as carefully as they were stored and preserved, they were falling apart just simply lying there in a box on a shelf. The meticulous work that these historians do to get these dresses back up and running for us to enjoy in museums and in exhibits is truly remarkable and in many cases greatly underappreciated. Speaking for myself, before learning all this, I didn't consider all the prep work that went into an artifact like this before it was ready for public enjoyment. There was even one dress I was shown that had beads falling off it as I was filming it. In any event, Mrs. McKinley had impeccable taste, and spent a lot of money showing it.

Before we boxed everything back up, and I headed out for the next town, they had one more item to show me. It was something I had never seen. It was something I didn't even know existed. It wasn't quite as dramatic as Mrs. Monroe's hair earrings, but it was equally as interesting just for the fact that is existed as a "thing" back in the day. It was a parasol accessory kit. It came in a beautiful display box, and contained the points, top, handle, and slider. They were all in perfect condition and a vivid coral color. They were used to give lady's parasol a new look or a facelift of sorts. I was told that coral was likely another favorite color of Mrs. McKinley's as they had a few other pieces and jewelry sets in the same color. All of the pieces were skillfully crafted and each was amazing works of art. Whether it was a brooch, a necklace or an earring, no detail was overlooked.

SUMMARY

The very fact that Ida McKinley made public appearances, despite her poor health, makes her unusual for her time. Period. I could end this summary right there. Many First Ladies appointed family members and friends to cover their hostessing duties in times of poor health and chronic ailment. Ida McKinley did not. She powered through campaigns, dinners, receptions and events, knowing that at any minute her condition could compromise the image of strength she projected in front of hundreds, if not thousands, of people.

She was a role model for other women in many areas. She was a fashion icon for her day, she found a way to use her knitting skills for charitable efforts and organizations, and she was highly educated and in her younger years before she fell ill, an adventurous woman. Her father was unusual for his time, because he wanted his daughters to be independent and not in need of a man to take care of them in life. This was a stark contrast to most fathers in that day, who were trying to marry their daughters off. Not only did Ida accept these unconventional skills and roles, she learned and performed them well; she flourished. After her husband was shot and killed she put on a surprisingly strong and brave face for the public and the processionals and ceremonies. Some First Ladies, in better health than she, did not have the wherewithal to do the same. She was a strong and talented woman. She was unusual for her time.

Travelogue Food Tip

Every once and a while you need to go for the known...the sure thing...the safe bet. Sometimes this choice is conscience and other times it's situational. Travel schedules and work schedules and appointments can come into play. In this case, I was driving down the road and on my way into Canton, and I saw a Bonefish Grill. I got the mussels and a Caesar salad. It totally hit the spot. Don't shy away from things you know that work just to get a new experience for the sake of saying you tried something new. Sometimes it pays off to go with the familiar.

CONCLUSION

Behind every great man is an even greater woman...or in this case...lady.

If George Washington had never met and married Martha Dandridge Custis, this book would be called something quite different. It may have been written in a different language, or perhaps never written at all.

If George and Martha Washington had never married, America would be a very different place... or quite possibly... not America at all.

Martha Washington was unusual for her time.

That's the way this book and this adventure started. There was more to each of their stories than their time in the White House. They were more than an oil painting on a wall or a chapter in a history book. They were women, daughters, sisters, aunts, grandchildren, and grandmothers. They were little girls, teenagers, young woman, girlfriends, wives, mothers and widows. They were (and are) real people who lived and loved, real people who won and lost. I hope that this first volume and these chapters have proven these statements to be true of Martha Washington, and all the First Ladies I've covered here in the 1700's and 1800's. They were all unusual for their time. I look forward to bringing you volume 2, and the 1900's and 2000's.

When I was first told about the C-SPAN project, I thought "what a cool idea, I'm in if they'll have me". I knew C-SPAN had an impeccable reputation. I had no idea that the project, and my contributions and experiences would make such a huge impact on my life and me as a person. As I mentioned in the beginning, I don't think anyone knew exactly what I would be doing when we embarked on this project, nor how intense it would get, and the tight production schedule within which we ended up working. Much to my appreciation, the series grew in an organic way. The U.S. Government shut down in the middle of the series, people got sick, guests had to cancel, holidays happened, babies were born, and life went on around us. The road gaveth and the road tooketh away. We got it done. Every woman was captured during the series, from Martha to Michelle. Every First Lady and hostess's story was told.

I would like to again take this opportunity to thank C-SPAN for allowing me the opportunity to be part of such a great team and such a historically significant project. It gave me a great sense of responsibility and professional self worth to bring this material back to Washington to be a part of the bigger live show. I appreciate the trust they put in me to go out, by myself, and get the stories from the field locations for these women, to help tell the stories of their lives. I gave my heart, soul, and sometimes, physical well being to this project, and it was worth it. My colleagues at C-SPAN and I used to joke about needing more hands on deck for this massive project, but that in the end there would be fewer hands patting ourselves on the back for the greatness we had achieved. I'm glad our jokes proved true in the end. It was not a large group of people that pulled this off. In the case of this project, it was definitely quality over quantity, and I am fortunate to have worked with some of the best in the business on these shows.

Each of these locations and each of these collections could have been dedicated to a show of their own. There is an amazingly large amount of material and a huge number of artifacts out there for most of these women. Since I started my work on these women I have been (and continue) learning that there is also an amazing amount of interest in these women and their lives. The people I meet and speak to cannot get enough of this stuff. Even as I go back and read what I have written, I realize how much more there is to talk about and see. There are still gaps that need to be filled in, and places I have not yet traveled to in pursuit of their stories. I'll get there. We'll get there together. As I said, in the beginning and as I mention in my speeches, I have walked tens of thousands of miles in the shoes of these women, and my feet are killing me. However, I am not too tired to keep walking.

I still have another volume to write that will start right where I left off in Volume One. We will begin with Edith Roosevelt, and continue on to whomever (man or woman) is married to the next President of the United States. While I write Volume Two, I will continue to deliver my public speaking program at live events all across the country, and grow that part of the FIRST LADIES MAN as much as I can. I will continue to travel to places that tell the stories of these remarkable ladies, and I will update my notes, journals and writings. My journey, as it concerns these women, is far from over. If you would like to continue this journey with me, you are all invited. Pack your bags, and let's hit the road.

Thank You

THE FIRST LADIES MAN would like to thank all of the locations that shared their people, places, collections, information and time.

COLONIAL WILLIAMSBURG

VALLEY FORGE NATIONAL HISTORIC PARK

INDEPENDENCE NATIONAL HISTORIC PARK

GEORGE WASHINGTON'S MOUNT VERNON

ADAMS NATIONAL HISTORIC PARK

UNITED FIRST PARISH CHURCH

ABIGAIL ADAMS HISTORICAL SOCIETY

MASSACHUSETTS HISTORICAL SOCIETY

THOMAS JEFFERSON'S MONTICELLO

JAMES MADISON'S MONTPELIER

THE OCTAGON HOUSE

THE DUMBARTON HOUSE

THE JAMES MONROE MUSEUM AND MEMORIAL LIBRARY

ASH LAWN-HIGHLAND

OAK HILL ESTATE

ANDREW JACKSON'S HERMITAGE

MARTIN VAN BUREN NATIONAL HISTORIC SITE

CEDAR GROVE PLANTATION

SHERWOOD FOREST

JAMES K. POLK ANCESTRAL HOME

MILLARD FILLMORE HOUSE

THE PIERCE MANSE

NEW HAMPSHIRE HISTORICAL SOCIETY

ANDOVER HISTORICAL SOCIETY

THE AIKEN HOUSE

FENDRICK LIBRARY

JAME'S BUCHANAN'S WHEATLAND

HARRIET LANE BIRTHPLACE HOME

MARY TODD LINCOLN HOUSE

LINCOLN HOME NATIONAL HISTORIC SITE

ABRAHAM LINCOLN PRESIDENTIAL LIBRARY AND MUSEM

PRESIDENT LINCOLN'S COTTAGE

ANDREW JOHNSON NATIONAL HISTORIC SITE

ULYSSES S. GRANT NATIONAL HISTORIC SITE

GRANT'S FARM

ULYSSES S. GRANT HOME

RUTHERFORD B. HAYES PRESIDENTIAL CENTER

JAMES A. GARFIELD NATIONAL HISTORIC SITE

ST. JOHN'S EPISCOPAL CHURCH

SMITHSONIAN INSTITUTION

NATIONAL MUSEM OF AMERICAN HISTORY

GARRETT COUNTY HISTORICAL SOCIETY MUSEUM

BENJAMIN HARRISON PRESIDENTIAL SITE

SAXTON MCKINLEY HOUSE

NATIONAL FIRST LADIES LIBRARY

WILLIAM MCKINLEY PRESIDENTIAL LIBRARY AND MUSEUM

RECOMMENDED
Reading

Books used during the series, travels and writing of this book:

The First Ladies Fact Book
by Bill Harris Revised by Laura Ross

Homes of the First Ladies
by William G. Clotworthy

Loves, Lies and Tears: An Intimate Look at America's First Ladies
Volume 1 by Jacqueline Berger

The First Ladies: An Intimate Portrait of the Women Who Shaped America by Feather Schwartz Foster

Rating the First Ladies: The Women Who Influenced the Presidency
by John B. Roberts II

Martha Washington: An American Life
by Patricia Brady

Abigail & John: A Portrait of Marriage
by Edith B. Gelles

Abigail Adams: A Writing Life
by Edith B. Gelles

My Dearest Friend: Letters of Abigail and John Adams
Edited by Margaret A. Hogan and C. James Taylor

The Adams Papers: Adams Family Correspondence *Volume 10*
Edited by Margaret Hogan, C. James Taylor, Sara Martin, Hobson Woodward, Sara B. Sikes, Gregg L. Lint and Sara Georgini

A Perfect Union: Dolley Madison and the Creation of the American Nation
by Catherine Allgor

The Adams Papers: Diary and Autobiographical Writings of Louisa Catherine Adams *Volumes 1 & 2*
Edited by Judith S. Graham, Beth Luey, Margaret A. Hogan and C.

James Taylor

A Being So Gentle: The Frontier Love Story of Rachel and Andrew Jackson by Patricia Brady

First Lady: The Life of Lucy Webb Hayes
by Emily Apt Geer

Harriet Lane Johnson
by Joan C. McCulloh

Destiny of the Republic: A Tale of Madness, Medicine and the Murder of a President by Candice Millard

Frank: The Story of Frances Folsom Cleveland, America's Youngest First Lady by Annette Dunlap

To be continued…

Andrew Och, The First Ladies Man

ABOUT
THE FIRST LADIES MAN
Andrew Och

Andrew Och is an award winning television and multi-media producer who has traveled the world with his pen, paper and camera. A Radio, Television and Film graduate from the University of Maryland, Andrew started his production career in music, recording and touring with his band in the 1980's and 1990's. Soon after that he added his camera to the mix and all the pieces fell into place. A storyteller from a young age, Andrew enjoys the art of communication, and will go anywhere in the world for more knowledge, greater understanding and a good story. He is a true documentarian of life.

Most recently, for the C-SPAN series – **"First Ladies: Influence and Image"**, Andrew spent over a year traveling to nearly every location that helped tell the stories of every First Lady of the United States of America. He covered Martha Washington through Michelle Obama and visited with people and places all across the country. From Colonial Williamsburg to Stanford University he was given an ALL ACCESS – BACKSTAGE PASS to some of the nation's most treasured collections and historical landmarks. He spent time in libraries and museums, homes and schools, birthplaces and cemeteries, train stations and churches. No stone was left unturned nor door left unlocked in his unique and historical journey to learn everything he could about these women before, during and after their time in the White House.

Historians, archivists and enthusiasts agree "Andrew's recent project and travels put him in a small and rare group of people." He is responsible for one of the most vast and complete collections of material and information about this unique sorority of women ever assembled. He is the First Ladies Man and he is excited to share the stories of his adventures.

Credits and Contributors

Publishing: Tactical 16, LLC
CEO, Tactical 16: Erik Shaw
President, Tactical 16: Jeremy Farnes
Cover Design: Kristen Shaw
Author Photo (cover): Austin Polasky
FLM Logo: Joe Wilk and Andrew Och
Web design - www.firstladiesman.com: Joe Wilk at Shadowfire Web Development

ABOUT THE PUBLISHER
Tactical 16, LLC

Tactical 16 is a Veteran owned and operated publishing company based in the beautiful mountain city of Colorado Springs, Colorado. What started as an idea among like-minded people has grown into reality.

Tactical 16 believes strongly in the healing power of writing, and provides opportunities for Veterans, Police, Firefighters, and EMTs to share their stories; striving to provide accessible and affordable publishing solutions that get the works of true American Heroes out to the world. We strive to make the writing and publication process as enjoyable and stress-free as possible.

As part of the process of healing and helping true American Heroes, we are honored to hear stories from all Veterans, Police Officers, Firefighters, EMTs and their spouses. Regardless of whether it's carrying a badge, fighting in a war zone or family at home keeping everything going, we know many have a story to tell.

At Tactical 16, we truly stand behind our mission to be "The Premier Publishing Resource for Guardians of Freedom."

We are a proud supporter of Our Country and its People, without which we would not be able to make Tactical 16 a reality.

How did Tactical 16 get its name? There are two parts to the name, "Tactical" and "16". Each has a different meaning. Tactical refers to the Armed Forces, Police, Fire, and Rescue communities or any group who loves, believes in, and supports Our Country. The "16" is the number of acres of the World Trade Center complex that was destroyed on that harrowing day of September 11, 2001. That day will be forever ingrained in the memories of many generations of Americans. But that day is also a reminder of the resolve of this Country's People and the courage, dedication, honor, and integrity of our Armed Forces, Police, Fire, and Rescue communities. Without Americans willing to risk their lives to defend and protect Our Country, we would not have the opportunities we have before us today.

Giant Squid Creations

Washington, D.C.

GIANT SQUID CREATIONS is the brainchild of Senior Executive Producer and President, Andrew Och. Andrew is an award winning television, music and multimedia producer who has been working in the United States and around the world for nearly 30 years. Giant Squid is a creative service that provides your projects an open-minded way of thinking that customizes and creates every project to fit the personal a professional wants, needs and desires of the client. Everything began for Andrew with musical rhythms, notes and the sound of drums. A lifetime of music and drumming has opened Andrew's eyes, ears and mind to the limitless world of multimedia. Anything and everything is possible with Giant Squid Creations.

www.giantsquid.us

CPSIA information can be obtained
at www.ICGtesting.com
Printed in the USA
LVOW04*1430100816

499838LV00015B/134/P